The publisher gratefully acknowledges the generous contribution to this book provided by the Literature in Translation Endowment Fund of the University of California Press Foundation, which is supported by a major gift from Joan Palevsky.

Publié avec le concours du Ministère français chargé de la culture, Centre national du livre. Published with the assistance of the French Ministry of Culture's National Center for the Book.

COOKING: THE QUINTESSENTIAL ART

CALIFORNIA STUDIES IN FOOD AND CULTURE
DARRA GOLDSTEIN, EDITOR

COOKING

THE QUINTESSENTIAL ART

HERVÉ THIS AND PIERRE GAGNAIRE

TRANSLATED BY M.B. DeBEVOISE

UNIVERSITY OF CALIFORNIA PRESS
BERKELEY   LOS ANGELES   LONDON

University of California Press, one of the most distinguished university presses in the United States, enriches lives around the world by advancing scholarship in the humanities, social sciences, and natural sciences. Its activities are supported by the UC Press Foundation and by philanthropic contributions from individuals and institutions. For more information, visit www.ucpress.edu.

University of California Press
Berkeley and Los Angeles, California

University of California Press, Ltd.
London, England

Library of Congress Cataloging-in-Publication Data

This, Hervé.
 [Cuisine. English]
 Cooking : the quintessential art / Hervé This and Pierre Gagnaire ; translated by M.B. DeBevoise.
  p. cm.
 Includes bibliographical references and index.
 ISBN: 978-0-520-25295-0 (cloth : alk. paper)
 1. Gastronomy—History. I. Gagnaire, Pierre, 1950– II. Title.

TX631.T5513 2008
641'.013—dc22   2007050920

Manufactured in the United States of America

17 16 15 14 13 12 11 10 09 08
10 9 8 7 6 5 4 3 2 1

The paper used in this publication meets the minimum requirements of ANSI/NISO Z39.48–1992 (R 1997) (*Permanence of Paper*).

CONTENTS

TWO INTRODUCTIONS

HERVÉ THIS   How can we reasonably judge a meal? How can we go beyond merely liking or disliking what is served to us? From my almost daily discussions with my friend Pierre Gagnaire and from my constant practice a good many years now of the discipline known as molecular gastronomy, I have come to see that the world of food is urgently in need of clearer standards of judgment.

The question is not a simple one. We must first decide whether a cook has mastered basic techniques. Cooking meat at a low temperature, for example, which is nothing other than a modern version of the ancient technique of braising, is very much in fashion today, because in this way even the toughest cuts can be made very tender while retaining their juices. But try putting a leg of lamb in an oven for several hours at a temperature of 70°C (158°F)—it will end up like cardboard. The cook who envisions a dish that melts in the mouth, yet arrives at this unintended result, deserves no praise. He must therefore succeed in achieving what he sets out to do.

And, then, of course, there are the hundreds of small touches that determine whether a dish is more or less pretty to look at: the way in which a vegetable is julienned, how a brunoise is arranged on a plate, and so on. In a word, care. Attention to detail.

But these things are not enough if we are to properly appreciate culinary art. It is as though one pretended to judge a Rembrandt drawing by looking to see if the ink had run.

Let us raise our sights, then, and try to create a new form of criticism appropriate to the talents of true culinary artists. Because we cannot avoid dealing with the question of "beauty"—a term that, in view of the difficulties it conceals, requires more quote marks than I have given it here—we need to adapt aesthetic analysis to the subject at hand. Theories of beauty have been elaborated for painting, music, sculpture, and literature, but not for cooking, which some deny is an art at all. Insofar as it concerns cooking, aesthetic theory is not so much backward as absent.

The work that you hold in your hands was originally meant as this missing treatise on culinary aesthetics. I hope that it may yet serve this purpose. But why make something dry and tedious when one can entertain instead? Why speak in grave, somber tones when a bit of humor will enliven even the most serious subject? Why deprive oneself of the pleasures of life, in all its exuberance, when discussing an art as sensual as cooking?

Having resolved, then, not to produce yet another perfectly boring book, I have been careful, following Jean Anthelme Brillat-Savarin's example, to barely touch on all those subjects that are liable to become dull and to do my best to convey in an appetizing and easily digested form all those ideas that seemed to me useful. In the light-hearted drama that I have imagined, technical aspects of science and mathematics are interspersed with aesthetic notions, because life itself—and cooking, in particular—are not, happily, purely technical activities. In life, as in art, everything is mixed together, everything changes, everything is tangled up with everything else. True knowledge always blends theory and practice.

A book that asserts the existence of a specifically culinary art cannot avoid giving examples. I have therefore set Pierre Gagnaire the difficult task of creating culinary works of art in order to give life to the various aesthetic ideas worked out by theorists of art in other domains that I have sought to transpose to cooking.

Like many other chefs whose creations I admire, Pierre denies that he is an artist, denies producing works of art—but this is nothing more than a becoming piece of modesty. Why should certain musicians, certain painters, certain sculptors accept the title, and not cooks? The struggle against received ideas will have to be carried on a while longer before this situation changes. I demand that gastronomic guides, for example, distinguish craftsmen from artists. If on finishing this book you are convinced of the necessity of this distinction, perhaps you will join me in insisting upon it.

Despite his own reluctance to consider himself an artist, Pierre generously agreed to illustrate some of the aesthetic ideas developed in the chapter dialogues. Obviously it was not a question of providing conventionally formatted recipes, with their measures and cooking times, that reduce the cook's task to simply carrying out a set of instructions. Instead, I asked Pierre in his In Practice sections to illuminate the process of culinary creativity—to explain his reasons for choosing one ingredient rather than another, for combining the elements of a dish in a certain way, for presenting it in a particular fashion. In the In Theory sections, I briefly introduce Pierre's culinary commentary and then, in the concluding Your Turn paragraphs, I encourage you to experiment on your own, to play with the ideas we have discussed.

The fact that Pierre sometimes speaks of Hervé, and vice versa, risks giving the impression that this business is just between the two of us.

Nothing could be further from the truth: everyone who shares our fascination with food and cooking is invited to take part in these discussions
of culinary art. How could we possibly exclude friends? Isn't cooking first
and foremost a matter of love?

PIERRE GAGNAIRE   It does seem to me that there is an element of
pretension, even vanity, in calling oneself an artist. I am more comfortable being known as a storyteller. Whereas Hervé has asked me to create what he calls "culinary works of art," I see myself as telling stories,
using the language of flavor to impart meaning and, where culinary tradition would have preferred that I go on stuttering, to articulate new ideas
as eloquently as possible.

Beyond words such as "art," "style," and so on, the task that Hervé
and I have set for ourselves in this book is the result of active collaboration over a number of years. In the course of our working sessions,
cooking meets science and, owing to our friendship, our separate purposes merge with each other. Science searches for knowledge, mechanisms, phenomena; the cooking that I dream of, on the other hand, must
give happiness, emotion. Hervé is obliged to shed his scientific reserve,
temporarily abandoning the quest to identify the causal mechanisms of
culinary phenomena, and to entrust me with the technical applications of
his research. For my part, I am free to draw upon his thinking in order
to compose novel dishes.

Cooking is often a matter of wanting to do something. Of seeing a
very beautiful fruit and wishing to create a setting for it, for example. Or
of eating an ordinary vegetable and seeking to share a little pleasure, a
little passion, by placing it at the heart of a culinary idea. Why should
one forego the pleasure of finding a place for even gelatinous emulsions
or three-dimensional "checkerboards"?

Most of our working sessions are devoted to exploring technical aspects of cooking, but Hervé and I have spent a considerable amount of time trying to understand the artistic—I still hesitate to use the word— impulses that animate so many of our culinary investigations. Along the way we have had to work at adapting aesthetic notions from other arts to the language of cooking. Hervé has played the obstetrician in all of this, bringing these ideas into our world and stimulating my desire to cook in new and different ways. I invite you to accompany us on our journey.

PART ONE

THE BEAUTIFUL IS THE GOOD

ONE

THE EXISTENCE OF A CULINARY ART

It is traditionally accepted that music is an art, that painting is an art, that theater is an art—no less than literature and, for more than a century now, the cinema. Why not cooking? Its essential function of providing nourishment has caused us to forget that, in the hands of a great cook, a meal is capable of touching us as a love song does, of giving us joy, occasionally even of moving us to anger. To the extent that it detaches itself from tradition (which works to consign it to the status of an artisanal trade or craft, based on repetition) and insofar as its purpose is to stir the emotions, cooking—which alone among the arts stimulates all of the senses at once—cannot be excluded from their company.

A CONVERSATION OVER DINNER

An apartment somewhere in Paris, white walls, beige carpet; an open window lets in the sounds of the city on an early fall evening. Four people are seated around a dinner table. They have just finished their meal.

JEAN   I can't quite agree with those who say that if you want to know something, you should look at it up close, but that if you want to love it, you should look at it from far away. These fat quails that Cécile prepared for us, stuffed with juniper berries—ummm, what a delight! I love them up close!

DENIS   Always talking, rather than simply appreciating your sensations!

JEAN   Go ahead, make fun of me all you like. As Leonardo da Vinci said, the more one knows, the more one loves.[1] And another thing: why some people refuse to consider cooking an art is beyond me.

CÉCILE   Refuse? Doesn't one speak of "the arts of the table"?

HÉLÈNE   Yes, but you've said it yourself: the *arts* of the table, the culinary *arts*. If there were such a thing as culinary art, it would be singular. The fine arts are traditionally confined to architecture and the plastic and graphic arts, though music and dance are sometimes admitted.

JEAN   None of the Greek muses represents culinary art.*

DENIS   And yet the pleasure that we've taken this evening in these quails is not somehow less elevated or more vulgar than the pleasure one experiences contemplating a picture or listening to a beautiful piece of music.

JEAN   Nicolas Boileau† put it well when he said that the art of the table bears only a distant relationship to the satisfaction of hunger.

---

*The nine Muses were daughters of Zeus and Mnemosyne, the goddess of memory: Clio, muse of history; Calliope, epic poetry; Erato, lyric poetry; Euterpe, music (particularly flute-playing); Melpomene, tragedy; Polyhymnia, hymns and pantomime; Terpsichore, dance; Thalia, comedy; and Urania, astronomy.

†NICOLAS BOILEAU (Paris, 1636–Paris, 1711; known to his contemporaries as Nicolas Despréaux): poet, satirist, and critic, friend of Racine and Molière, whose influence helped shape the literary tastes of eighteenth-century French classicism.

DENIS   Another quotation! But it isn't pertinent. We're not speaking of the art of the table, but of culinary art. We're not speaking of the beauty of the napkins or the silverware. What matters are Cécile's quails!

HÉLÈNE   You're right, Cécile's quails *are* what matters. And we're indebted to her for the happiness she's given us.

The evening continues, but Cécile has closed the window and we hear nothing more.

TWO DISHES

ONE BEAUTIFUL TO LOOK AT AND UGLY TO EAT, THE OTHER UGLY TO LOOK AT AND BEAUTIFUL TO EAT

IN THEORY

The first exercise for the cook: to demonstrate that culinary beauty has nothing to do with the appearance of a dish. A work of art is not composed primarily to be looked at, unless it is a picture. Does one go to a concert to see the orchestra members? Or does one go to hear the music better?

The two recipes that follow constitute the desired demonstration, thanks to which gourmets need no longer dwell on the visual beauty of a dish. Let's try to see further than our eyes, and learn instead to see with our mouth.

IN PRACTICE

To make something that is pretty to look at, there are any number of tricks of the trade that may be employed: arranging the vegetables on a plate just so, cutting the fish In a certain way, adding a cream or some other sauce, piling up the elements of a dish rather than juxtaposing them. The essential thing is to set the stage, to construct the dish without trying to conceal its component elements. This way your friends have the feeling that your love for them is genuine, that you are taking care of them.

JOHN DORY WITH SOUTHERNWOOD

John Dory is a beautiful fish to look at—when it is cooked for a suffi-ciently brief time, its flesh is pearly white. To enhance the visual effect I cut it at an angle, in rather thick slices; a perpendicular cut, no matter how perfect, is less interesting to the eye.

I season the slices with salt before cooking them in some chilled but-ter, in a nonstick pan. The butter should be heated just until it begins to foam and turn an attractive shade of brown: here again there's beauty. The fish must then be "frightened"—cooked for no more than fifteen sec-onds on each side—and served in the pan, which has been deglazed with beer or Riesling.

Some twenty years ago, I had the idea of cooking John Dory with South-ernwood, a herb that came to me in dried form from the area around Gap, in the Hautes-Alpes. Southernwood is a cousin of savory and sage, and contains many essential oils, which may be why even a small quantity is enough to make the dish inedible. It gives an absolutely appalling flavor—oily, overpowering, pharmaceutical: *not* good. I gave up experi-menting with it at once!

OYSTERS WITH SPANISH HAM

This dish calls for a few fatty oysters. If none are available, you can use a combination of milky and lean oysters.

Open the oysters, take them out of the shell, and arrange them on plates. Strain the liquid from the shells, mix it with some very finely diced gray shallots and sherry vinegar, and pour over the oysters. Put the plates in the refrigerator.

When ready to serve, slice some well-aged Spanish ham—Jabugo, for example, whose flavor is characteristic of the black-footed pigs of the Iberian Peninsula from which it comes, and of their acorn-based diet. Slice the ham as thinly as possible and serve at room temperature: the fat will ooze out of the ham.

For some of my guests, who find the appearance of oysters disturbing, the visual effect is unpleasant, to say nothing of all that fat oozing out. Nonetheless, attempting to improve the look of this dish would be a mistake: a more refined presentation, multiplying the number of ingredients, would ruin its distinctive flavor.

When everything is said and done, what makes something beautiful to eat? In this case the reverberation of the two combinations of flavor is memorable: the one enriches the other. The effect is a bit like what one encounters in *Huîtres à la louquenqua,* a dish from the Bordeaux region, in which oysters are paired with flat spicy grilled sausages.

Here the sausage is replaced by ham, which is more interesting because of its notes of aged fat. The sherry vinegar and the shallots, whose familiar association with oysters lends a reassuring touch, balance the fattiness of both the oysters and ham. When the proportions are well judged, this is a very lively combination.

YOUR TURN

Try to think of ingredients that are beautiful to look at but ugly to eat, and things that are ugly to look at but beautiful to eat. What makes them beautiful? What makes them ugly?

TWO

ARTISANAL VERSUS ARTISTIC CUISINE

A clear distinction needs to be made between craft and art in cooking. The hallmarks of craft are workmanship, repetition, tradition. Art, by contrast, demands emotion, creation, expression.

AN ARGUMENT ABOUT BEAUTY—AND THE GOOD

A week later, again in the evening. The same four friends, this time in Cécile's restaurant. The room is simple: stone walls, tile floor. The meal is coming to an end, around a long table, covered with a coarsely woven white tablecloth, before a chimney so large that a person could fit inside. Only the dessert plates, water carafes, and a bottle of late-harvest Gewürztraminer remain on the table. The condensation on the outside of the bottle shows that it has been chilled, and just opened.

CÉCILE   And here to conclude, we have a selection of sorbet quenelles: pear, *fromage blanc,* and grapefruit!

JEAN   What a feast! A salad of summer truffles, crisp sorrel, and finger-ling potatoes; a fillet of lake trout with thyme and lemon; a creamy foam of red currants with mugwort, served in a cup like a cappuccino, with, uh . . . ah yes, a clear lobster jelly and a Junot tomato; a crispy puff pastry containing two kinds of cuttlefish, small *chapirons* served whole and sliced *blanc de seiche;* then a squab salad with lasagna and zucchini chutney—

CÉCILE You're forgetting the braised fillet of sea bass on a mixed salad of aromatic herbs.

DENIS   Right you are. And then for dessert there was Bavarian cream with coconut milk, apples prepared in several different ways, Mirabelle plum jelly with pomegranate seeds, a tonka bean sabayon with poached fresh peaches and emulsified grape juice, hazelnut cake, an orange mousse, fresh figs with cumin caramel, chocolate cake—and now the quenelles.

JEAN (*ironically*)   After all that, why ask whether there is such a thing as culinary art? Cécile has demonstrated its existence by her very cooking.

HÉLÈNE   To make Jean happy, I looked for an apt quotation and found one from Madame de Staël: "Why ask the nightingale the meaning of his song? He can explain only by starting to sing again; only by giving oneself up to the impression he creates can he be understood."[2]

DENIS   An amusing and poetic sentiment—to which I am utterly opposed because it denies the possibility of understanding.

JEAN   You take the same line as Brillat-Savarin,* who said, "Animals feed themselves; men eat; but only wise men know the art of eating."[3]

---

*JEAN ANTHELME BRILLAT-SAVARIN (Belley, 1755–Paris, 1826): lawyer and economist who held various public posts. As a deputy to the Estates-General of 1789 he played

HÉLÈNE   I like that, but I'd like it better if he had said, "Animals feed themselves, human beings know the art of eating." First, I don't care for his distinction between men and wise men; and then he leaves out women—

DENIS   Yes, but to come back to Madame de Staël, there are many other things I'd reproach her for. First of all, I'm always wary of arguments from authority, on the one hand, and of formulas on the other. Simply because Madame de Staël—someone I hardly know—said this, and simply because she said it in an elegant way, I am expected to accept it as true. All right, Jean, let me quote someone to you for once, someone in my line of work: Descartes. His first precept of scientific method was "never to accept anything as true that I did not clearly know to be such."[4] And then the idea of acquiring knowledge by surrendering oneself to sense impressions. This is a lazy way of living one's life. By simply letting oneself go, one avoids the trouble of trying to understand—

JEAN   Your old obsession: the search for understanding.

DENIS   Yes, otherwise we are merely dupes. Descartes, Brillat-Savarin, Boileau, Madame de Staël—these are only names we mention in conversation to flatter ourselves. Do any of us really know who these people were?

---

a secondary role, but his honorable conduct won him election to the Tribunal of Appeals, then as mayor of his native town of Belley, in the Rhône-Alpes, in 1793. Charged by the Revolutionary Tribunal with "moderatism," or a lack of sufficient enthusiasm in carrying out the aims of the Revolution, he sought political asylum in Switzerland and then in the United States. He came back to France in 1796 and took up an appointment to the Court of Appeals under the Consulate, thereafter dividing his time between his judicial duties and writing.

His works include *Aims and Purposes of Political Economy* (1802); fragments of an unpublished work on judicial theory, written in 1818; *Historical and Critical Essay on the Duel* (1819); a report to the Société Royale des Antiquaires the following year on the archeology of the department of the Ain; and his celebrated treatise of gastronomy, *The Physiology of Taste,* published in Paris in 1825.

HÉLÈNE (*in an ironically learned tone*)   René Descartes, seventeenth-century philosopher and mathematician, creator of a method of scientific thought exposited in the *Discourse on Method* (1637); coiner of the phrase "Cogito, ergo sum" ("I think, therefore I am"—the first absolute certitude), father of analytical geometry, author of a treatise on optics, uh—

DENIS   Bravo! But you see how brief your description is. My friend Jean Largeault, the philosopher, likes to say that erudition is a pretentious way of not thinking. I don't say that of you, Hélène. But how sure *are* you of what you claim to know?

HÉLÈNE   First name, René, no question there. Nor about Descartes. Philosopher and mathematician: very well, he was also interested in physics, but I make up for this lapse by citing his treatise on method, the title of which I am equally sure of—

CÉCILE   I think I know what Denis is getting at, but I haven't read this famous *Discourse on Method*. What's it about?

DENIS   You're right to admit your ignorance—unlike those who seek to give the impression that they understand the works of this or that philosopher, when in fact they've only heard the name. This is nothing more than a form of snobbery.

HÉLÈNE   It's true, I may know Descartes and Madame de Staël, but I know nothing about the great cooks of the past. Apart from the story of Vatel*—

---

*VATEL (born Fritz Karl Watel; Paris, 1653–Chantilly, 1671): Swiss maître d'hôtel who began his career as household steward for Nicolas Fouquet, the royal inspector-general of finances, passing then into the service of the house of Chantilly. In April 1671, the Prince de Condi entrusted him with responsibility for organizing a three-day feast in honor of Louis XIV. At the supper on the second evening there was not enough roasted meat, owing to an unexpectedly large number of guests, and later the fireworks display was ruined by cloudy weather. On the morning of the third day, mis-

JEAN   Who wasn't a cook at all, but rather a maître d'hôtel—a household manager, or steward!

CÉCILE   Just the same, I'm often embarrassed by how little I know. On the other hand, perhaps for this very reason, I find that philosophical reflection is often very helpful to me in thinking about cooking. For example, in planning our dinner this evening I made use of a quotation from André Gide that Jean gave me a while ago and that I wrote down in one of my notebooks: "A work of art is an idea that one exaggerates."[5] The whole meal this evening is based on this idea: I exaggerated the number of dishes, the number of ingredients of each dish, the combinations of flavors and correspondences between them, the transitions between courses. And to prevent the meal from being nothing more than a succession of one dish after another, I borrowed Denis's idea that each dish ought to be a sort of act of love.

JEAN   Your dinner made me realize that great cooking raises the question both of simplicity and of tradition. You speak of love, but I'm not sure that my great-uncle Jacques, for example, would have welcomed the embrace. Jacques was not an adventuresome sort when it came to food—he wanted his green beans well cooked, for example, not crunchy. Which raises in turn the question of art and craft.

CÉCILE   I don't see the connection.

JEAN   There's a distinction, you see, between art and craft. Someone who paints a wall, for example, is applying a certain technique—he is a craftsman. In this kind of work the artistic component is weak: if the paint runs or if the color is poorly mixed, the result will be mediocre, but these are technical details. When everything is said and done, a painted

---

takenly believing that the fresh fish he had ordered would not arrive, he ran himself through with his own sword.

wall is only a painted wall. The craftsman doesn't matter—he disappears once the job is finished.

On the other hand, think of a painter like Cézanne, who went back day after day to Mount Sainte-Victoire, near Aix-en-Provence, painting the same scene over and over again, always in a different way. Cézanne was concerned with art, rather than craft, and he emerged from anonymity because the public came to admire his work. In this case it was a matter of communication, not of a job well done.

CÉCILE   Of communication?

JEAN   Communication, yes. Naturally, the artist paints because he likes to paint, but there are a thousand other reasons for wanting to paint: because the mountain is beautiful and one wishes to preserve an image of it, say, which amounts to communicating with oneself; or because one wishes to share a feeling, to communicate with others. A painter may paint because he wants to express his feelings, or else because he has to make a living, or because—

CÉCILE   And you think it's the same in cooking?

JEAN   Of course. Think of the plate of steak and French fries that you eat quickly for lunch, or the side order of green beans, soft rather than crunchy. This is the work of a craftsman. Whether it's good or bad, it's meant mainly to keep your body going.

HÉLÈNE   Hold on, it's more complicated than that! If you like your green beans soft rather than crunchy, it's because your upbringing has led you to prefer them this way. In other words, the green beans speak to your mind as well as your body.

JEAN   I don't say that craft has nothing to do with one's background, with being brought up in a particular culture. Consider this wooden chair that Denis and Cécile just bought in Saint-Marie-aux-Mines, in Alsace. It's a sturdy, well-made chair, complete with a traditional heart-shaped back—a solid piece of craftsmanship. The furniture maker has put all his training and skill into it, but he has done nothing more than reproduce the design of every Alsatian chair that has ever existed or, at least, that has existed for several centuries. This, too, is a product of culture.

Still, the relationship between art and craft is a complicated one. Look at this groove that runs along the edge of the seat: it may not be found on every Alsatian chair. Perhaps the craftsman added this touch because he liked the way it looked. Certainly there is beauty in artisanal work— and happily so! But craftsmanship and artistry aren't the same thing, and one can hardly claim that the craftsman's individual signature—in this case, the groove—is enough to justify us in calling the chair a work of art.

CÉCILE   So you *are* saying that when I eat steak and French fries in a bistro, it's an agreeable experience because the dish has been well executed from a technical point of view. And that I'm nourishing my body, not my mind—because there's no communication with the mind of the cook in any of this.

DENIS   The artisanal cook must, of course, be capable of cooking the steak the way you like it, of seeing to it that the French fries have just the right crispiness, and so forth. There's a good deal of technique in this, but little art. By contrast, what you prepared for us this evening is something else altogether. First of all, you wished to please us. And then, even though our bodies weren't starving for nourishment, we ate rather a lot. This is an interesting phenomenon: what kind of hunger do we feel in this case?

JEAN   Good old Denis—the analytical mind in action.

DENIS   Which doesn't preclude subtlety or the ability to synthesize, mind you—

CÉCILE   In any case, I think you must be right, even if we don't know very well how to describe what it is that distinguishes art from craft. Our friend Henri, who lives in the heart of the Vosges, near the forest ridge, creates stunningly beautiful pieces of sculpture out of tree trunks. Some of these pieces resemble chairs, but Henri isn't trying to make chairs; the works he produces are the fruit of his inspiration. What he does isn't craft, it's art.

JEAN   Exactly. There are certain restaurants, such as yours, Cécile, to which one goes not to provide the body with fuel by filling up the stomach, but to satisfy an intellectual need. One goes to such restaurants for the same reason that one goes to the concert hall or the opera: the chefs at these places are searching for beauty in cooking.

DENIS   Not the good?

HÉLÈNE   You're right, one ought to say that they're searching for the good—since otherwise one risks confusing it with visual beauty. In this connection I have much more than Madame de Staël to give you. I have a whole raft of things for Cécile in my bag. Jean, would you please hand it to me? Thank you. On the way here I went by Geneviève's bookshop and bought everything she had on art. One of the most beautiful books that I found is this one, *Treatise on the Philosophy of Painting* by Shitao–*

CÉCILE   How lucky we are to have this bookshop in the neighborhood! Geneviève lets me sit there and read old cookbooks as long as I like. I came up with several of the ideas for our dinner this evening there, in fact. But I wouldn't have thought you'd find a book on painting in her shop.

HÉLÈNE   Oh, that reminds me. I met an odd sort of fellow there, neither handsome nor ugly, or rather, I couldn't really tell you how he looked. The only thing I noticed were his eyes. It was as though they had stars in them.

---

*SHITAO (also Shih t'ao; Luizhou or Qingjiang, 1642–Yangzhou, 1707): Calligrapher, poet, and painter who on becoming a Buddhist monk assumed the name "Friar Bitter-Melon." His work, devoted chiefly to landscapes and plant motifs, expresses the immensity of the world, the beauty of life, and other complex themes with striking simplicity. Shitao was also the author of an influential *Treatise on the Philosophy of Painting* (1707).

JEAN (*teasingly*)   Starry eyes! How romantic!

HÉLÈNE   You're wrong to make fun, Jean. Even your idol Brillat-Savarin speaks of twinkling eyes—look, I also picked up a copy of his *Physiology of Taste*. In the introduction, Brillat-Savarin tells of being encouraged by a friend to publish his book, an idea that he resists. When the friend points out that it would restore the good name of gourmands, he replies: "This one time you're right! It is incredible that they have been misunderstood for so long, the poor fellows! I suffer for them like their own father . . . they are so charming, and have such twinkling little eyes!"[6]

JEAN   Well, what about that! You, Denis, the scourge of superficial learning—you must be in seventh heaven!

HÉLÈNE   I haven't finished telling you about the fellow in Geneviève's bookshop. He was watching me poke around the shelves and then, without saying a word, he handed me a book. An old book that wasn't worth much. I was rather surprised—so much so, in fact, that I took it from him without even looking to see what it was about.

CÉCILE   Show me the book, would you? Hmmm . . . yellowed jacket, foxed pages. Handwritten recipes. No date. The title is *The Quintessential Art*. It reminds me of an old cookbook from the eighteenth century called *The Gifts of Comus*,[7] which says that cooking is the art of quintessentializing sauces. Can I borrow this? Perhaps it will give me an idea or two for our meal next week.

HÉLÈNE   And here are the notes I took before coming this evening. First, a line from Ernest Renan:* "The worth of a man is in proportion to his capacity for admiration."[8]

---

*ERNEST RENAN (Tréguier, 1823–Paris, 1892): French writer and historian who abandoned an ecclesiastical vocation to devote himself to the study of Semitic languages and the history of religions. Renan's exegetical labors strengthened his rationalist con-

CÉCILE (*leafing through the book*) Oh, look! Here on page 22 I find something about Renan.

DENIS   What a funny coincidence, finding a mention of Renan just when Hélène is talking about him. Although—

JEAN   Although what?

DENIS   Although coincidences are like beauty: often they exist only in the minds of those who notice them. For example, did you know that when more than twenty-three people are brought together—

JEAN   Two football teams plus a referee, in other words.

DENIS   That's right. Well, it turns out there's a better than 50–50 chance that two members of the group share a birthday. Or, to take another example, it's almost certain that I know someone who knows someone I happen to meet in the street. Suppose I know 500 people, each of whom in turn knows on average 500 people: 500 times 500 means there are 250,000 people removed from me by one person; and if one adds another link to the chain, 500 times 250,000 makes 125,000,000 people—twice the population of France!

HÉLÈNE   Since you're so fond of the Far East, Denis, I found a quotation for you from Okakura's *Book of Tea:** "Those who show themselves

---

victions, expressed in *The Life of Jesus,* which caused a great sensation on its appearance in 1863, and *The Future of Science* (1890). In *Memories of Childhood and Youth* (1883), he explained how he lost his faith.

*KAKUZŌ OKAKURA (1862–1913): Japanese intellectual who contributed to the development of the arts in his native country. In 1890 he helped to found the Tokyo Academy of Fine Arts, of which he was named director. He later founded the Japanese Academy of Fine Arts and directed the Department of Asian Art at the Museum of Fine Arts in Boston. Okakura published several books, but it is chiefly for his *Book of Tea* (1904) that he is remembered in the West today.

incapable of feeling in themselves the smallness of great things are not able to recognize in others the greatness of small things."[9] That will answer those who refuse culinary art the status of true art. I also took a note in reading the preface to Shitao's treatise on painting: "The notion of art varies depending on the culture: in the Chinese tradition, art is nothing other than perfection in the imitation of reality."[10]

DENIS   A dreadful opinion!

CÉCILE (*continuing to leaf through Hélène's book*)   Oh look, it says here that *"the last word in cooking occurs on the third Thursday of October."* That's strange. What do you think it means?

JEAN   It means you must make dinner for us that evening! One that will be still more extraordinary than the one tonight—

HÉLÈNE   Impossible!

CÉCILE   We'll see. In any case, it's a good idea. Let's get together in two weeks then. At our apartment this time.

A PERFECTLY ARTISTIC DISH

IN THEORY

Culinary art cannot be the endless repetition of the same dishes, nor can it be overly attached to tradition. Art, by contrast, involves the idea of creation, of novelty. Ingredients, both old and new, must form the basis of dishes that are continually being reinvented. Cooking becomes culinary art only if the cook refuses to tolerate repetition from year to year, season to season, or indeed day to day!

IN PRACTICE

A "perfectly" artistic dish? I'm afraid that would require a good deal more pretension than I'm capable of. Instead, let me give you an idea of how my treatment of a particular dish—in this case one involving pigeon—has changed over the years. As you will see, my style as a cook has evolved through the accumulation of small discoveries.

If you happen to take a braised turnip and some pine nuts, for example, and wrap them with streaky bacon from Colonata, in Tuscany—this is what I call a discovery: suddenly, as if by magic, you are confronted with a very interesting combination of flavors. I don't know why, but my first instinct is to try to construct a well-balanced dish around such combinations. At the beginning of my career I wasn't very familiar with farm produce, but I had no inhibitions: I set about transforming these ingredients, which meant little or nothing to me, in every way imaginable.

In December 1976 I took over the reins of my family's restaurant, the Clos Fleuri, near Saint-Étienne. I wasn't very experienced yet, but already I was beginning to take a little pleasure in my work. At that time I still shared the kitchen with my father, and my forays beyond the confines of tradition were a way of asserting myself—tactlessly, and rather disrespectfully, I'm afraid. Nevertheless, my haphazard experiments turned out to be a great asset, because they led me to ideas that I couldn't have found in the cuisine I grew up with.

So much for discoveries. As for my style as a cook, my guests are often the ones who point it out to me. I think that a style becomes perceptible only if the cook goes a bit further than others do, in a particular direction.

A PIGEON DISH OF FIFTEEN YEARS AGO

Long ago I used to roast a pigeon whole and very rare; I let it rest, then removed the breast fillets, leaving the skin on. Using the carcass and thighs and some Port or Maury (a wine from Roussillon), I made a sauce. Then I reheated the breasts in a little fresh fat until they were pink, and let them rest again until it was time to assemble the dish.

At this point the breasts were cut with a knife into very thin slices, a sort of carpaccio that I served with a scallop mousse—a preparation having a very delicate consistency, obtained by pressing the scallops through a sieve, in the great tradition of classical French cooking. To this I added a large langoustine (*Nepthrops norvegicus*), sautéed in butter, with mustard.

In this dish, then, there were three separate elements. What bound them together? The way in which the dish was assembled. A "normal" cook would have put the mousse in the middle of the plate, with the pigeon set off to one side and the langoustine to the other. That didn't suit me, because the elements remained independent of one another. To give meaning to a dish like this, you have to organize these elements, instead of leaving it to your guests to tell the story for you.

In this case my style consisted in a particular way of cutting the breast fillets, into very thin slices, and placing them astride the mousse on one side, with the langoustine straddling the mousse on the other side. I still needed something that would link the pigeon and langoustine together— a few leaves of spinach, for example! This meant rejecting the classical culinary principle that a dish can accommodate no more than three items: beyond that number, one was taught, the diner is liable to become lost and confused. Not at all—what confuses the diner is a lack of thoughtfulness and effort on the part of the cook!

As I say, the inspiration for this approach came from the fact that I wasn't content to reproduce what had always been done. But it was also, and especially, due to the fact that I felt sure that with enough effort and imagination the right linkages—or chords, to use a musical image—could be found. It was a question of trying to make the principal and secondary elements of the dish harmonize with one another.

Obviously I started out in a rather baroque way, piling things up on the plate and devising combinations that were slightly surreal but nevertheless well balanced. With the spinach leaves, for example, I used to add a few pomegranate seeds, shavings of raw ham with a bit of fat in it, a small sautéed slice of apple, and so on. I also used to add licorice to the cooking juices of the pigeon, along with some praline paste, milk, cream, chilled butter, and a dash of lemon juice, so that the sauce, unexceptional on first encounter, would release successive waves of flavor—in other words, I used anything other than wine, which most cooks would have contented themselves with. As I say, familiar ingredients and traditional cooking have always bored me!

Serving this dish on an ordinary plate didn't satisfy me either. Why not use a shallow soup dish equipped on one side with a small bowl, for example? And cut the langoustine in three pieces? The problem with this kind of restless experimentation, however, is that you've got to stop somewhere. Where do you draw the line? It was only in mastering my trade that I learned to refine and pare down, to stop adding and accumulating.

At the time, food critics asked why anyone would want to serve langoustine with scallops and pigeon. The juxtaposition of what Americans call "surf and turf" is unusual in French culinary tradition; during my apprenticeship, for example, I was never exposed to the idea. I was taught to make pike quenelles with an ordinary fish sauce, or a piece of beef with a béarnaise sauce. In this style of cooking there is only one central element, accompanied by a garnish, which is secondary. The worst example of it, I think, is the slice of wild game terrine served with some sort of jelly on the side. Surely we deserve better than this!

Some people are content to perpetuate tradition; others are not. My destiny was to rebel against classical cuisine, to try to change it. Pigeon, lan-goustine, scallops: this was one of those fortunate instances where trial and error led to an interesting result. I tried pairing the pigeon with whiting instead of langoustine, but the iodized notes of the fish were disagreeable— or rather, *I* found them disagreeable. Langoustine, on the other hand, has a sweet, mild flavor with a hint of vanilla. Obviously not everyone will agree. And, of course, first impressions can be changed: with enough effort, I might be able to make the combination of whiting and pigeon work to my satisfaction, but not simply by putting the two things together. As I say, this is a matter of personal aesthetic taste. Another cook might be per-fectly happy with a straightforward juxtaposition.

What would happen if the langoustine (also known as Dublin Bay prawn or Norway lobster) were replaced by rock lobster? Or by Breton or Maine lobster, or Australian rock lobster? Or by slipper lobster? Keep in mind that these crustaceans are not interchangeable. The rock lobster has a milder flavor than a Breton lobster, for example.

As I say, I used to coat the langoustine with mustard in order to give the dish a sharper edge, and to emphasize that foods don't have to taste like what they are. At all events, the way in which the ingredients of a dish are treated is something that must be decided by the cook. A lan-goustine is a fine thing in and of itself, but instinct and experience have taught me to distrust creatures that are reputed to be "beautiful," because this isn't always true—and because the cook can give them a measure of soul, of sensibility, that by themselves they lack.

LAST YEAR'S PIGEON

Last year I decided to do something quite different: the pigeon was still roasted whole, but the cooking of the breast fillets was finished with some sweet red peppers. The visual focus of the dish was therefore more on the pigeon itself, because the red peppers accentuated the brutal, bloody ap-pearance of a bird that has not been overcooked—all the more since it has a gamy, slightly untamed flavor to begin with, especially when it hasn't been bled.

TODAY'S PIGEON

The pigeon on my menu continues to change: why should one be satisfied with a single way of preparing it? I can no longer stand the thought of using chocolate, for example, because I've seen it served this way a thousand times. Fresh ideas are what is needed, not conventions.

Grégoire Sein, the executive chef of my London restaurant, Sketch, recently gave me a tamarillo to taste. The tamarillo is a Brazilian fruit that resembles a plum, with an inedible skin and a very beautiful color, between orange and burgundy. I hadn't tasted one for a long time. It has a very juicy pulp and a flavor that is very long in the mouth, a little bitter, even acrid. Sein suggested giving it a salty taste, rather than play upon its natural sweetness, and I came to think he was right. In any case, the acrid edge had to be softened.

It occurred to me to serve the tamarillo crushed and uncooked, in order to further emphasize the bloody aspect of the pigeon. The tamarillo therefore replaces the lemon juice that I had used to moisten the pigeon just after roasting. But it does more than this: it takes its place in the line of duck dishes made with fruits—peaches, cherries, or even pineapple—in which the balance of flavors is essential, without allowing the sugar of these fruits to dominate.

Well, why stop there when things are going so well? One might think of using the tamarillo to glaze the pigeon with a sweet-and-sour sauce. Or serving the pigeon barely roasted, with black pepper and spicy tamarillo. Or adding some crystallized grapefruit, or wine lees, or a nice red-currant jelly, or . . .

There are so many possibilities, any one of which acquires meaning only after a patient effort has been made to adjust and perfect the recipe, considering it with detachment, assessing, correcting, reflecting. Cooking, to the extent it involves organizing and structuring gustatory sensation, can't be considered a manual trade. It isn't enough to place one's fingers on the piano: one must start out with a song in mind.

YOUR TURN

Cooks who know how to describe their compositions are often the ones who produce the most beautiful works, at least in the minds of judges at culinary competitions (as I know from my own experience serving on such juries). This is not something that should be made into an absolute rule, however, for there are genuine artists who don't know how to talk about their creations and who speak only through their art.

Try coming up with your own recipe for pigeon. To make things a bit more challenging, try describing your dish in advance to some friends, who then will taste it and decide how well the result measures up to your conception.

THREE

TRADITION AND LOVE

Since the beginning of the twentieth century, artist-chefs have sought to throw off the yoke of the French restaurateur Auguste Escoffier. Along with many collaborators who often go unmentioned (notably among them Édouard Nignon, Thomas Gringoire, and Louis Saulnier), Escoffier codified the rules and techniques of classical cuisine, giving many dishes their familiar names while, at the same time, restricting the range of artistic possibilities. Some chefs have reacted by exploring new culinary directions more or less systematically, forgetting that the pursuit of novelty for its own sake is without interest. Culinary artists must remember that tradition has its own uses and virtues, and that when we eat we are consuming a whole culture.

FAREWELL TO TRADITION?

Denis and Cécile's apartment, two weeks later, the third Thursday of October. Night has fallen and it is raining. Inside, the kitchen and living room have been ransacked. Denis and Cécile scurry about, trying to put everything back in place. The table has not been set for dinner. The doorbell rings.

DENIS   I'll get it. Jean, come in. Hélène hasn't arrived yet. But don't expect a feast: the apartment was robbed this morning after we left.

CÉCILE   It turns out the old book was mistaken—I haven't had time to prepare anything for dinner! I don't even know what I've got left on hand.

DENIS   Here's Hélène.

CÉCILE   I hope you're not hungry, Hélène, otherwise I'm afraid you'll be disappointed. The burglars took a small amount of money I had in a drawer and a laptop computer. Now I see that they took the silverware and cleaned out the refrigerator and pantry. That leaves us with the fresh bread we bought coming home and—oh, look, here's a duck terrine and some stewed onions. Apparently they didn't have time to visit the cellar, so we've got some wine, and there's enough to make a dessert. What should we do: have a picnic or go out to eat?

HÉLÈNE   Let's stay here. I found something surprising in the old book—you forgot to take it with you the last time.

CÉCILE   Let me put everything on the table and then you can tell us.

HÉLÈNE   First, on page 32, I find a quotation from the book you mentioned last time, *The Gifts of Comus,* published in 1742 and attributed to François Marin, cook for the Duchess of Gesvres and later maître d'hôtel in the service of the Maréchal de Soubise: *"The science of the cook consists in decomposing, in making meats digestible and in quintessentializing them, in drawing out the nourishing and light juices. This kind of chemical analysis is indeed the whole object of our art."* This passage is inserted between two recipes, with the note "see page 33." And on page 33 we find—

CÉCILE   Wait, I'm spreading some of the terrine and compote on a piece of toast for you. Salt and pepper?

DENIS   And I'll lighten your task by opening this bottle from the cellar, which eluded me for a long while: a Puligny-Montrachet, Les Pucelles.

JEAN   1955–a famous year! Exactly two centuries after Brillat-Savarin's birth.

HÉLÈNE   Ah, here's the passage on page 33:

> *Jules Maincave: French chef who was killed in action during the First World War. "The art of French cooking," Maincave observed, "remains deplorably confined to a dozen recipes; the same dishes appear on our tables, rechristened a hundred times, with names that mask their mediocre uniformity. For three centuries, we have had few truly new dishes in France. First of all, I denounce the two fortresses of modern cuisine: combinations, and herbs and spices. Tradition excludes some of them, while authorizing many others. For example, oil mixed with vinegar forms a classic sauce, but the thought of mixing rum with the juice of pork is considered heretical. Why? The same is true of seasonings—we are pitiably limited. We still use bay leaf, thyme, parsley and so on, whereas the progress of modern chemistry would permit us to use roses, lilacs, lilies and the like. There is nothing more delicious, in my opinion, than beef cooked in kümmel, garnished with sliced bananas and filled with gruyère; or than a puree of sardines with Camembert; or than whipped cream with cognac-flavored tomatoes; or than a chicken roasted with lily."*[11]

DENIS   The trouble with this view is that novelty is so easy to come by. Imagine a table with a series of ingredients listed in a column: turbot, truffle, sweet pepper, fried potatoes, Camembert, raspberry, and so on. And then the same entries arranged in a row. When one examines the squares of the table, at the intersection of the rows and columns, one finds the various possible combinations, such as Camembert with raspberry.

HÉLÈNE   That limits the number of ingredients to only two—

DENIS   No, this table is only meant to suggest the sort of thing you can do. Using a computer, you could construct tables in more than two dimensions.

JEAN   How can you get more than two?

DENIS   Look at that chessboard behind you. It's like the table: on the plane of the board you've got squares, in two dimensions—in other words, you need two numbers to describe the points of the space. Take, for example,

	TURBOT	TRUFFLE	SWEET PEPPER	FRIED POTATOES	CAMEMBERT	RASPBERRY
TURBOT	TURBOT TWO WAYS	TRUFFLES WITH TURBOT JUICES	SWEET PEPPERS WITH TURBOT	FRIED POTATOES FILLED WITH TURBOT	CAMEMBERT WITH TURBOT	RASPBERRIES WITH TURBOT
TRUFFLE	TURBOT WITH TRUFFLES	TRUFFLES WITH TRUFFLE GARNISH	SWEET PEPPERS WITH TRUFFLES	FRIED POTATOES FILLED WITH TRUFFLES	CAMEMBERT FILLED WITH TRUFFLES	RASPBERRIES WITH TRUFFLE JUICE
SWEET PEPPER	TURBOT WITH SWEET PEPPERS	TRUFFLES WITH SWEET PEPPERS	SWEET PEPPERS STUFFED WITH SWEET PEPPERS	FRIED POTATOES AND SWEET PEPPERS	CAMEMBERT WITH REDUCED SWEET PEPPER JUICE	RASPBERRIES WITH A BRUNOISE OF SWEET PEPPERS
FRIED POTATOES	TURBOT WITH FRIED POTATOES	TRUFFLES WITH FRIED POTATOES	SWEET PEPPERS WITH FRIED POTATOES	FRIED POTATOES TWO WAYS	CAMEMBERT FILLED WITH FRIED POTATOES	RASPBERRIES WITH FRIED POTATOES
CAMEMBERT	TURBOT WITH CAMEMBERT	TRUFFLES WITH CAMEMBERT	SWEET PEPPERS WITH CAMEMBERT	FRIED POTATOES WITH CAMEMBERT	CAMEMBERT WITH CAMEMBERT	RASPBERRIES WITH CAMEMBERT
RASPBERRY	TURBOT WITH RASPBERRIES	TRUFFLES WITH RASPBERRIES	SWEET PEPPERS WITH RASPBERRIES	FRIED POTATOES WITH RASPBERRY SAUCE	CAMEMBERT WITH RASPBERRIES	RASPBERRIES WITH RASPBERRIES

the square C5 on the chessboard. The letter *c* could be written as 3 since it is the third letter of the alphabet. Imagine now placing another chessboard on top of the first, and a third one on top of the first two, and a fourth on top of those, and so on. In short, you make a stack of chessboards. Any square would then be designated by three numbers: the number of the column, the number of the row, and the number of the chessboard. Each square would therefore correspond to three elements. Using our simple two-dimensional table, for example, the square 3, 4, 6 would correspond to sweet pepper, fried potato, and raspberry.

JEAN   What an awful combination—

CÉCILE   Don't say that. I can very well imagine a dish combining these three things. Actually, darling, your system doesn't suffice: still more elements would be needed.

DENIS   You can add as many as you like. Instead of thinking of squares on boards, think of a series of numbers. For example (3, 4, 6, 12), where the number 3 designates turbot, 4 pepper, 6 raspberry, and 12 cream. The number of numbers in such a list is unlimited.

HÉLÈNE   None of that settles the question of which combinations are good.

DENIS   Like Cécile, I believe that everything is good; it is only a question of expertise, knowing how to put things together.

HÉLÈNE   How do you explain, then, that tradition has selected particular combinations—that certain wines, for example, are thought to go better with certain dishes? How is it that duck confit goes so well with white navy beans, as in a cassoulet? Or peach with a coulis of raspberries and vanilla ice cream, as in a peach Melba? Or rabbit with garlic, white wine, and rosemary? Isn't it the same with chords in music? C and G go together, but C and B, and C and F sharp, are dissonant, if I remember rightly.

DENIS   You are confusing two different things. First, there is the question of tradition, and then there is the question of beauty, or rather of the good, as we have agreed to call it.

Regarding tradition, I wrote down an interesting quotation from the English chemist Sir John Meurig Thomas in one of my notebooks. Darling, hand me the blue one, would you—right there behind you. When he wrote this, Thomas was director of the Royal Institution,* a cross between the Palais de la Découverte and the Académie des Sciences here in Paris. Here he is speaking of a friend, the Russian chemist Kirill Ilyich Zamaraev, who had recently died:

> It was during this period, in 1993, that I discovered our common love of tradition. To some thinkers, tradition is an irrational inheritance from the dead past, a mere residue of obsolete customs and beliefs, which an enlightened society should discard as an impediment to reason and progress. But tradition, we both agreed, is necessary to society, necessary to the continuity of rational as well as irrational thought; and it is the very bedrock upon which scientific research and material progress

---

*THE ROYAL INSTITUTION: Part scientific museum, part scientific research institute, it was founded in London in 1800 by Benjamin Thompson (1753–1814), who had earlier been ennobled by George III with the title of Count Rumford. Born in America, Rumford was accused of espionage in 1788; he subsequently sought asylum in England, where he took British nationality before going abroad to advise the Elector of Bavaria on military and other matters. Shortly after returning to England in 1798, Rumford drew up plans for the Royal Institution of Great Britain with Joseph Bank, president of the Royal Society. Rumford is said to have discovered the phenomenon of convection (in a pot of water that is heated from below, the water rises up through the center and then, on cooling, falls back down along the sides of the pot) when he burned his mouth while eating a thick soup (in a clear bouillon, by contrast, convection does not take place since only the upper layer cools by contact with the air, by conduction). Rumford took an interest in many culinary questions, and as a young man published a 400-page essay, *On the Construction of Kitchen Fireplaces and Kitchen Utensils Together with Remarks and Observations Relating to the Various Processes of Cookery and Proposals for Improving That Most Useful Art* (1776).

is built. Advances in scientific studies are made by constant reference to, and calibration against, prior thoughts and traditions. I can still see the glint in Kirill's eye when I placed him on the spot in the famous lecture hall from where Faraday delivered more than a thousand lectures-demonstrations, the same spot [where] Mendeleyev, Helmholtz, Cannizzaro, Schrödinger, Pierre Curie, and Dumas* had also held forth.[12]

*DIMITRY IVANOVICH MENDELEYEV (Tobolsk, 1834–Saint Petersburg, 1907): Russian chemist who devised a table for classifying the chemical elements at a time when chemistry was continually discovering new elements (carbon, iron, sodium, hydrogen, oxygen, and so on) and searching for a way to order this growing list. Mendeleyev's table ordered them from the lightest to the heaviest, from left to right and from top to bottom, putting chemical elements having analogous properties, such as sodium and potassium, in the same column. Noting the presence of empty squares in the table, he predicted the existence of as yet unknown chemical elements along with their expected atomic masses and properties. The subsequent discoveries of these predicted elements earned Mendeleyev everlasting glory—but not the Nobel Prize.

HERMANN VON HELMHOLTZ (Potsdam, 1821–Charlottenburg, 1894): German scientist who introduced the notion of potential energy (a marble at the top of a mountain will roll to the bottom, transforming its potential energy into the kinetic energy of movement) and stated the principle of conservation of energy. He also studied the mechanisms of hearing and measured the speed of nerve impulses in the brain.

STANISLAO CANNIZZARO (Palermo, 1826–Rome, 1910): Italian chemist who introduced a number that bears the name of another Italian chemist, Amedeo Avogadro, corresponding to the number of atoms in twelve grams of carbon-12. He also made important discoveries concerning chemical synthesis.

ERWIN SCHRÖDINGER (Vienna, 1887–Vienna, 1961): Austrian physicist responsible for the equation that bears his name describing the behavior of particles as well as the absorption and emission of light by atoms.

PIERRE CURIE (Paris, 1859–Paris, 1906): Widely known as the co-discoverer with his wife, Marie Curie, of radium, it is often forgotten that earlier, with his brother Jacques, Pierre Curie had discovered the phenomenon of piezoelectricity, exploited today by a great many devices, including portable gas lighters (compressing certain kinds of crystal produces a difference in electrical potential between two opposed faces, which in turn generates the spark that ignites a flammable fluid). Pierre Curie also studied the modifications of the magnetism of bodies as a function of temperature,

JEAN   It's a sort of fetishism, isn't it, this story of the lecture hall? It reminds me of the time you showed me the crystals that Pasteur separated
by hand, under the microscope, to demonstrate the existence of left-handed
and right-handed molecules—a sort of avatar of the myth of a golden age,
which would have us believe that the old is better than the new.

Sorry, I prefer my modern comforts to the rusticity of the past: thanks
to running water I no longer have to walk miles with a bucket to get
water from a well; electricity gives me heat and light in all seasons, without which I'd have to chop wood; new medicines allow me to live longer
than before; I prefer glasses with thin lenses made from titanium-based
alloys to the old thick lenses; computers rather than quills and ink, and
so on.

The same is true with regard to wine. As recently as a decade ago,
many Alsatian wines kept for only a few years before maderizing, and
often produced migraines. Since then winemakers have learned to control the use of sulfur, and improved methods of vinification now yield
wines that keep much longer.

DENIS   But I didn't say that—

CÉCILE   There have been many improvements in cooking as well, Denis. A century ago cookbooks always contained a chapter warning against
various forms of adulteration: plaster of Paris mixed in flour, sugar doc-
tored with various lime compounds (gypsum, chalk, and so on), milk
diluted with water; I'll spare you the slurry liquid used to add color to
coffee!

---

before devoting himself, together with his wife, to the study of radioactive phenomena, which won them the Nobel Prize for physics in 1903.
    JEAN BAPTISTE ANDRÉ DUMAS (Alès, 1800–Connes, 1884): French chemist who
determined the atomic mass of several chemical elements. Dumas was among the first
to use chemical equations and to discuss the notion of chemical function.

•

HÉLÈNE   This is a long ways from the question of tradition. Couldn't we say that a certain path of historical development—

JEAN   In other words, actual experience—

HÉLÈNE   —led to the way we cook today, with all its virtues and defects? We can, if we like, continue to cook by repetition, in the traditional manner; but we can also change, abandoning what displeases us and devising a sort of custom-made tradition for ourselves. If we don't change, well, that's a personal decision. And if we do change, that's a personal decision as well. I notice that the quote from Jules Maincave in *The Quintessential Art* is followed by this aphorism from the Chinese novelist Lu Wenfu: *"To forget the past is a grave error; to neglect the future would be a greater error still."*[13]

DENIS   Another argument from authority!

HÉLÈNE   Perhaps—but history does teach lessons, you know. We are all creatures of culture. What Jean calls "fetishism" is also a recognition of the fact that we belong to a community that has a history, values, traditions. Criticism is not impossible, nor is change, but we'll never be able to erase the fact that our past precedes us. Regional cuisines, yesterday and today, are understood by the people who grew up with them. When a traditional dish is served to us, we understand that part of what we are eating is tradition. When we eat choucroute, for example, we know that we're eating something from Alsace. The story we are being told is clear, and therefore easily understood. This is what I call legibility.

DENIS   The surprising thing is that traditional dishes give us pleasure. After all, whether it's cooking or science, why should we like tradition? Hélène, another glass of Puligny? Jean, I know you're thirsty.

CÉCILE   This is related to the question we discussed last time: even when our bodies are not hungry for nourishment, we can still eat quite a lot.

HÉLÈNE   Your curiosity will be satisfied. My book gives the answer:

> *Cooking, by initiating chemical and physical reactions, places the health and life of the diner in the hands of the cook. Tradition provides a measure of safety for the cook, who, being aware of the dangers of various foods, while yet being unable to subject the chemistry of nature to his control, is assured of the harmlessness of what he makes by reproducing those dishes that have been served before and that have not poisoned eaters in the past. In cooking, then, imitation and tradition are guarantees of security. Every innovation must be carefully assessed and considered.*

JEAN   Cécile, did you realize that by serving us this terrine you were taking our lives in your hands?

HÉLÈNE   Hold on, that's not the end of it. There's a reference to page 40, where the author says that cooking has two purposes: nourishing the body and nourishing the mind:

> *Nourishing the body is a matter of providing it with nutriment, in suitable chemical form for the nutriment to be assimilated. This is essential in societies that suffer from a shortage of food, but not in societies where famines no longer threaten public health.*
>
> *Nourishing the mind is something different. It is the mind that balks at the idea of being served vinegar, egg yolk, and oil, carelessly thrown together in a bowl; this same mind prefers that the oil be carefully dispersed in the form of droplets into the water of the egg white and the vinegar, which have previously been mixed together, thus creating an "emulsion" called mayonnaise.*
>
> *It is the mind that demands the combination of sour cabbage with smoked pork in the east of France, a combination that in the form of choucroute garnie the Alsatian finds pleasing. More generally, the mind is satisfied by tradition because we do not eat out of a desire for nutriment, but out of a desire for love.*

JEAN   Exactly! And this is the answer to our other question. How is it that we can eat a lot even when our bodies aren't demanding to be fed?

Answer: because it's not food we're hungry for, we're hungry for the love of the person who's cooking.

DENIS   Biologically, you are right. Biologists like Theodosius Dobzhansky* have argued that everything having to do with the animal world—of which human beings are members—ought to be interpreted in evolutionary terms.

HÉLÈNE   Why evolutionary?

DENIS   Because it's biological evolution that has made us what we are today. Moreover, we need to ask ourselves whether culture itself isn't a biological fact. Let me explain—

JEAN   Please do!

DENIS   Why do we eat in the company of others? Because human beings, like other nonhuman primates, are social creatures: we live in cities because, biologically speaking, we are programmed to live in groups. And we gather to eat together because this behavior has been selected for over millions of years of evolution. We take what we call pleasure in eating with others because our brain rewards us when we do: cerebral circuits were gradually established, over many generations, that register the sensation of pleasure when circumstances place several or more of us around a table. Indeed, we seek to organize our lives in such a way that we have

---

*THEODOSIUS DOBZHANSKY (Nemirov, Russia, 1900–San Jacinto, California, 1975): Russian-born biologist who studied zoology in Kiev and, on moving to the United States in 1927, became interested in population genetics, studying ladybugs. He discovered that successful species tend to have a wide variety of genes that, while they do not appear to be useful to any particular individual, confer an evolutionarily valuable diversity upon the species as a whole. In *Genetics of the Evolutionary Process* (1970) and other works, Dobzhansky argued that this diversity enables the species to adapt effectively to changes in the surrounding environment.

frequent opportunities to eat with others. And it's for much the same reason that we are prepared even to eat things we don't like.

JEAN   You're in a mood for paradox this evening, I see!

DENIS   Not at all. Think of the infant. One readily observes that human and nonhuman primate newborns—chimpanzees, for example—like sugar, but few other tastes. If one puts a sweet solution in their mouth the day they are born they smile, whereas a bitter solution makes them grimace. Many children show a preference for sweet foods as well. How does it happen, then, that as adults we are happy to eat a toasted piece of unsweetened bread spread with a duck terrine, which has a powerful taste, and an onion compote, which has a surprising, slightly acid flavor?

HÉLÈNE   Foods that, as infants, we wouldn't have liked?

DENIS   Right—and, what's more, we take pleasure in drinking beverages that no child would drink. This phenomenon is sometimes called the "beer and tobacco effect." Children like neither beer, which is alcoholic and bitter, nor tobacco, which is acrid. And yet many of them will grow up to drink beer and smoke tobacco. Whether they do or not depends on peer pressure. A young person who doesn't drink beer and smoke tobacco is typically rejected by friends who do. This rejection is a form of biological punishment, since human beings are sociable by nature. When young people drink beer and smoke tobacco, they weigh the biological reward of acceptance by their peer group against the gustatory punishment of drinking and smoking substances that they find unpleasant. And it is the biological reward that wins out. This phenomenon has too often been underestimated!

CÉCILE   And what am I to make of all of this in the kitchen?

DENIS   You already take it into account, unconsciously, but you can do so deliberately as well. As Hélène pointed out, tradition is "legible" in the sense that certain dishes or ingredients immediately remind us of the regions with which they are associated: choucroute signifies Alsace, just as cassoulet calls to mind the Southwest, buckwheat crêpes Brittany, cream Normandy, garlic the South, and so on. If you serve someone a dish that he knows from having grown up in a certain place, you give him a biological reward, a confirmation of belonging to a certain culture. Which poses the question of culinary innovation: how can we innovate in cooking when evolution seems to condemn us to tradition?

JEAN   If I understand you correctly, the answer is contained in what you have just said. When we eat something new—the original creation of a culinary artist, for example—we will receive a biological reward only if we understand the meaning of the dish. In that case there is a meeting of minds between cook and diner—

HÉLÈNE   This book is full of surprises. On page 43 I find the following: *"The Romans claimed to be different from the barbarians. In ancient Greece, the Spartan lawgiver Lycurgus, memorialized by Plutarch,* was reputed to say, 'We do not sit down at table to eat, but to eat together.'"*[14] And below there's a note: *"As Boris Dolto† observed, 'When you are in love, you eat everything that is put in front of you.'"*[15]

DENIS   When I met Cécile, a few years ago, I really did eat everything—

CÉCILE   Stop your teasing! But, you know, I often think of my Alsatian grandmother and the wonderful dishes she made. Looking back, I'm not sure she really was such a good cook. It wasn't that. When I was little I

*PLUTARCH (Chaeronea, before 50–Chaeronea, after 120): Greek writer who traveled in Egypt, lived on several occasions in Rome, and was a priest of Apollo at Delphi. His literary work influenced many writers and philosophers, Michel de Montaigne and Jean-Jacques Rousseau among them.

†BORIS DOLTO (Sebastopol, 1899–Antibes, 1981): Russian émigré who created an important school of physical therapy; married to the French psychoanalyst Françoise Dolto.

used to love spending time in the kitchen with her and watching her work. She would talk to me about what she was doing. She was forever trying to improve her recipes, to add a little more of this, a little less of that, so that everyone would be happy. And it's true, even though we didn't all like the same things, the whole family loved her food—because what she gave us was love. It was something more than mere attention to detail.

DENIS   It was a way of bringing the family closer together, of satisfying the sociable instinct of the group. Once again the biological reward—

HÉLÈNE   This theory of sociability and biological reward troubles me. It seems to imply that we are only animals. To reduce a human being to a monkey—

DENIS   I don't reduce humans to monkeys; I say only that we mustn't forget our animal origins.

JEAN   Ah, the old opposition between nature and nurture.

HÉLÈNE   Jean, how did you guess? That's exactly the topic that *The Quintessential Art* takes up next.

CAMEMBERT AND RASPBERRIES

IN THEORY

One might suppose that the height of implausible culinary combinations is reached with Camembert, a prince among salty products, and raspberries, which occupy an exalted place in the sugar kingdom of desserts. Nonetheless it should not be forgotten that there is bitterness in the cheese and acidity in the fruit. This is why Morello cherry, a cousin of the raspberry, is traditionally paired with goat cheese, and fig jam with Franche-Comté.

IN PRACTICE

Camembert and raspberry? I see no particular difficulty. Still, as so often, there is an essential question: what kind of Camembert and what kind of raspberries? There is a difference, after all, between ammoniated Camembert, runny and soft Camembert, and chalky Camembert. The same is true with raspberries, which may be more or less watery, more or less sweet, more or less fragrant, and so on.

RASPBERRY CAMEMBERT WITH LOVAGE

Take a round of Camembert and cut it in two, like a sponge cake. Then cook the pulp of the raspberries with a little sugar, some finely diced celery, lovage leaves, a little tarragon. Spread this mixture over the two faces of the Camembert, wrap it with cellophane, and let it sit in the refrigerator for three days.

I've never actually tried doing this myself, but I'm sure that it would work perfectly. Or at least I know, from my many years in the kitchen, that this sort of composition would suit my aesthetic—perhaps I should say, more modestly, my taste—perfectly.

The underlying intuition is nonetheless worth scrutinizing more closely. Raspberries in the middle of the summer have an acidity and water content that soften up the cheese, just as cherries do in the case of a clafouti. The lovage, which substitutes for a salad course, has a very strong anise flavor, with a hint of cumin, that enriches the flavor of the Camembert. The sugar in the fruit is anecdotal in a different way: it tames the flavor of the dish, offsetting the acidity of the raspberry without making it disappear. Note that this acidity is important—it combats the chalkiness of the Camembert.

This is a line of attack that I often pursue: when the quality of an ingredient leaves something to be desired, I try to divert it, to turn it in another direction. Even a chalky Camembert can be transformed into an asset if it is properly handled. As I say, we must do away with the idea that an ingredient has to be "beautiful" in order to be worth cooking.

YOUR TURN

Which fruits would you pair with your favorite cheeses? A harder question: which vegetables would go with these cheeses?

FOUR

THE QUESTION OF NATURE

There is a sort of intellectual negligence in believing that nature is good, and a sort of dishonesty in promoting this belief in order to make it easier to sell food products. Nature is neither good nor bad: it is both the springtime that brings forth vegetables and fruits, and the winter that brings starvation. The human race has continually searched for ways to protect itself against the natural environment. If we wear clothes and live in houses, it is because the idyllic state of nature that we are forever imagining is far removed from reality.

We should think twice before concluding that chemistry is the work of the devil, for chemistry, like the other sciences, aims at producing knowledge. And is knowledge not the highest achievement of the human mind?

THE COOKED AND THE RAW

The evening continues in Denis and Cécile's apartment. Hélène is reading a passage from The Quintessential Art, *on the opposition between nature and artifice.*

In cooking, it is sometimes said, one should respect nature—and yet what if respecting nature isn't good for us? Raw carrots are too hard for people with fragile teeth; certain white beans are dangerous in their raw state because they contain anticoagulant compounds called lectins; and a crushed nutmeg can kill a person who eats all of it because the powdered seed contains a toxic molecule called trimyristicin.

Cooks really have less reason to worry about the quality of nature's products than farmers, who aim to provide them with superb vegetables, or livestock breeders, who aim to provide them with healthy and tender meats. Cooks would do better to concern themselves with the happiness of their guests.

The idea that one should cook using "natural" foods is another illusion. The ancestor of the wheat we know today was natural, but it was also a stunted plant that produced only a few dry, scrawny seeds. The ancestor of the modern bull was an emaciated creature. The wild carrot is a pitiful thing. Since the earliest times humanity has sought to domesticate vegetables and animals. By crossing the most productive individuals it has been possible to obtain today's wheats, for example, with their plump, rounded seeds. They are full of flour for making bread—and anything but natural! The same is true of beef, pork, tomatoes, peppers, pears, and, yes, apples. Have you ever tasted one of those small wild apples you sometimes come across in the woods? They are horribly astringent and bitter. In short, it's been ages since we've eaten anything natural.

Naturalness is no less a fantasy in cooking. Indeed, nothing could be more false, more absurd, or more unjustified. In the same way that we wear clothes rather than go around naked, that we live in houses rather than sleep outside, we cook our foods not only to tenderize and purify them, but also to give them flavors that they don't have in their natural state. Cooking is a completely artificial activity, as the dictionary attests: "Artificial: made by human skill; produced by humans; not natural."

Still, it may be asked, do foods really need to be prepared? The periodically recurring temptation to believe that we can eat vegetables raw and animals on the hoof has now become an institutionalized fashion that tries, with the utmost insincerity, to promote itself by creating public anxiety over the toxicity levels of certain cooked foods and the loss of vitamins and other nutriments during cooking.

What is forgotten in all of this is that nature is not good.

CÉCILE   There—in saying that nature is bad—the book goes too far. Without nature we wouldn't be here to talk about it! I admit that cooking is artificial, because it is the product of human technology and art, but it doesn't follow from this that nature isn't good! Would any of us prefer a steel-reinforced concrete pylon in front of his building to a hundred-year-old oak?

JEAN   We'd all prefer the oak—

DENIS   Except when its leaves fall and clog the gutters, when its branches break off in a storm and fly through the roof, or when its roots spread and push up the paving stones! I like the oak when it's not too close to my home. And undoubtedly you feel the same way: you like your nature under control, which is to say artificialized.

HÉLÈNE   The text continues:

Living on top of one another in cities, crammed into subways and trains and buses, stuck in traffic jams, we yearn for the great expanses of forest, plain, and mountain. We prefer the green of the grass to the gray of concrete. The idea that we love nature is drilled into us.

When it comes to food, this unreasoning emotion leads some people to suppose that they show their respect for nature by eating raw vegetables. But why? Why should we eat raw vegetables rather than cooked vegetables? Let's take a hard look at the facts of the matter. John Stuart Mill—

JEAN   Wait a minute. For once, Denis, I am wholly in agreement with you. Here we have another famous name, but it's only for show, to impress. I mean, I've heard of Mill, of course, but I'd be hard-pressed to tell you anything more about him than that he was an English philosopher.

HÉLÈNE   Not to worry. On page 50 there is a footnote identifying Mill.

JEAN   Hmmm . . . associationism, induction based on a law of universal causality, moral utilitarianism. I don't really understand any of this. The book answers the question, but not in any useful way.

HÉLÈNE   Hold on, there's also this note: *"Utilitarianism: philosophical doctrine that makes utility the principle and norm of every individual action."*

JEAN   That's no clearer!

HÉLÈNE   That's because you've forgotten the philosophy you studied in school. Broadly speaking, utilitarianism distinguishes between physical pleasures ("vulgar hedonism") and pleasures of the mind. To make this distinction it uses a test that consists in presenting people who are deemed "competent to judge" with an example of each kind of pleasure: the mental pleasure is remembered longer, even if it requires some effort. For example, reading Brillat-Savarin's *Physiology of Taste* requires some effort, but the pleasure you take from it stays with you. Playing sports is another example. The aim of utilitarianism is to maximize the sum of higher-quality pleasures in society as a whole, rather than individual pleasures.

Shall I go on? There's a long quotation from Mill:

*JOHN STUART MILL (London, 1806–Avignon, 1863): British philosopher and economist who made major contributions to associationism and liberalism. Mill founded induction on a law of universal causality and, in ethics, developed the doctrine of utilitarianism.

> In sober truth, nearly all the things which men are hanged or im-
> prisoned for doing to one another, are nature's every day per-
> formances. Killing, the most criminal act recognized by human laws,
> Nature does once to every being that lives; and in a large propor-
> tion of cases, after protracted torture. . . . Nature impales men, breaks
> them as if on the wheel, casts them to be devoured by wild beasts,
> burns them to death, crushes them with stones like the first Chris-
> tian martyr, starves them with hunger, freezes them with Cold, poi-
> sons them by the quick or slow venom of her exhalations.[16]

JEAN   In other words, nature is the hemlock that poisons us, the wild beast that attacks us, the cold that freezes us, the heat wave that kills the elderly, the plague that ravages whole populations, the rot and decay of foods, the mosquitoes—

HÉLÈNE   And there's this from Mill as well: *"Conformity to nature has no connection whatever with right and wrong."*[17] The author of our book comments:

> Everything considered, nature is neither bad nor good: it is indisputably
> what enables us to live, and it is also what kills us. And so we must
> learn to enjoy it, while trying to reduce as far as possible the suffer-
> ing it causes. It is also what makes us human, something many people
> fail to realize. If we wear clothes, it is in order to protect against the
> cold. If we bathe, it is in order to avoid disease. And if we cook our
> foods, it is because we know they are contaminated on the outside
> (and sometimes on the inside: think of the parasites found in pork
> and horsemeat) by microorganisms that are not always benign.

CÉCILE   Not always benign, no—but not always malign either. When I was at cooking school I was warned against only the dangers of micro-organisms, food contamination, and so on. Of course, young cooks must be taught not to poison their guests. But they also need to be taught that domesticated microorganisms are responsible for bread, wine, vinegar, cheeses, sausages—

JEAN   This is exactly the issue over which France and Italy find themselves in disagreement with countries such as the United States, which take the view that food products must be 100 percent clean, thoroughly sanitized. European countries argue that the presence of benign microorganisms in a raw-milk cheese, for example, will prevent pathogenic microorganisms from developing.

CÉCILE   I agree—there's no reason to go overboard on hygiene!

DENIS   The reflexive bias in favor of nature is dangerous, and chemistry is the victim of it. Vague talk of a natural equilibrium, or harmony with nature, is accompanied by a belief that nature must be obeyed, which is insane.

CÉCILE   Why insane?

HÉLÈNE   The book answers your question once again, with yet another quotation from Mill:

> As the nature of any given thing is the aggregate of its powers and properties, so Nature in the abstract is the aggregate of the powers and properties of all things. Nature means the sum of all phenomena, together with the causes which produce them; including not only all that happens, but all that is capable of happening; the unused capabilities of causes being as much a part of the idea of Nature, as those which take effect. Since all phenomena which have been sufficiently examined are found to take place with regularity, each having certain fixed conditions, positive and negative, on the occurrence of which it inevitably happens; mankind have been able to ascertain, either by direct observation or by reasoning processes grounded on it, the conditions of the occurrence of many phenomena; and the progress of science mainly consists in ascertaining these conditions. When discovered, they can be expressed in general propositions, which are called laws of the particular phenomenon, and also, more generally, Laws of Nature.[18]

DENIS   In other words, one must reserve for the word "nature" a meaning like "That which occurs without human intervention, or without deliberate and intentional intervention." But to come back to the dangers of diet, it's surprising that microorganisms should be singled out. After all, lead salts poisoned the Romans—to the point of triggering the decline of the Empire. Shouldn't cooks also be taught to be wary of certain metals as well?

CÉCILE   It's true—the disappearance of copper pots and pans, which have been replaced by stainless steel, has caused the dangers of copper to be forgotten. I remember the "regreening vats" that one of the chefs I apprenticed under used to use: we cooked green vegetables in them to preserve the color they were expected to have!

DENIS   Of course—copper from the vat replaced the magnesium found inside chlorophyll molecules, producing a fluorescent green molecule, actually greener than the green of the vegetables themselves.

CÉCILE   I've never understood this business. We used to say that when one cooks green beans, for example, the chlorophyll must be "fixed," but I've never seen chlorophyll leeching into the cooking water. What's going on here?

DENIS   It's simple enough. Green vegetables are green because they trap light and use its energy to synthesize—chemically synthesize—various molecules that are vital to their growth and reproduction.

JEAN   Natural chemistry in a sense!

DENIS   Yes, everything is chemistry—well, not really, that's a silly thing to say, since chemistry is a science, a way of searching for knowledge, and a plant has no need to know the chemical reaction that activates its development. Here again, though, I would point out that chemical reactions are neither good nor bad in themselves; they are what they are. Good and evil must be sought elsewhere. At all events, green vegetables manufacture their tissues from light because they contain little sacs called chloroplasts.

JEAN   Trying to impress us with your fancy words, are you?

DENIS   Sorry, that's what they're called, these little sacs in plant cells in which chlorophyll molecules are stacked up—chloroplasts. The molecules themselves—made up of carbon, hydrogen, oxygen, and nitrogen atoms, which form small platelets with what looks like a tail—absorb light and transform it into chemical energy. At the center of these platelets, four nitrogen atoms surround a magnesium atom.

When you cook green beans, the magnesium atom ends up being detached from the chlorophyll molecule, which then becomes something called pheophytin, and the beans turn brown. By contrast, if you cook them in the presence of copper, the copper replaces the magnesium and the beans retain their beautiful green color. But copper in sufficiently great concentrations is toxic. What used to be called "copper rust"—verdigris—was a cause of poisoning in the past. Similarly, kitchens today that still use copper pans for making fruit preserves are careful to remove the preserves after cooking, because the acidity of the fruits (which exists even though its taste is masked by the sugar) degrades the copper, which then seeps into the preserves. The copper of the preserving pan therefore has chemical properties of its own.

To come back to the question of natural and artificial, vegetables are "natural" despite the magnesium in their chlorophyll. Does that make them good?

JEAN   The answer is obviously no. Take hemlock, which very closely resembles the wild carrot: it's a deadly poison (the Athenians used it to kill Socrates, you'll recall, allegedly for having corrupted the youth of the city). The death cap fungus, a mushroom that schoolchildren are taught to recognize, is lethal as well. You may remember the incident a few years ago here in Paris, when the kitchen of a luxury hotel was fooled by *Gy-*

romitra esculenta, a toxic species known as "false morel" for its resemblance to the actual one, and everyone dining there one evening came down with food poisoning!

This is why the vogue for natural products frightens me: my life is in the hands of cooks—when they use herbs, they really have to be sure they know what they're doing. And it's no good trying to justify the use of unfamiliar herbs by saying that our ancestors used them: our ancestors lived shorter lives than we do, and their health was worse!

CÉCILE   This is something I've worried about for a long time, for example when I see so-called edible orchids at the market at Rungis, and all the strange herbs you find there: which ones are truly edible—I mean, with no danger whatever—and which ones aren't? I wonder if my fellow cooks are really aware of the risk to which they are exposing their guests when they cook with such things?

DENIS   Of course, we know that previous generations were not instantly poisoned by these plants, but that doesn't prove that they're harmless. None of them has been as thoroughly analyzed as pharmaceutical products are today. Would they pass the toxicology tests that new medicines must undergo in order to be approved? By no means all of them, I'd wager. The crosiers of certain ferns have a delicious flavor of hazelnut, but they are nonetheless severely carcinogenic. Even certain methods of cooking are dangerous. Did you know, for example, that the surface of meat cooked over a charcoal fire accumulates highly carcinogenic benzopyrenes from the smoke?

Obviously not all ferns carry this risk; still, one has to know which ones are safe to eat and which ones aren't. And obviously not all grilled meats are full of benzopyrenes; still, one should be careful to cook the meat in front of the fire, or to one side, and not above it.

CÉCILE   The point is that we have to learn to cook more intelligently. For example, cooks in the nineteenth century used *coquilles,* shell-shaped

pieces of metal that were positioned in such a way that the meat was between the fire and the metal, which served as a reflector, speeding up the
cooking. Putting a dripping pan beneath the meat in order to catch its
delicious juices was another smart idea!

JEAN   All this takes us a long ways from culinary art!

CÉCILE   Not really. If we kill our guests, there won't be anyone left to
admire our "works," as you call them.

HÉLÈNE   Wait! At the end of the page I just read, there's this: *The last
word in cooking is found at the Louvre"—*

JEAN   Which you know well. I've got an idea. How about if you and I
meet there tomorrow?

CÉCILE AND DENIS   What, no last word in cooking for us?

HÉLÈNE   Okay, let's all meet there tomorrow—at the entrance to the
pyramid.

COOKING THE UNCOOKED

IN THEORY

Why should cooks allow the products of agriculture, livestock farming, and
fishing to be served as they are, without any further ado? If we call these
products "ingredients," it will be easier to see that cooking amounts to something more than merely making the right choice at the butcher's or fish-

monger's or greengrocer's shop. It requires planning, artistic imagination—and, quite obviously, the act of cooking itself.

IN PRACTICE

The strawberry is the classic example of a fruit that is almost always eaten raw, since cooking it usually produces disappointing results. And so it makes sense to look for ways to avoid this outcome, which is due to nothing more than a lack of effort and imagination. Here are three ideas.

SHELLFISH WITH COOKED STRAWBERRY VINAIGRETTE

Try using the juice from cooked strawberries to flavor shellfish. Combine the strawberry juice with lemon juice and olive oil to make a sort of vinaigrette, which can be served warm, if you like.

FOIE GRAS WITH COOKED STRAWBERRIES

You can also cook the strawberries, and then add some lemon juice and a brunoise of green apple and crushed raspberry, to make an accompaniment for a thick slice of foie gras.

UDON WITH RAW HAM AND COOKED STRAWBERRIES

A Japanese-flavored *amuse-bouche* can be obtained by combining udon (wheat-flour noodles) and raw ham with strawberries that have been cooked and seasoned with soy sauce and wasabi.

Strawberries and other fruits of the same type, such as peaches, are sometimes of such poor quality that they have to be modified in some way, just as gherkin cucumbers are pickled in vinegar (green apricots benefit from this sort of treatment as well). In all these cases, one exaggerates the defect in order to make a virtue of it.

This idea forms the basis of a large part of my cooking: when I'm dissatisfied with a certain ingredient, I find a way to distort it, to turn it into something else. Early in my career It was the cooking of a certain food that I didn't like, and so I tinkered with the recipe. The distortion is never gratuitous: there's always an idea behind it—not an intellectual idea, but a sensual idea, without which cooking is only a formal game.

You're not happy with the cooked strawberry? Tweak it.

YOUR TURN

Are there certain products, such as cooked strawberries, that you find disappointing from the point of view of flavor? Think about the reason for this flaw and try to imagine a way to turn it into an asset. Wondering about what makes something bad is sometimes more useful than wondering about what makes it good. The philosopher Jean Largeault makes much the same point with regard to the usefulness of bad books: by forcing us to decide why they are bad, they show us what we really think.

FIVE

THE RECOGNITION OF A CULINARY ART

Can one speak of a specifically culinary aesthetics? There will always be, alas, those who believe that aesthetics must involve what is beautiful to look at, whereas cooking produces what is beautiful to eat. Writers on gastronomy have not ceased to encourage this way of thinking. In recent times, the French critic Maurice Edmond Sailland, known as Curnonsky, was particularly responsible for the idea that the good in cooking is entirely a question of the ingredients and has nothing to do with the work of the cook—or, as we should say, the artist.

STYLE

Hélène and Jean are waiting for Cécile and Denis at the entrance to the pyramid in the courtyard of the Louvre, in order to set out together in search of the "last word in cooking" enigmatically mentioned in The Quintessential Art.

HÉLÈNE   There you are, finally! (*Aside, to Cécile, with an air of complicity*) Jean came by my place to get me.

DENIS   Have you had a chance to figure out where we are supposed to go inside?

HÉLÈNE   The book says to go look at a picture by Louis Boilly, a painter of the eighteenth—wait, here are his dates: 1761–1845. The painting is called *Le Gourmand*. A friend of mine is a conservator here—I asked him where to find it. Follow me. Ah, that's it right there.

CÉCILE   But—it's Brillat-Savarin!

HÉLÈNE   Yes, you're right. The book has a short biographical entry, with this comment: *"Let us be clear: the beautiful in cooking is not what is beautiful to look at, but what is good. The visual beauty of a dish is only a very small component of what is beautiful to eat, which is to say of the good."*

DENIS   Precisely what we were saying a while ago.

JEAN   It's right—

DENIS   What's right?

JEAN   The book.

DENIS (*abruptly*)   Well, I'm not going to allow myself to be strung along any longer. We've been too quick to agree with what this book says, because it confirms our ideas about culinary art—forgetting that we don't know where the book comes from, who wrote it, or anything else. And yet it schedules appointments for us—

JEAN   But it's right about the influence of sight. A friend of mine who works in Bordeaux experimented recently with coloring white Bordeaux wines: experienced tasters, all of them young wine professionals, unanimously described wine that hadn't been colored using words for white objects, and wine that had been colored red using words for red objects—

lilac, banana, tobacco, and so on in the first case; caramel, pepper, red fruits, black fruits, and so on in the second. And yet the experimenters had verified, through a series of prior tests using dark glasses, that the red coloring had no influence on the perceived flavor of the wine.

What's more, my friend and his colleagues analyzed thousands of tasting notes and found that red wines are unfailingly described with words for dark objects, and white wines with words for clear objects. The world of oenology is still reeling from this discovery!

CÉCILE   Every cook knows that visual appearance is important, and that color influences taste. Spinach extract has long been used to color mayonnaise, for example. I once amused myself by making fruit pastries with beets: everyone thought they were made with black currants! To say nothing of mayonnaise colored with saffron. one hardly notices the saffron, but the perception of the flavor changes completely, because the color changes.

DENIS   All this proves that visual perception is an important component of flavor, but it doesn't change the fact that what is beautiful to look at is not the same as what is beautiful to eat, which is to say the good. And what is the good?

JEAN   Curnonsky answered the question a few decades ago: "Things are good when they taste like what they are."

HÉLÈNE   Jean, did you read that over my shoulder?

JEAN   Excuse me?

HÉLÈNE   How did you know that the book mentioned Curnonsky?

JEAN   I didn't.

HÉLÈNE   Another coincidence! It says here:

> Curnonsky: Maurice Edmond Saillant, born in Angers in 1872, died
> in Paris in 1956. Writer, journalist, and gastronome, he adopted the

pseudonym Curnonsky when the humorist Alphonse Allais suggested that Saillant take over writing his column "La Vie drôle." Franco-Russian friendship was the fashion of the day: "Why not-sky?" asked Allais. From the pig-Latin for "why not"—cur non—Saillant came up with the name Curnonsky. Saillant made his living as a ghostwriter for Colette's husband, Henri de Jouvenel (who wrote under the pen-name Willy), and many other literary figures. Over a period of seven years, beginning in 1921, together with Marcel Rouff, he examined the regional cuisine of France in a series of twenty-eight pamphlets that were later collected under the title La France gastronomique: Guide des merveilles culinaires et des bonnes auberges françaises. *These gastronomic tours (or "gastronomades") of the country made him famous. In 1927, Curnonsky was voted "Prince of Gastro-nomes" in a poll conducted by the newspaper* Paris-Soir. *"Things are good," he maintained, "when they taste like what they are."*

Just take a look at this and see if I'm lying.

JEAN   I swear, I didn't read this passage. I was merely quoting a well-known phrase.

CÉCILE   In any case, this is a misguided notion. Here we are standing before two canvases, both of which depict Mary and the infant Jesus. The fact that they are competently executed representations isn't enough to make them beautiful. They are beautiful because both artists have given a personal, artistic interpretation of a familiar theme.

In cooking, if we were to follow Curnonsky, all roast chickens would be roast chickens and nothing more—there would be only one sort of good. I believe, to the contrary, that works have value, in my profession as in painting, in proportion to the care that has been lavished upon them, to the personal touch of the artist. Two cooks will make very different roast chickens because they have different sensibilities. The choice of the chicken is not insignificant, of course, but the main thing is the way of roasting it, the ingredients that the cook chooses to add—

JEAN   This is an aesthetic choice—

HÉLÈNE   By "aesthetic" do you mean that the ingredients are what make a roast chicken beautiful?

JEAN   No, I'm talking about a culinary aesthetic, an aesthetic of the good—not of what is beautiful to look at. Take, for example, statues of spun sugar or pulled sugar, or ice carvings. Some of them are beautiful to look at, but you can't eat them! This is sculpture, not cooking.

DENIS   I agree with you. Curnonsky's opinion neglects the work of the cook: the taste of a green bean will depend on the person who cooks it. And besides, it would be very surprising indeed if cooks were to refrain from cooking the green bean—but this would be the only possibility if it is to have the flavor of a green bean, for the flavor changes with cooking. In fact, simply cutting vegetables releases enzymes that slightly alter the flavor to begin with.

HÉLÈNE   All that brings us back to the question of culinary art.

JEAN   The question is settled, since we all agree that it exists!

HÉLÈNE   No, it's not settled. If it were, we'd have an aesthetic theory of cooking. There are any number of such theories for music, literature, and painting, but not for cooking—as if one can't speak of what one eats, out of a sort of reverence for the thing that is eaten. A superstitious vestige of the famines of the past, perhaps?

CÉCILE   You mean that we should speak of periods and schools and styles in cooking, just as in—

HÉLÈNE   Of course! We know that spices were important in the Middle Ages. We know that in the sixteenth century, cooking was still conceived as the search for a quasi-medical sort of equilibrium, or balance, between the four Aristotelian elements and the qualities associated with them: air/dry, earth/cold, fire/hot, water/moist. Thus it was thought to be necessary to nourish hot temperaments with cold foods and vice versa. In other words, dishes had to be composed according to dietary rules of equilibrium governing hot and cold foods on the one hand, and dry and moist foods on the other. This is why still today, at the beginning of a meal, one eats melon (a cold food) with black pepper (a hot food). Nonetheless, so long as cooking was a matter of repetition—

DENIS   Prudent repetition, mind you, since one wished to avoid chemically dangerous experiments.

HÉLÈNE   Yes, but so long as familiar routines were repeated, with familiar ingredients, cooks couldn't compose freely. A little as though people thought that it was dangerous for musicians to play certain notes, or that painters risked blindness in seeing particular scenes or particular combinations of color. The effect was to retard the development of culinary art!

DENIS   And as a result cooking was left with a series of popular dishes, suitable for small children, a bit like the story of Little Red Riding Hood or the song "Frère Jacques." Steak and French fries has a certain infantile charm, but it's not on the same level with an opera by Mozart or a concerto by Bach.

CÉCILE   That's going too far! There are lots of other dishes besides steak and French fries! I remember once visiting Pierre Gagnaire's kitchen and seeing a piece of gelatinous stock in a dish, half of it dark and the other half white. I asked Pierre what he was going to do with it. His idea was to put a translucent green cylinder on top of the jelly—a green apple tuile, as I recall, filled with some sort of crabmeat preparation. Now, if your theory were correct, the story told by this dish would have been centered on the crabmeat, since there was more crabmeat than anything else on the plate. But not at all! Pierre had built everything around a button mushroom, which appeared in the form of a rosette on top of the crispy green tuile. It was the flavor of the mushroom that was at the heart of the story, not the crabmeat.

The story therefore had a hero—the mushroom—and a supporting cast: the jellied stock, the crabmeat tuile, and a risotto whose recipe is known only to Pierre. The dish unfolded in the mouth like a peacock's tail, blossoming with each bite to create the simultaneous perception of distinct flavors. But these flavors were pastel—not fluorescent, like the ocelli on the peacock's tail. The moment I became aware of the mushroom's presence, I understood the story that was about to be told.

Wouldn't you say, then, that this kind of cooking is abstract?

HÉLÈNE   The dish you've described seems to me modern, but not abstract: one hears the mushroom's gustatory timbre, as it were—just as one recognizes the characteristic sound of a trumpet—instead of perceiving its flavor, which is complex. The legibility of the dish is assured by the recognition of this timbre.

JEAN   Was it good?

CÉCILE   Delicious. Besides—

JEAN   Excuse me for interrupting, but it occurs to me that certain culinary artists play on the emotions evoked by their region. One thinks, for example, of Michel Bras, who serves a dish he calls "Shadow and Light" that tells of his home town of Aubrac, in the Massif Central, with its great clouds chasing across a sunlit sky. Or Olivier Roellinger, in the port town of Cancale, in Brittany, who uses the spices brought back by the sailors of the region to create a picture of its windswept dunes and hills. In a certain sense, the cooking of these chefs is "figurative": it shows what it evokes. Michel Bras depicts shadow and light visually, using monkfish, which is very white, and an elaborate arrangement of very dark olives. But the flavors of this dish evoke shadow and light as well: the monkfish has an almost milky flavor, whereas the flavor of the olives is almost as dark and powerful as its color.

Alongside this figurative cuisine, there is another kind, which we may call abstract—

HÉLÈNE   It really isn't a question of being abstract. When a child sings "Frère Jacques," we smile because we remember the melody from our own childhood. Denis would say that there is a biological reward in belonging to a group that recognizes the melody. By contrast, if I make indistinct cries and noises, which mean nothing to my listeners, they don't consider it music, much less beautiful music. In the same way, if culinary art is a form of communication, it must make itself understood. A chef who simply throws things together wouldn't be understood, and his guests would say that his food isn't any good. This reminds me of a dinner I had in a restaurant called Laurie Raphaël in Quebec City—

JEAN   You know Canada?

HÉLÈNE   I love it, why?

JEAN   Me too. I'm going there next October. If you'd like—

DENIS   And Laurie Raphaël?

HÉLÈNE   Oh yes, the chef there is Daniel Vézina, a very talented cook who insists on using local products. Vézina's cooking isn't traditional, it's modern; but each of his dishes is constructed around an ingredient from Quebec. For example, I had pan-seared foie gras and macaroni with Perron cheddar, fiddlehead ferns, and morels. The foie gras came from a farm called Le Canard Goulu in Saint-Apollinaire; the Perron cheddar is a locally made raw-milk cheese, and so on.[19] Just as *Syrinx,* the famous piece for flute by Debussy, recounts mythological adventures, Vézina's food is an emotional response to the land. It tells a story.

CÉCILE   I agree. The cook doesn't assemble ingredients at random, any more than artists in other domains do. He chooses them with care, because he has something to say, because he has a feeling for how they should go together. For the diner, no less than someone who listens to a story or reads a book, there's a need to understand. A story that's dis-

jointed, that rambles on and strays too far from the usual conventions of storytelling, is incomprehensible and therefore disliked.

HÉLÈNE   That's what I meant by saying that cooking has to be legible.

JEAN   Some may resist the idea that culinary artists must take care to organize their stories properly, in order to achieve a particular purpose. But it's clear that the general construction of a dish matters as much as the details of its presentation. For example, I'm not always sure how to "read"—that is, eat—dishes that consist of several separate elements. Imagine a piece of meat in one part of a very large plate, a vegetable in another, a cream sauce somewhere else. Where does one begin? In cooking, as in music, things can't be presented just any which way; the composer has to organize the notes in a definite sequence. Similarly, a painter doesn't randomly distribute patches of color; he organizes his composition in such a way that the viewer's eye moves across the canvas in accordance with a particular intention. Obviously the eye can follow a different path than the one suggested by the artist, but if he knows what he's doing he has worked out all the possible paths in advance. In a figurative picture, the eye more or less automatically perceives the juxtapositions of the various objects, because we know that above a pair of legs there will be a torso, that at the end of branches there will be leaves, and so on.

CÉCILE   In constructing a dish I always try to keep in mind that cooking isn't what one sees, but what one eats—

DENIS   And that we lack a language for describing the sensations we have when we eat. With regard to flavors, by the way, Curnonsky's claim that things are good when they taste like what they are is a sort of guarantee of legibility: if we taste a roasted chicken when we eat a roasted chicken, we know how to decode the dish, how to interpret it—in this case, as an imitation of nature. But imitating nature can't be the basis of anything more than a very impoverished aesthetic. The cook is simply saying, here's a roasted chicken.

CÉCILE   And where's the style in that?

HÉLÈNE (*looking down at the book*)   Exactly!

CÉCILE   What?

HÉLÈNE   This book is starting to make me superstitious. Just now, at precisely the moment you brought up the question of style, I was reading this quote from the American art historian Meyer Schapiro: *"By style is usually meant the constant form—and sometimes the constant elements, qualities, and expression—in the art of an individual or a group."*[20] And then this: *"In general the description of a style refers to three aspects of art: form elements or motifs, form relationships, and qualities (including an all-over quality which we may call the 'expression.'"*[21] And this: *"Investigation of a style is often a search for hidden correspondences explained by an organizing principle that determines both the character of the parts and the patterning of the whole."*[22]

DENIS   We do seem to be thinking along the same lines, don't we? But perhaps it's not so very surprising—after all, we've been acting on the book's suggestions. It encouraged us to come to the Louvre, so we came to the Louvre. It was inevitable, then, that we should speak of style.

HÉLÈNE   But this isn't the only coincidence: just a few minutes ago Jean was quoting Curnonsky, and the book mentioned him as well. And then there was that strange fellow who pressed the book on me in the first place. And the fact that it isn't really a proper book; it's more like a scrapbook or an album, with remarks on aesthetics interspersed with recipes. Just the same, there's nothing ordinary about it. Why don't we try a little experiment? Let's see what happens if I turn the page and— there we are! Another one of these strange remarks: *"You will find the last word in cooking at Les Eyzies-de-Tayac-Sireuil."*

DENIS   This time it's not next door. Isn't Les Eyzies in the Dordogne?

JEAN   Yes, it's a superb place—and this year's Salon International du Livre Gourmand takes place in Périgueux next week. Would you care to join me?

CÉCILE   There are several famous prehistoric sites nearby. I'm afraid we'll discover only the origins of culinary art at Les Eyzies, not its future.

HÉLÈNE   I'm tempted: the national museum of prehistory is there, and there's also the cave of Font-de-Gaume, the shelters at Cro-Magnon and Laugerie-Haute—

JEAN   We're decided then.

WHEN COLOR FOOLS
THE SENSE OF TASTE

IN THEORY

Because sight is an important sense, it is tempting to suppose that the play of colors in a plate of food is essential, when in reality it is only a minor component of degustation. Indeed, visual perception can be misleading in culinary matters: coloring the filling of a fruit pastry blue, for example, may lead us to believe that it is made with black currants, when it is really made from apple; coloring a white wine red may lead us to detect aromas of red fruits and licorice, when otherwise we would have found notes of lilac, banana, and tobacco. We need to taste further than our eyes can see!

IN PRACTICE

Vadouvan is a spicy onion-based paste made with curry leaves, fenugreek, mustard seeds, and garlic. It's a very fragrant product, but when cooked it has the disadvantage that its color spreads throughout the dish, like cherries in a clafouti. A disagreeable shade of dark brownish red fools the sense of taste.

I first encountered this phenomenon with a line-caught turbot that I roasted whole, and the same problem arose recently with a duck dish: the vadouvan "cooks" the skin and permeates it, flavoring the flesh or meat without, however, imparting any visual beauty.

TURBOT RUBBED WITH VADOUVAN AND ROASTED WHOLE, WITH QUARTERED PEARS AND GREEN CUCUMBER JUICE

Rub the fish with vadouvan, then cook it in butter and finish it in the oven, braising with onions, chives, orange peels, parsley, and a dash of white wine, Vermouth, or Côtes de Jura, a wine that I find goes very well with pears.

The pears must be very ripe, almost overripe. They are cut into quarters, with the skin left on because this is where most of their flavor is. The pear pieces are sautéed in butter with brown sugar and balsamic vinegar. Cook them until they begin to discolor: the flesh should taste sweet and sour and the skin should have a tan color when the dish arrives at the table.

The pears are served with the green peel of a cucumber, which is cut off in strips together with a nice layer of the flesh of the vegetable. These strips are coarsely chopped and macerated with rice vinegar and salt. After maceration, the dice are washed and mixed in with the pears.

Finally, the juices rendered by the fish are strained through a chinois or other such device, together with any encrusted matter that has been scraped from the braising pan, and thickened with a bit of honey. The honey mustn't be cooked, since otherwise it will acquire the flavor of mead.

This recipe owes its effects mainly to the vadouvan, a mixture that is notoriously difficult to handle, but in the right proportions—no more than a very small amount should be used in any case—it gives the turbot a deceptive color without destroying the flavor of the fish. Here, success depends entirely on the subtlety of the combination.

Everything else serves to bring the dish alive: after all, the cook's art above all is a matter of mastering techniques of cooking and seasoning. And, of course, there's always the question of how far can one go without going too far. The bitterness and astringency of the cucumber go very well with the pears because of the cucumber's anise flavor. Together, the pears and cucumber prolong the flavor of the turbot in the mouth, so that first one registers the flavor of the fish, then that of the vadouvan, and finally that of the pear and cucumber. The proportions of these ingredients determine the sequence of flavors, with each one coming at the right moment.

YOUR TURN

If certain ingredients need to be handled with caution, they also invite us to enjoy them in moderation. Look around in your kitchen for ingredients that you normally avoid using and reduce the proportions, having first decided what you want to combine them with.

THE APPEARANCE OF THINGS

IN THEORY

Cooks have played with colors since the Middle Ages: saffron, cochineal, and spinach extract are all classic coloring agents. Does this amount to a kind of cosmetic art? This question is hardly new, since some ancient philosophers held the view that art itself is wholly a form of deception—while admitting that beauty has something of the divine about it.

IN PRACTICE
HADDOCK WITH PARSLEY EXTRACT

Place thin slices of haddock in a baking dish, with spring water and olive oil, and heat them in the oven until they have slightly stiffened. In this way the fish conserves its saltiness while taking on a superb orange, bluish, pearly white color.

Next spoon some parsley juice—which has a powerful, very herbaceous flavor—on to a plate and lay the haddock slices over this intensely green sea to create a dramatic and shimmering contrast of colors. You might also think of adding a few pomegranate seeds and a bit of chopped hard-cooked egg, seasoned with the cooking liquid of the fish.

YOUR TURN

Playing with colors is fun, especially when they're not what we think they are. What's the true color of an egg white? Yellow! And the true color of an egg yolk? Orange—or green, it is said, in the case of hens that eat June bugs in the spring! Deception is less important, of course, than creating new sensations.

A POST-BEBOP RECIPE FOR LOVERS OF TRADITIONAL JAZZ

IN THEORY

Innovation is often controversial: what offends the sensibilities of some is enthusiastically received by others. Behind the apparent incoherence of novel interpretations, in cooking as in music, one often finds the usual rules, only pushed further than we are used to.

IN PRACTICE
DUCK AND RED TUNA

The pairing of these two items may well seem incoherent to many people. But if the cook has done his work well, the result should be pleasing even to lovers of traditional forms of cooking.

You begin by taking a nice, fat duck and cutting the breast fillets into thin slices, which are then marinated in pear brandy with melted butter drizzled over the meat (the butter rapidly congeals, covering the duck during the marinade phase).

Next, heat in a pan the juices left over after slicing the duck and cook the marinated breast fillets in them. Once the butter has melted and the meat has firmed up a bit, remove the slices and cut them into smaller pieces. In the meantime, cut the raw tuna into large cubes and coat them with a sugar syrup that has been caramelized and then "uncooked" with soy sauce.

Now put the duck pieces in shallow bowls that have been warmed in the oven, and then the cubes of tuna on top. Reheat the reserved cooking juices of the duck until the liquid comes to a boil, and then season it with salt, pepper, and lemon juice; finally, stir in compound chocolate

(couverture, with at least 36 percent cocoa butter) and fresh butter in order to create a lovely, emulsified sauce—silky, long in the mouth, with a
pronounced flavor—that is added to the dish just before serving.

One ends up, then, with the uncooked fatty flesh of the tuna, the cooked
meat of the duck, and the sauce, which coats both of them. It's a complicated dish, which some people don't like because they don't find enough
in it that is familiar. They'll have to travel a bit further along this road
that goes from the classic to the new, but the cook can make the journey
easier for them by lavishing great care on the technical aspects of the
dish. The caramel coating of the tuna is crucial, no less than the serving
bowls themselves, which must be perfectly adapted to the story being
told by the dish. I omit the obvious technical details: the quantity of duck
juices, for example, must be measured as exactly as possible, for if the
sauce is to accommodate the contrasting textures of the tuna and the
duck, there must be enough to cover both of them.

YOUR TURN

It's not easy for recreational cooks to compose freely, but it's worth making the effort. Think of the formal rules that usually guide you in your
cooking, and then eliminate some of them in order to derive a new set
of rules with which you can exercise your imagination.

PART TWO

CLASSICAL IDEAS OF BEAUTY

SIX

THE ORIGIN OF BEAUTY

Art is inseparable from the problem of constraints. The prehistoric artist had to contend with the irregular surface of stone walls; the modern artist has made the handling of perspective easier by painting on flat canvases. Victor Hugo was a master of the alexandrine; later poets freed themselves from the impediments of the twelve-syllable line while adopting other metric rules. Art no longer has the virtue ascribed to it in prehistoric times: no one today believes that capturing the image of an object or creature confers a physical power over the thing represented.

TRANSPOSITIONS

Back from Les Eyzies, Jean telephones Denis.

JEAN   Hello, Denis? So, you and Cécile finally decided not to make the trip?

DENIS   We really should have come along with you and Hélène. It's been nothing but trouble here.

JEAN   You're spoiled for bad luck! First, the robbery—

DENIS   And then, while you were gone, some guy ran a red light and rammed into us. The car's a wreck, I've got a slipped disk and have to wear a neck brace, and Cécile's right arm and leg are badly bruised.

JEAN   Oh my!

DENIS   And that's not all. Cécile's depressed: she says she can't do any-thing right in the kitchen anymore, that everything she makes turns out badly—all her measures are wrong, everything is undercooked or over-cooked, seasoned too much or not enough—

JEAN   She'll get over it—we all go through periods like that.

DENIS   That's what I told her, but, believe me, it didn't help matters one little bit! Her cooks don't understand what's going on. And since she's frustrated, she's become rather short-tempered. She doesn't feel she's in control of her own kitchen anymore. The cooking is losing its style—its legibility, if you like, to use Hélène's expression. How did it go with Hélène, by the way?

JEAN   Don't even mention her name. Here I was counting on our hav-ing some time alone together, and she brings a girlfriend along.

DENIS   A girlfriend?

JEAN   Yeah, a foolish woman who talked only about prehistoric cave painting and population migrations—she doesn't even like to eat. Ruined my trip *and* my meals.

DENIS   And the museum of prehistory, how was that?

JEAN   Rather a surprise, actually. First, Hélène lost her book—

DENIS   Her book?

JEAN   The one on cooking as the "quintessential" art. She'd laid it aside, next to us, in the museum cafeteria, and then it disappeared. Stolen.

DENIS   Who would have wanted a worthless old book like that?

JEAN   Beats me. Afterward I visited the museum alone.

DENIS   Alone? What about Hélène and her friend?

JEAN   Her friend dragged her off to meet some conservator she knew, so I was left to go around the museum by myself. I couldn't stay long because I had to go to the Salon International du Livre Gourmand. It's about a twenty-five mile drive to Périgueux, along a winding road, and I had to be there in time to meet some honey producers.

DENIS   So Les Eyzies was a waste of time?

JEAN   As far as being alone with Hélène is concerned, yes, a complete waste—which is too bad, because she's really pretty. But as far as the question of culinary art is concerned, not at all. Les Eyzies is a very interesting place if you're trying to transpose the ideas of the other arts to cooking—my new hobby!

The point of primitive representation, you see, was to act upon the world: cavemen and shamans depicted objects of the external world over which they wished to exert control; they painted bison so that hunting would be successful, predators in order to be protected against them, and so on.

DENIS   And how do you transpose that to cooking? Not even the most superstitious person today would entertain such an idea. Only a chef who's completely loony could imagine that making a certain dish would change the world around him.

JEAN   Well, what about "neoshamanism"—making believe that cooking has such an influence?

DENIS   Why would anyone bother?

JEAN   Okay, shamanism is a dead end—but still there are aspects of cave painting that could be revived. For example, the graffiti one sees on buildings today are a sort of modern avatar, and there are painters who are now going back to painting on unprepared surfaces, not unlike the rock walls of caves.

DENIS   What do you mean?

JEAN   At the museum in Les Eyzies, the guide mentioned one of your favorite authors, the American evolutionary theorist Stephen Jay Gould, who said that art arises from constraints: the essence of every picture is the frame that delimits it. He also quoted Meyer Schapiro: "The student of prehistoric art knows that the regular field"—he was talking about the flat surface of the picture—"is an advanced artifact presupposing a long development of art."[23] It took a long while to go from paintings on the unprepared ground of stone walls to paintings on a canvas stretched over a frame.

The same thing is true of cooking: Cro-Magnon man didn't eat on plates. Even in the Middle Ages, solid foods were served on trenchers—large slices of bread—and one ate the whole thing.

DENIS   You mean that all cooking goes back to a slice of bread and butter—that the sandwich and hamburger are prehistoric? But what about bowls? They're very ancient.

JEAN   They are, yes—but the plate we know today, with its raised rim, is rather recent. The guide was very interesting. A funny sort of guy, tall, who knew a great deal about both prehistory and ancient art. He pointed out that in classical antiquity the status of a work of art was ambiguous. On the one hand, it was held to be inferior to nature, because it did nothing more than imitate—rather like Curnonsky said cooking should do. At the same time, art was superior to nature because, by erasing the defects of natural productions, it produced a new image of beauty.[24] I'd forgotten the story of the Greek painter Zeuxis, who was said to have painted grapes so realistically that even the birds were fooled. In order to represent Helen of Troy, Zeuxis took as his models the five most beautiful maidens of the city of Croton, in Sicily, selecting the most beautiful aspect of each.[25] What would be the culinary analogue for this?

DENIS   Hmmm. Ah, I know. When Cécile cooks a chicken, she prepares it in such a way that you really smell the chicken; otherwise, she says, you don't fully appreciate the flavor. Yes, that's it. On the one hand, there's the roast chicken that everyone makes, which is akin to the ordinary representation of a model by simply reproducing her features—à la Curnonsky. And then there's the roast chicken that certain cooks are able to make by selecting from the facts of nature those that will make the young girl appear more beautiful than all other young girls—a roast chicken that's more flavorful than all other roast chickens.

JEAN   Oh yes, I almost forgot, something bizarre happened. You know, the guide—

DENIS   What about the guide?

JEAN   He gave the book back to me at the end of the tour—the book that had been stolen. He took me aside, and said: "You've been warned. Don't leave it lying around, and don't start fooling around with numbers." And then he left.

DENIS   Warned against what?

JEAN   That's what I wondered later. But at the time I was so taken aback that I let him leave without questioning him further, and afterward I wasn't able to find him in the crowd.

WHEN THE FLAVOR CHANGES
WITH THE COOKING OR THE CUT

IN THEORY

As we have seen, the notion of a uniform, invariable ingredient is a fantasy. No two strawberries are alike—it's the way they are cooked that matters. One of the major difficulties of the culinary art is that cooks must take into account the variability of their ingredients. Imagine the plight of a musician whose instrument doesn't give the same note each time it is played. This is why cooking students are instructed to continually taste the dishes they are preparing. This is not only a matter of correcting the seasoning, of adding more or less salt—above all the cook must check to be sure that the sensation produced agrees with the original conception.

There are any number of possibilities to be explored. Let's begin by considering the effects of cutting meat, seafood, and vegetables in different ways.

IN PRACTICE

The idea that flavor changes with the manner of cooking or the cut is hardly new. It is well known that meats, for example, have a different flavor depending on whether they are cut with or against the grain. Think of a leg of lamb: it may be cut parallel to the bone, yielding slices that range from well done to rare; or, more intelligently, perpendicular to the bone, which allows the diner to travel through all the various degrees of doneness, as it were, from the crispy brown crust on the outside to meat that becomes progressively more tender the closer it is to the bone.

The same is true for vegetables. One of the clearest cases is that of Belgian endive braised whole and then cut up into thin slices: the result will differ considerably depending on whether one slices it lengthwise or crosswise.

In the first of the two recipes here, it is the size of the radish that is of crucial importance.

ESPARDEIGNES AND *PISTES* WITH SLICED CELERY AND RADISH

This recipe is based on two rather unusual kinds of mollusks. *Espardeignes,* a species of sea cucumber (*Stichopus regalis*), are found off the coast of Provence in France and Catalonia in Spain. The sexual organs of this creature, small, soft, rectangular in shape, look a bit like the beach shoes known as espadrilles, and their texture is similar to that of rock lobster or scallops. Pan-frying gives them a somewhat rubbery (though not firm) texture, with a flavor that is long in the mouth.

Pistes are small squid, similar to sea cucumbers, but not quite so rugged-looking; they have a rubbery texture as well, but smoother, more like a marshmallow. You sauté them in clarified butter, along with the organs of the *espardeignes,* and deglaze the encrusted juices with the liquid reserved after opening their shells (the raw mollusks are also served separately, on toasted bread).

Finally, a piece of chilled butter is whisked into the gelatinous liquid obtained by deglazing, to create a reassuringly smooth, silky sauce.

In the meantime you peel the celery stalks, removing the fibrous outer coat, and thinly slice them. The radishes are cut crosswise into thin slices, which are then combined with the celery slices. Pouring the warm emulsified sauce over them changes their flavor, through a sort of instantaneous cooking.

This dish is very difficult to pull off. The sliced radishes and celery stalks must be cooked, but only for an exceedingly brief time, so that the texture of the slices is not altered. Learning to do this requires intuition and practice—it's not something that can really be taught.

Similarly, in cooking the sea cucumbers and the squid, the sauce turns out as it should only if the cook is extremely vigilant: one mustn't use too much of the juices of these mollusks, because they have to be emulsified in the end, as I say, by adding some fat along with a little fruit juice or alcohol.

WARM SLICED HARD SAUSAGE WITH *SARASSON*

When we were little, my father used to treat us to a simple dish made with a very lean, hard (salami-style) sausage that had been aged in ash. He poached it over low heat for several hours, then cut it obliquely into thick slices that were served with *sarasson,* a kind of cream cheese typical of Auvergne that is seasoned with chives and a dash of vinegar.

In this case, I propose serving a more traditional, fattier sausage, cut into thin slices. Some of these slices are heated to make them slightly more firm. You could also cut the two types of sausage (fatty and lean) into a small dice, mixing and flavoring them with a very astringent juice extracted from watercress. Along with nice, thick slices of toasted bread, the *sarasson* serves to tie them together.

YOUR TURN

The preceding recipes have by no means exhausted the possibilities of serving different cuts of a particular item—whether meat, fish, vegetable, or fruit—together. One might imagine, for example, carving half of a leg of lamb parallel to the bone, and the other half perpendicular to the bone; and serving a slice of uniformly cooked meat together with one displaying all the gradations from roasted brown to rare. Or serving round slices of tomato mixed with diced tomato, and so on. Any other ideas?

SEVEN

BEAUTY BY NUMBERS

Number has been an enduring source of fascination for centuries. The ancient Greek belief, in particular, that numbers govern the world led to the invention of the musical scale. In cooking, numbers can guide the artist as well—but let us not be so naive as to suppose that today, any more than in ancient times, art can be had so cheaply!

PYTHAGORAS IN THE KITCHEN

Cécile and Hélène are standing at the counter of a café across from the Sorbonne. Outside it's pouring rain.

HÉLÈNE   The weekend was a complete failure. Jean's a fool. I invited Sylvie to come with us down to Les Eyzies, and once we got there he paid no attention to us. He said he had some meetings in Périgueux and didn't have time. What's more, my book was stolen.

CÉCILE   I know, Denis told me. But apparently Jean says that you and Sylvie went off to see a conservator without giving a thought to him.

HÉLÈNE   We left him alone for all of five minutes! You can't trust what this guy says. And he's continually complaining. Fortunately the book was recovered by a guide, who said something strange when he gave it back. He seemed to be some sort of visionary, to judge from Jean's description of him. He told Jean that we'd been warned, and that we mustn't concern ourselves with numbers—as though he knew that I was going to give this lecture today, on the Pythagorean school and numbers in relation to beauty!

CÉCILE   This is a subject that very much interests me, because there's a certain tradition in cooking that insists upon balance, harmonious construction—

HÉLÈNE (*looking at her watch*)   Oh, we've got to be on our way. Are you ready? My students will be getting restless.
Later, at the Sorbonne, Hélène is finishing her lecture.

HÉLÈNE   Finally, there is this engraving of Pythagoras from the eighteenth century—a latter-day impression of what he looked like, since no contemporary image has come down to us. Born on Samos about 570 B.C.E., Pythagoras died around 480 in Metapontum. A mathematician and philosopher, he founded a mystical school of mathematics that bears his name. His life is shrouded in legend, and his teaching, which seems to have been exclusively oral, was transmitted by rival groups of followers, some of whom attached great importance to secrecy.

I suppose that everyone remembers the Pythagorean theorem? No? Well, it's not difficult. Consider the following image of a square that contains another, smaller square as well as four identical right triangles around the inside square. Let's call the lengths of the three sides of one of these triangles *a, b, c,* respectively.

Look at the top side of the large black square. Its side is equal to $a + b$, since you have the length a of the long side of the triangle at the upper left, and the length b of the short side of the same triangle, which is equal to the short segment on the upper right of the large square (as you can see by rotating it clockwise by 90 degrees).

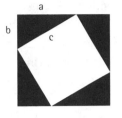

The area of this large square is therefore equal to $a + b$ multiplied by $a + b$, which is to say $a \times a$ plus $b \times b$ plus two times $a \times b$. Is there anyone who doesn't see this? Look at this other figure.

Here you see the square $a \times a$ at the upper left, and the square $b \times b$ at the lower right. This leaves two rectangles, each of which has one side equal to a and the other equal to b, or an area equal to $a \times b$.

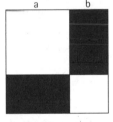

All right, now let's go back to the first figure. Here you see that the area of the large square is equal to $a + b$ times $a + b$. This area can be decomposed into four right triangles plus a square, each of whose sides is equal to c, which is the hypotenuse of each of the right triangles. The area of this smaller square is equal to $c \times c$. And the large square whose area is $a + b$ multiplied by $a + b$ is equal to $c \times c$ plus four times the area of each right triangle, or simply two times a rectangle with sides a and b. Combining these two demonstrations, we obtain the result that $a^2 + b^2$ is equal to c^2. This is the Pythagorean theorem.

Naturally, we have no way of knowing whether this is how Pythagoras actually made his discovery. What mainly interests us today, in any case, is the fact that Pythagoras and his disciples, the Pythagoreans, thought that the world was constructed on the basis of number. For example, suppose that plucking an open guitar string gives a pitch note of C. If you reduce the length of the string by half and pluck it in open position you will still get a C, only it will be one octave higher. What the Pythagoreans observed was that strings that were shortened in a simple ratio, such as 1/2 or 2/3, produced notes that seemed to go together harmoniously with the note played by the string in its full length. Thus a C harmonizes with another C as well as with any G. It is from the Pythagoreans that we inherited the pitch notes of the diatonic scale, with a few minor modifications.

The Pythagoreans believed that this concept of harmony was the key to the world, which numbers explained. This is undoubtedly why the discovery of numbers that could not be expressed as simple fractions gave rise to a philosophical crisis. Take, for example, the square root of 2—that is, the number which, multiplied by itself, yields 2. It is approximately 1.414213562 . . . , with an infinity of decimals that never repeat themselves, unlike simple fractions. This is what is called an irrational number, because the rational numbers—so called because they were thought to satisfy reason—are fractions whose decimal expansion is periodic: for example, 24 divided by 7 gives 3.428571428571428571 . . . You see the repetition?

The fact that the square root of 2 isn't a simple fraction was a philosophical catastrophe: how could one admit the possibility that the length of the diagonal of a simple square might not be what was then considered a number? The mystery of irrational numbers came to form a body of occult, or hidden, knowledge whose revelation carried with it the risk of death.

The idea that the world is constructed in accordance with number influenced artists and philosophers alike, from ancient times up until the Renaissance and beyond. The Greek sculptor and architect Polyclitus, born in either Sicyon or Argos in the fifth century B.C.E., developed the notion of a canon—a set of rules for determining the ideal proportions of the human body. In holding that numbers are at the heart of the idea of aesthetic perfection, Polyclitus helped to lay the basis for Greek classicism: "Beauty comes about, little by little, through many numbers."[26]

The treatise *De architectura,* composed in the first century of the common era by the Roman architect Vitruvius, nourished European classicism from the fifteenth century onward, through both manuscript and printed copies and edited versions. Vitruvius upheld the ideal of symmetry, which he defined as the "appropriate harmony arising out of the details of the work itself; the correspondence of each given detail among the separate details to the form of the design as a whole."[27] This is a very Pythagorean idea: once again, correspondence and harmony are interpreted in terms of number.

With the Greek physician Galen, who was born in Pergamum in 129 C.E. and who died in either Rome or Pergamum near the turn of the third century, a whole medical tradition that sought balance in numbers—sorry, our time is up. We'll stop here, thank you. Until next week then.

Leaving after the students, Cécile and Hélène are followed by the proctor, who closes the lecture hall. They pass through the main gate of the Sorbonne and continue talking. The rain has stopped.

CÉCILE   That was marvelous, the end of your lecture on the Pythagoreans. Do you think it would be possible to use numbers to compose dishes?

HÉLÈNE   You mean according to numerical sequences: one portion of one ingredient, two of another, three of a third, and so on? Or with quantities that would stand in particular relations to one another?

CÉCILE   Why not? After all, the chef Émile Jung, at Le Crocodile in Strasbourg, uses a principle of multiplication in organizing his compositions: one part violence, three parts strength, nine parts sweetness. Or one might use the prime numbers: 2, 3, 5, 7, 11 . . .

HÉLÈNE   But would that help you come up with something good?

CÉCILE   I don't know—at the moment I'm ready to give anything a try. Ever since our conversation about tradition, I find I can't go on doing the same old thing any longer—but at the same time I seem to have lost my creativity, my knack for invention. I'm a bit lost just now. And this business about the last word in cooking hasn't helped. I don't even know how something should taste any more, or how to combine things in the right way, or what the exact seasoning should be—hey, watch out!

Two motorcyclists jump the curb onto the sidewalk.

HÉLÈNE   Those guys are crazy! The first one came within an inch of hitting us!

CÉCILE   And the second one tried to grab your bag!

HÉLÈNE   Why? I mean, there's nothing in it anyone would want—

CÉCILE   Except perhaps the book that was stolen and recovered—did Jean give it back to you? Strange things have been happening ever since that book fell into your hands.

HÉLÈNE   Since it was placed in my hands, you mean. (*She looks inside her bag.*) No, it's still there. And what a strange little book it is. Wait a minute—this slip of paper wasn't there when it was taken from me at Les Eyzies! There's something written on it: *"The last word in cooking is found at the Musée Camondo."* Another mysterious rendezvous!

CÉCILE   I know this museum—it's in a magnificent mansion that looks out onto the Parc Monceau. The kitchens are extraordinary, but I don't see why—

HÉLÈNE   Listen, this time it's your turn to show me around. Okay?

CÉCILE   Denis has to come along—I promised him I'd take him there one day. Besides, I've been uneasy since the break-in at our apartment. How about three o'clock Tuesday afternoon?

PLAYING WITH NUMBERS

IN THEORY

Let's forget for the moment that numbers and flavor belong to completely separate realms—after all, no one can measure flavor. Let's pretend that numbers do in fact rule the world, by means of a sort of secret harmony that can be revealed in the kitchen, only not on pain of death.

IN PRACTICE

THE THREE DISKS OF SPRING

Here I propose to use three different disk-shaped jellies. Why three? I find odd numbers more elegant, less direct, somehow more conclusive—at least until one gets to five.

Under the first disk I put a mound of duck; under the second, some mango chutney; under the third, small raw shrimp. Everything is arranged on the same plate.

The combination of duck and shrimp may seem a pointless bit of affectation. But that's because you're thinking of ordinary shrimp. In this recipe I use tiny, very fatty blue shrimp, whose meaty flavor reminds me of the flavor of a fatty duck.

As for the jellies, you might consider making all of them shades of red: the first using black currants, say, the second red currants, and the third red cabbage. But one could also imagine making one jelly with red beets, another with carrots, and a third with red sweet peppers.

YOUR TURN

This recipe is an invitation to experiment with the cooked elements of a dish. Try arranging two, three, four, or five elements. Where would you put them on the plate? Do you find a certain arrangement is more appropriate for two elements? For three or four? Does symmetry appeal to you? Asymmetry?

EIGHT

THE IDEA OF FLAVOR

The ancient Greeks regarded art with a certain ambivalence. For Plato, there was something reprehensible about the notion of imitating nature: art was possible only if habit and routine were excluded. Artistic value was reserved for works that revealed truth, which is to say the good. Over the intervening centuries our thinking about beauty in music, literature, sculpture, and painting has evolved—but hardly at all in cooking.

THE IMITATION OF NATURE

Coming out of the Musée Camondo, Denis gives a kiss to Hélène, who then departs.

CÉCILE   You've done nothing but talk to Hélène since the moment we got here!

DENIS   What do you mean?

CÉCILE   You haven't said a word to me; you've been with her the whole time. You asked her how she was feeling—

DENIS   But she's been sick, come on!

CÉCILE   You see, there you go again. You leave early every morning, I hardly ever see you anymore—

DENIS   But you come back home late at night! I'm sitting there, at home, waiting for you.

CÉCILE   At home? Last night you were out with Jean and you didn't come by the restaurant.

DENIS   I was with Jean, yes—we went out to get a quick bite to eat.

CÉCILE   And after that?

DENIS   After that? Jean left and I came home. Really, this is a bit much.

CÉCILE   A bit much—who's constantly talking to me about Hélène? About her nearly being run over on the sidewalk coming out of the Sorbonne, about her food poisoning, about whether she has anyone to take care of her—I've had it!

DENIS   Cécile!

CÉCILE   Cécile's going to the restaurant. Alone.
She leaves.

DENIS (*to himself*)   Well, what can you do? I guess I might as well go back inside and visit the rooms we didn't see. The second floor seems worth a look.
He comes to a painting of a man in a white toga with bare feet, stand-

ing before the sea, surrounded by younger men: Plato* and his students at the Academy. Denis reads the accompanying description:

The ancient Greeks opposed art (*téchnē*, or reasoned technical skill) to routine, habitual activity. In this view, art was incompatible with endless repetition: each work had to be a fresh instance of creativity. Nonetheless, the Greek conception of what constituted a work of art betrays a certain ambivalence. Plato, in particular, considered it to be a simulacrum—an imitation (*mimēsis*) of an ideal reality, and therefore something reprehensible.[28] Imitation being the reproduction not of a reality (a form or idea), but of an appearance (*phainómenon*) or image, art is removed not once, but twice from the truth. Plato held furthermore that this kind of mimetic art was to be distinguished from an art that reveals what is hidden, the true (*alétheia*), an idea developed by Aristotle, who identified beauty with the Good, which brings pleasure.[29]

DENIS *(to himself)* "The Good" again—with a capital *G!* Here's what I'll do: I'll copy out this description, add a bit of commentary, some ideas for culinary transpositions and so forth, tie it all up with a pink ribbon, and drop it off at the restaurant. Maybe that will calm Cécile down.

---

*PLATO (Athens, *ca* 429–Athens, 347 B.C.E.): Greek philosopher, born into an aristocratic Athenian family. As a young man, he had hoped for a political career. After studying under Socrates he traveled in Egypt (according to tradition, at least) and Sicily before coming back to Athens, where he founded a school of philosophy, the Academy. On later visits to Sicily he tried unsuccessfully to advise the tyrant Dionysius II.

Plato wrote some thirty philosophical dialogues, in many of which Socrates leads his disciples and his opponents, by means of skillful questioning, to admit the contradictory character of what they claim to know. In this way Plato sought to attain knowledge of Ideas—the Good, the Beautiful, the True, and so on—archetypes to which the intellect has only limited and partial access, forcing it to give way to myth and conjecture.

Let's see, what use could Plato be put to in cooking? Imitation, imitation . . . That's it: Curnonsky's principle that things are good when they taste like what they are had already been formulated by the Greeks, more than two thousand years earlier. On the other hand, the notion that a roast chicken must reveal something hidden isn't one you encounter very often. But why shouldn't a culinary artist attempt such a thing? It means that the flavor of the roast chicken would have to reveal to the person who eats it something that he didn't suspect.

Now, to make this conform to the style of our book on the quintessential art of cooking, I'd have to add a note on Plato. Ah, there's a dictionary of art on the desk: Delacroix, Kandinsky, R—I've gone too far. P, hold on, Proust—and his famous story of the madeleine: "In one of his early works, Marcel Proust wrote that he was reminded of his childhood one day while eating a small *biscotte*. Later, in the first volume of *In Search of Lost Time*, he transformed the rusk into something more evocative, a madeleine." An odd idea. Could any use be made of it in cooking, I wonder?

Right, I was looking for Plato. And now I've gone too far back, unless—Montesquieu,* his view of art, let's see. Now here's an idea that could be applied to cooking: bringing out more aspects of a thing than one had hoped to find. Cécile went through a period like that once: I used to call her "Cécile More"! And then it's also a reply to Plato, who wanted a work of art to reveal something.

Finally, here's Plato. Let me write this down.

---

*CHARLES-LOUIS DE SECONDAT, BARON DE LA BRÈDE ET DE MONTESQUIEU (Bordeaux, 1689–Paris, 1755): French writer noted for his intellectual rigor and liberal sympathies, whose works include the *Persian Letters* (1721) and *On the Spirit of the Laws* (1748). In the *Essay on Taste*, unfinished at his death and published in 1757, he wrote: "Thus one will always be sure of pleasing the mind by causing it to see many things, or more than it had hoped to see."

Okay, that still leaves the question of what a work of culinary art can reveal. And whether such a work really reveals the same thing to everyone. A madeleine, well, that spoke to Proust, because he used to eat madeleines when he was little, but does it speak to anyone else?

Denis goes back downstairs, crosses the hall, and passes in front of the dining room. A sign announces the title of a lecture: "Dietary Behavior in Primates." He quietly takes a seat in the back row.

SPEAKER   ... and if both the human newborn and the young primate give a look of pleasure when they taste a sugar solution, whereas they wince with disgust when they taste something bitter, for example, this is because taste sensations—sweet, bitter, sour, and many others—have an innate meaning for us: we associate them with pleasure or disgust.

From this point of view, the behavior of humans is similar to that of animals. Horses and cows lick salt stones, and we add salt to foods as well, so they won't seem bland.

Research I have carried out in collaboration with primatologists demonstrates that our species reacts to sugar in the same way as our cousins in the monkey family: fruits, many of which are sweet, provide the primate organism with the energy it needs. Bitterness, by contrast, is associated with toxic alkaloids found in certain vegetables, and therefore is often rejected by young animals.

Why do we also like to eat comparatively flavorless foods such as fats and starches? It turns out that we have receptors that detect the presence of fats—a recent discovery, though we don't yet understand how such signals are processed by the brain. And although we don't have receptors for detecting starches, it seems that we learn to recognize their texture through a sort of conditioning: once we notice that we feel full after eating starches for the first time, we then unconsciously associate being full with the detection of starchy matter in foods.

Cooks need to keep in mind this innate sense, which is based on a species reflex. And pastry chefs could make greater use of sugars other than sucrose: glucose, fructose, and lactose are promising candidates. On the other hand, since our organism and, in particular, our sense of taste have been forged by evolution, we ought to find molecular combinations in the diet of primates that our species also recognizes as intrinsically pleasing. For example, if we were one day to discover why certain flavors or odors seem innately agreeable to us, from an evolutionary point of view, we should be able to predict the existence of other such sensations. The same is true for juxtapositions of familiar and unfamiliar flavors. For example, why did Europeans immediately like vanilla, which is not naturally present in their environment, when they first encountered it? There is certainly an evolutionary reason for this that is important to understand. Similarly, the question arises whether certain molecules are present in the mother's womb that are immediately recognized by the fetus.

Closely related to this innate sense is what might be called a physiological sense, by means of which the organism detects compounds that it needs in order to function. This sense operates upon salt, and probably many other molecules as well. For example, fats are necessary for the organism, which uses them to make cell membranes, particularly . . .

Denis looks at his watch, then gets up and walks back through the kitchen, where a large sign above the stove poses the question: "Should reductions boil or only simmer?"

DENIS (*to himself*)   Another odd question. Maybe Cécile can answer it. Now to write up my remarks and drop them off at the restaurant on the way home.

MAKING A FOOD TASTE LIKE WHAT IT IS

IN THEORY

This exercise brings us right to the heart of classical cuisine: the cook must give a food its "proper" taste. Obviously a modern cook must also be capable of reproducing older styles, for virtuosity isn't restricted to a particular period. It isn't entirely honest to invite the cook to play this game, however, for we know in advance that *the* flavor of a food does not exist, and that the only thing that matters is the idea that the cook forms of its flavor. Experience shows that the most talented chefs are able to force the rest of us to reconsider ideas that we had taken for granted.

IN PRACTICE

To make something taste like what it is: this sums up an entire culinary school of thought. The recipe calls for eggplant? Then you have to bring out the flavor of the eggplant, period. If you're making a lamb dish, it must taste like lamb, and so on. This is a narrow-minded approach to cooking: why shouldn't we be able to taste both the eggplant and the lamb; or the lamb, the eggplant, and a thousand other things? It's as though musicians were to limit themselves to making only a C heard when playing a C. Why should musicians shut their ears to the resonances produced among neighboring notes at the moment the C is sounded? By the same token, why not allow a C to be heard too, when other notes are played? These are the two paths that I wish to explore here.

ROYALE OF FRESH ANCHOVIES SERVED WITH A CHILLED *MARINIÈRE* OF NORMANDY OYSTERS, SMALL SCALLOPS, WILD CLAMS, AND PERIWINKLES WITH SORREL-THICKENED MACKEREL JUICES

The *royale* is prepared in the classical manner: a small egg flan made with anchovies and accompanied by oysters from Normandy, which are milder than ones from Brittany, milkier, less imposing, and which do not take up the whole gustatory space of the dish.

In this presentation, the shellfish, opened and served raw, swim in the juices of the mackerel, which are agreeable only if the mackerel is extremely fresh. The fish must be well cleaned, cut into sections, and cooked in olive oil over low heat (taking care not to let it brown); then add some dry white wine, flaming it to burn off the alcohol, and a little water.

Let the fish simmer in the liquid for an hour. Then strain the liquid, without pressing the fish, in order not to "muddy" the flavor. Reduce it a little and thicken it with sorrel, either sorrel leaves or some puréed sorrel.

The point of the exercise is to bring out the flavor of the mackerel. One might quibble over the use of anchovies and make the flan with carrot juice instead, since this has a milder flavor. In any case, it is the mackerel that dominates this composition; as for the other ingredients, one is only playing with textures. The sorrel contributes a note of acidity—a second door that opens behind that of the mackerel.

BUTTON MUSHROOMS ON A TUILE OF CRABMEAT

The button mushroom has a very delicate flavor, weak but subtle. How can we make it really taste like a button mushroom? All the ingredients that are combined with it here act as flavor boosters: their purpose is to help the mushroom to express itself.

Begin by making a jelly with mushrooms that have been heated in a pan without any liquid other than a little lemon juice in order to keep the color nice and white. The water that has been sweated out of the mushrooms during the cooking is reserved, strained, and then combined with gelatin and a little lemon juice. Put it in a shallow dish, where it forms a thin sort of base, not unlike the plinth of a statue.

Now make a tuile with juice squeezed from green apples, a little egg white, flour, and butter. The dough is transferred to a baking sheet and cooked at 180°C (about 350°F). Then, while still hot, it is molded into a half-cylinder (recalling the shape of a roofing tile—hence the name) and left to cool.

Fill this tile with crabmeat that has been cooked in boiling salted water (be careful not to put the cooked crabmeat in the refrigerator, since this would cause it to lose all its gustatory value) and place it on top of the mushroom jelly.

Finally, place mushroom petals on the top of the crabmeat tuile to announce that the dish has been erected in honor of the *champignon de Paris* (as the humble button mushroom is rather grandly known in French). Perhaps one should even say Champignon de Paris!

YOUR TURN

The recipe for *champignon de Paris* with crabmeat adds another degree of difficulty to the initial task: bringing out the flavor of a delicate product.

Select an ingredient having a weak flavor, unlike the truffles and caviars that inflate check totals at flashy restaurants, and try to imagine a way to highlight and intensify its delicate effect. In these exercises of culinary art, there is no set of answers to check your results against when you are done—but feel free to submit your work to the judgment of your family and friends: as the English say, the proof of the pudding is in the eating!

MAKING A FOOD TASTE
LIKE SOMETHING IT'S NOT

IN THEORY

The preceding two recipes amount to imaginative variations on the false
idea that foods must taste like what they are. The next two recipes are
more honest in a way, at least to the extent they are based on a true idea,
that foods can be made to taste like something they are not. The paradoxical thing is that the results are neither better nor worse: despite their basis
in truth, the success of these recipes depends entirely on their execution—
a sign, perhaps, that aesthetic interpretation is often only a sort of justification that runs after the artist without ever managing to catch up. The
essential thing is that we try to combat the misconception that things are
good only when they taste like what they are.

IN PRACTICE

The proof that things are also good when they taste like what they aren't
is provided by these two langoustine tempuras. In both cases there is langoustine and, better still, it is fried in the Japanese manner. Yet the character of each dish is completely different.

I had experimented with tempura myself before actually tasting the
real thing in Japan. There I was disappointed to discover that the frying
produced a rather soft crust; and yet my version, with its crispy crust—a
sharper, cleaner texture—wasn't so far removed from the spirit of the genuine Japanese article.

The langoustine, for its part, is a marvelous creature, but often disappointing because, again, it's a bit soft. Tempura frying firms up the flesh.
Even langoustines that aren't of the highest quality profit from this treat-

ment, which yields a pearly white meat, close to perfection. "C'est de la plume," as Roland Barthes used to say.

I've made langoustine tempuras any number of different ways, with chutneys, crystallized fruits, Nora pepper, and so on; but I quit making them altogether when the vogue for Japanese-Californian fusion arrived.

BRITTANY LANGOUSTINE TEMPURA WITH LEMON THYME WHIPPED BUTTER AND STEWED ZUCCHINI WITH WHITE GRAPES

For the tempura batter you need rice flour and a little water. The main thing is to make sure that the batter has got the right density, so that it thoroughly coats the langoustines without being too heavy. And it has to be well chilled. The langoustines are dipped in the batter and then fried in two stages: the first frying imparts heat to the langoustine; the second serves to adjust the color and crispiness. Remove the pieces from the oil when the crust has become a light brown and the flesh inside is pearly white. The challenge here is to get the color and the texture just right for both the langoustine and the crust.

The whipped butter that accompanies the tempura is obtained by heating some butter in a casserole along with white wine, lemon juice, a little water, the liquid from the langoustines, lemon thyme, and a dash of starch. Once the thyme has yielded its flavor and fragrance, whisk the butter mixture a first time, and then a second time after it has cooled, in order to obtain a smoother consistency. The starch prevents the butter from congealing once it reaches the table.

A very small amount suffices, for the fattiness of the butter compounds that of the frying oil. The white wine, lemon juice, and lemon thyme are added to offset this effect, giving the sauce a lighter, more lively quality. Heating the lemon thyme sharpens the impression of the dish as a whole.

The stewed zucchini stand in contrast to the sauce, lending fullness to the dish and carrying it into another realm. In this case, the zucchini are cut into large dice and then rapidly sautéed in olive oil until they begin to change color. You then add some jam made from dried tomatoes, mixed with a dash of ketchup and an astringent, dark green olive oil, to obtain an emulsion that greatly lengthens the flavor of the zucchini in the mouth.

All in all, the dish is shimmering, pleasing, monumental. The fatty notes produced by the frying may seem a bit off-putting, but, as I say, they are balanced by the other ingredients.

Today, I would be inclined to modify the initial conception by serving the langoustine with something sharper, a sweet-sour sauce, for example. The idea recently occurred to me of combining grapefruit juice, lime, and Nana mint from Morocco, thickening this mixture with gelatin and then, at the last moment, adding chives, wasabi, and rice vinegar. The effect is spicier, livelier, more striking.

BRITTANY LANGOUSTINE TEMPURA
WITH A SPINACH AND APPLE-JUICE FONDUE

This tempura is very different in both style and flavor—further proof that langoustines are good when they don't taste like what they are. Here the tempura is done with very small langoustines, leaving the extremity of the shell on. You dredge them first in corn flour, then in a lightly beaten egg, and pan-fry them in clarified butter.

What makes this tempura entirely different is the fondue that accompanies it. Once again, however, the secondary element is by no means incidental, for the dish could not exist without it. In this case it involves using spinach, which is blanched, then strained and chopped, and finally cooked again with a little chilled butter and reduced apple juice, which coat the spinach. You then form the mixture into a sort of quoit, or disk, using a drum-shaped timbale.

This preparation recalls a simpler one that used to be popular, made by cooking the spinach in water and then sautéing the disks in hazelnut butter. Its effects owe nothing to the salt-sweet contrast of the first tempura recipe. Here it is a question of flavors supporting a combination of textures—the crispy firmness of the langoustine and the silky tenderness of the butter-coated spinach.

Which one of these two recipes gives us the true flavor of langoustine tempura? Neither! There are as many flavors as there are well-constructed recipes. None of them has *the* flavor of langoustine tempura.

As for the langoustine itself, in each case its flavor has been so mixed with that of the other ingredients that it holds its own—nothing more. Even the virtuoso langoustine can take its seat in the orchestra: no ingredient, not even the most prestigious, is entitled to assume a permanent role as a soloist. For one thing, the prestige of a product is not something that is fixed once and for all. Various kinds of trout, for example, are found in such large supply today that their price has fallen and they have become commonplace on restaurant menus. What is more, if every product were a soloist, the cacophony would be overwhelming. This is the inevitable consequence of accepting the false idea that things are good only when they taste like what they are—unless, of course, one is content to go on perpetuating a tradition of rustic simplicity in cooking, for which there is equally little justification.

YOUR TURN

Try devising your own tempura recipe—explaining your reasons for combining certain ingredients rather than others and for presenting the result in one way rather than another. Don't hesitate to commit your ideas to paper.

HOME COOKING VERSUS BANQUET CUISINE

IN THEORY

It is said that an idea is interesting if its opposite is interesting as well. The two recipes that follow are a synthesis of the preceding ones and serve to demonstrate that a theory of culinary aesthetics must be developed further before it can deliver definitive conclusions—whether reactionary, romantic, outdated, imperialist, or what have you—with regard to the question of what is good in cooking.

IN PRACTICE
HOME-STYLE GREEN BEANS

Green beans taste like green beans when they're cooked in boiling salted water to the point that they lose their crunchiness. This is how they're served at home.

Here there is no need to worry about overcooking: the beans' fiber having been broken down, you don't bite into them, you chew them like a kind of juicy baby food. The pure cooked flavor of the beans fills your mouth. Pour a little melted butter, not too hot, over the beans, which themselves shouldn't be served too hot, lest their flavor be killed by the heat.

In this case, as a cultural matter, the origin of the product is important. In France we are used to eating the thick Baraquet bean, not the needle-thin bean that comes from Kenya.

FANCY GREEN BEANS

The green bean served on formal occasions is very thin, the kind we have in France in early summer, cooked just until crunchy, and therefore very green. It may be accompanied with a juice or coulis of various types (vegetable, shellfish, or meat). The important thing is its tone, its crisp greenness. Here the center of interest has shifted in the direction of freshness, which adds another dimension to the flavor.

The crunchiness associated with this style of cooking would be unbearably annoying and pretentious at home, where meals are meant to be nourishing in a calm, comfortable way. Here one touches on an essential aspect of the cook's profession: the need always to seek to strike the right tone, avoiding affectation and arrogance at all cost.

YOUR TURN

Naturally, there are many gradations between home cooking and banquet cuisine: there is cooking for dinner parties or holidays at home, restaurant cooking, country cooking, city cooking, and so on. Can you imagine different recipes for green beans for each of these styles of cooking?

NINE

ARISTOTLE AND SUBTLETY

Aristotle, following Plato, held that art consists in the imitation of nature. In his *Poetics,* however, Aristotle considers in greater detail what constitutes a work of art and lays particular emphasis on the need for coherence. His aesthetics suggest innumerable paths for culinary art to follow, as the other arts have done in their own different ways.

———

AN ART OF THE EXTRAORDINARY

At Hélène's apartment. The place is a mess, books everywhere. The table is covered with open notebooks.

CÉCILE   Hélène! Denis is a dear! Do you know what he did? He went back to the Musée Camondo after we left and wrote down some notes for me about Plato's theory of art.

HÉLÈNE   Can I see?

CÉCILE   Of course.

HÉLÈNE   Oh—but this is really bizarre: this whole description of Plato is also in *The Quintessential Art*. And the final question too!

CÉCILE   You mean that he copied everything from the book?

HÉLÈNE   No, he couldn't have. But look here on page 95, it's the same.

CÉCILE   Amazing!

HÉLÈNE   Yes, it *is* amazing. A lot of amazing things have been happening lately. They all seem to be connected somehow: the fellow who first put the book in my hands, the burglary, the stolen book, the strange encounter with the guide at the museum in Les Eyzies, the two guys on motorcycles—it's almost as though there's someone behind it all. But who?

CÉCILE   This business is getting on my nerves—I can't seem to do anything right in the kitchen anymore. And all these discussions about art—they're very interesting, but they've thrown me completely off balance. I used to cook intuitively. Now, I'm forever trying to adapt aesthetic ideas to my cooking, and it's only making me more and more confused. I'm clinging to technique, which isn't proving to be much help.

HÉLÈNE   You've still got love to hold on to. I mean, you know how much Denis cares about you—and you, you're always trying to make others happy. That's the main thing, isn't it?

CÉCILE   I suppose so—but beyond that, it's a void. These stories Plato tells about the true and the good are all very fine, but it's been two days now that I've been trying to come up with flavors that will "reveal" something, and so far I've got nothing to show for it; or rather, I do—I've got my customers saying, "You really taste the apple" or "You really taste the duck." Which isn't necessarily a compliment. One of my teachers used to say that you should have to search for the flavor of tarragon in a tarragon sauce—it shouldn't be the first thing you notice. Otherwise your cooking lacks subtlety.

HÉLÈNE   What do you mean exactly?

CÉCILE   You know those images that you look at and all you see is a jumble of colored shapes? But then you let your eyes wander for a while, and eventually a three-dimensional image appears. Magic Eye pictures—

HÉLÈNE   Autostereograms, you mean. I love them! At first I had a hard time, but I found a book that tells you how to look at them: there are these black dots above the image that you have to line up, by squinting, and then the three-dimensional image leaps out at you. But what does this have to do with cooking?

CÉCILE   I remember another one of my teachers saying that the flavor should only become apparent after you've thought about it for a while. Take wine, for example. If you're immediately overwhelmed by the smell of banana or sweet pepper, there's no point drinking it—you might as well eat a banana or a pepper. By contrast, if you drink a glass of wine and you smell something delicate, without knowing what it is, you rack your brains trying to identify the sensation. You keep asking yourself, What is it? What could it be? And then all of a sudden it hits you: "Sweet pepper!" The light bulb suddenly goes on upstairs. In cooking, the theory of tarragon sauce operates on the same principle: you have to use just enough tarragon for this moment of illumination to occur—

HÉLÈNE   So that what was hidden suddenly stands revealed?

CÉCILE   That's it! The tarragon serves as a sort of a path. You're a dear. Oh, I'm so pleased—I had the idea in me and I didn't even know it.

HÉLÈNE   This itself is a very Platonic idea: in the dialogues, Socrates questions his listeners in order to show them that their knowledge of certain things—the elementary truths of geometry, for example—is innate, that what seem to be discoveries are things that they knew all along.

CÉCILE   You must excuse me, I've got to run off to the restaurant—finally I have an idea for tonight's menu! The food critic of a major newspaper is coming.

She kisses Hélène and leaves in haste. After walking for about ten minutes, lost in thought, Cécile arrives in front of the dark, modern façade of her restaurant. The door opens as she approaches.

A YOUNG COOK   Chef, this letter was dropped off for you.

CÉCILE   Thank you. Ah, it's from Denis (*who has written at the head of his notes*): "My darling, since you liked the information I gave you about Plato so much I went to the library to do some research on Aristotle. Here's what I've come up with. I couldn't resist adding my own commentary."

Aristotle (Stagira, 384 B.C.E.–Chalcis, 322 B.C.E.). Greek philosopher renowned for his encyclopedic knowledge. A disciple of Plato at the Academy, and later tutor to Alexander the Great, Aristotle founded his own school at Athens, in 335, the Lyceum, also called the Peripatetic School for his habit of teaching while walking.

He was the author of a great many treatises on logic, politics, biology, physics, and metaphysics, among other subjects.

Aristotle was much concerned with aesthetics, which he claimed did not involve the pleasures of hearing, smell, and sight.

This is bound to seem strange to us today. The modern theory of evolution, due to Darwin, holds that the characteristics of living beings are the result of selection: only those creatures that are adapted to their environment survive. If biological evolution has made us capable of taking pleasure from smelling and tasting, this must be because the pleasures

of hearing, smelling, and tasting are indispensable to the survival of the human species. It is hard to see how these faculties could not be related to the appreciation of beauty, which
is itself a product of evolution.

*Regarding the problem of beauty—which is better written here
without the uppercase B, for he disagreed with Plato in the matter of Ideas—Aristotle maintained that the arts "are all, viewed as
a whole, modes of imitation."[30] "It is clear," he says in the Poetics,
"that the general origin of poetry was due to two causes, each of
them part of human nature. Imitation is natural to man from childhood, one of his advantages over the lower animals being this,
that he is the most imitative creature in the world, and learns at
first by imitation. And it is also natural for all to delight in works
of imitation."[31]*

Imitation of what? Nature, according to Aristotle, who got the
idea from Plato; much later it was adopted by our friend
Curnonsky. Perhaps it needs to be elaborated a bit? The
painter imitates nature in depicting mountains, rivers, people,
and so on; but many other things could be imitated as well.
Thus, in cooking, one arrives at tradition, the cult of the land,
and baby food, made from starches and other soft foods.

Imitation: in painting, as we have said, there have been many
pictures of Mary with the infant Jesus, all of which give an
individual interpretation of the theme, sometimes by recre-
ating in their own way earlier pictures of Mary and Jesus. In
cooking, too, many cooks repeat famous dishes from the
past—game pies and flans like *L'Oreiller de la Belle Aurore,
Le Lièvre à la royale façon du sénateur Couteaux,* and so on—
while giving them a novel interpretation. One can recreate,
or imitate, and at the same time create something new.

*Aristotle also pointed out that music is composed of a melody and
a rhythm—instances of what Platonist philosophers call Forms.*

"Forms" needs some explaining. For philosophers, a form is not only the idea of a geometrical shape, such as a square or a circle, particular instances of which we see every day; it may also be the idea of a melody (the movement in a song between high notes and low notes), or a rhythm (a regular *ta ta ta* or, by contrast, the *ta ta ta tum* of Beethoven's Fifth Symphony)— or a flavor: the flavor that comes to mind when you think of asparagus is a form, as is the flavor of a vinaigrette. Individual instances of a form can be modified. Varying the use of peas in a dish, for example, in order to present several different versions of it, is a way of playing with the form (or idea) of "pea."

The poet, Aristotle said, must not only have a general conception of the work he intends to compose; he must also make sure that it hangs together, selecting incidents with a view to telling a coherent story; and he must see to it that everything is plausible and necessary, so that nothing will interfere with the pleasure of the spectator.[32] "There should be nothing improbable among the actual incidents. If it be unavoidable, however, it should be outside the tragedy. . . ."[33]

If Racine and other classical French authors were able to follow these rules, couldn't culinary artists today do the same thing?

Establishing a general idea is simple enough: the cook must construct the dish, which is to say arrange its principal elements, colors, tastes, smells, temperatures, consistencies, and so on. As for coherence, just as a dish would be nutritionally imbalanced if it contained only starches, such as pasta, rice, potatoes, or lentils, so too it would be incoherent if the ingredients were so hard you broke your teeth trying to eat them. Incoherence can arise for any number of reasons—a dish is too salty or too spicy, too heavy or too light, and so on.

With regard to the question of plausibility, Aristotle held that "the poet's function is to describe not the thing that has happened, but a kind of thing that might happen, [that is] what is possible as being probable or necessary."[34]

What inspiration does this idea hold for a modern cook? In literature, the implausible possibility is a coincidence the like of which occurs only very rarely. In the kitchen? Imagine a cook who is sufficiently ingenious to concoct an outsized pea (using individual peas to construct an object having the shape, color, and taste of a pea, but the diameter of a plate—after all, giant peas *could* exist in some world other than ours). The question nonetheless remains: was Aristotle right to criticize such an undertaking? Surely not, for the artist inevitably breaks free of the rules that the philosopher seeks to impose.

As for seeing to it that nothing interferes with the diner's pleasure, I recall once being served a dessert in a glass that was so narrow at its base the spoon couldn't get reach the bottom. That really interfered with my pleasure!

According to Aristotle, poetic language is above all a transgression of the norms of everyday language.

I propose this translation: culinary art is not the same thing as everyday cooking; instead, it is the possibility of constructing dishes and meals that are out of the ordinary. This reminds me of something that Pierre Gagnaire frequently says: "When I'm constructing a dish, I'm setting a scene." Setting a scene means creating a work of art that rescues the diner from the banality of everyday life. Even a humble radish can play a role in the culinary concert of a dish if the artist has scored all the other instruments properly, just as a simple triangle can contribute to a musical work. The question remains: is the analogue of a Greek tragedy a single dish or a meal?

Aristotle insisted upon the distinction between form and content.

What would be the corresponding distinction in cooking? Would beef be the content and roasting the form? This doesn't take us very far. Better, perhaps, to interpret it as a question of form and content in relation to flavor. That would be more interesting.

Aristotle held that "the many are better judges than a single man of music and poetry; for some understand one part, and some another, and among them they understand the whole. There is a similar combination of qualities in good men, who differ from any individual of the many, as the beautiful are said to differ from those who are not beautiful, and works of art from realities, because in them the scattered elements are combined. . . ."[35]

This is Zeuxis's old idea. Can it be applied to cooking?

A work of tragedy involves kátharsis *(purgation): it must create within the spectator powerful and uncomfortable feelings (pity and fear), so that the downfall of the protagonist brings about the cleansing of these emotions by pleasure.*

Hunger replaced by satiety? All cooking accomplishes this result, however, so it can't serve as the basis for a distinction between everyday cooking and culinary art. We'll have to come up with something better than this. Darling, I leave it to you!

A VOICE (*from the kitchen*)   Chef, can you come? Monsieur Pomme has just arrived with his produce!

AN AUTOSTEREOGRAPHIC DISH

IN THEORY

To "suggest" is a subtle way of saying things that please the mind. Naturally there's a risk that a suggestion is too subtle, so that it goes unnoticed, but that is hardly a reason for not trying. What would a culinary autostereogram look like?

IN PRACTICE

I often try to play with culinary analogues of the hidden image that autostereograms suggest: we taste a dish and find we are unable to say exactly what its flavor is—and then suddenly the flavor identifies itself, almost without our knowing it.

The cook can easily create this autostereographic effect with anything that has a licorice flavor: cèpes, nutmeg, cocoa, mint, as well as unusual flavors such as those of mandarin oranges and orange peel.

The autostereographic effect is an old idea of classic French cooking: it used to be said that in order for a tarragon sauce to be successful, you had to search for the flavor of tarragon. This is obviously an inadequate culinary theory, however, as one can see by considering the example of a shortbread cookie made with roasted flour and coated with chocolate.

The cookie itself has a smell of chocolate, and the chocolate coating has a smell of chocolate. At the end of a meal, diners are saturated with flavors—sometimes to the point that they can no longer stand the extremely dense flavor of chocolate. What is wanted is only the merest suggestion of this flavor, which is what a shortbread cookie made with roasted flour gives: once the desire has been suggested, the chocolate covering, which is very thin, is there to satisfy it. Obviously, the shortbread cookie must be constructed in such a way that the chocolate coating is perceived only after the cookie!

Moreover, not all culinary ingredients behave the same way as tarragon. Whereas more than a relatively small amount of this herb (as with lavender, thyme, oregano and the like) becomes oppressive, a considerable amount of mandarin orange must be present in order for its fragrance to be perceived. This is probably a question of the relative concentration of odor and taste molecules, but it may also be a question of perception. For science to decide one day.

SCALLOPS AND FOIE GRAS IN WALNUT OIL

Certainly there are cases where the cook himself is buffeted by waves of flavor: having carefully organized the ingredients of a dish to obtain the flavors that he has in mind, the unexpected occurs. This happened with a dish that I served in December 2004, using walnut oil with scallops and foie gras. Ginger usually does not go well with walnut oil, but in this particular dish it worked very well, because it created a role for itself in the story told by a variety of lettuce known as *sucrine*.

YOUR TURN

We've already tried our hand at bringing out the delicate flavor of products such as button mushrooms. Now let's do the opposite: take products having a strong flavor, such as spices, and try to determine how much to use so that their flavor does not appear right away.

A VERY TRADITIONAL RECIPE

IN THEORY

We all have our own conception of traditional cooking: for some it is a vol-au-vent; for others, a tenderloin of beef larded with strips of bacon. Etymologically, tradition is that which is transmitted. Can ideas and practices from six centuries ago, six years ago, and six days ago be equally well transmitted? How about six minutes ago?

IN PRACTICE
POT-ROASTED VEAL KIDNEYS JEAN VIGNARD, BAKED MACARONI WITH CHEESE, AND WATERCRESS SALAD

The chef I apprenticed under forty years ago was named Jean Vignard. His cooking was very traditional, indeed provincial. This kidney dish in his honor is based on an idea that recalls the very traditional sort of cooking that I learned starting out.

Is the recipe itself traditional? Goethe said that one can never reproduce Greek poetry, but only take inspiration from it in order to create something new, which nonetheless retains some of the flavor of ancient models. Today the old cuisine is lost; to imagine bringing it back is a fantasy. Still, echoes of it persist. Perhaps this is what tradition is, properly understood.

For this recipe the veal kidneys must be very white; once the central nerve has been removed, you roast them in a casserole. Throw out the fat rendered in the course of cooking, add some chilled butter, and deglaze with Port. The kidneys are then sliced and served with baked macaroni and cheese, napped with the reduced Port sauce, and a watercress salad.

The recipe is no good if the kidneys are mediocre. Without kidneys of the highest quality, it's a lot of work (and heart and soul) for nothing.

There's a certain nostalgia in this dish for a slower, less stressful time. Cell phones didn't distract us from the important business of eating; one wasn't ashamed of putting a napkin around one's neck and tucking in to a plate of food.

The macaroni and cheese can be served in a rustic, earthenware baking dish that's been used many times before—and looks it. There's no place for phony elegance here. The loving warmth of the kidneys and macaroni conveys the comforts of tradition, which makes us feel snug and secure. Not the least of the ways cooking can show love is by giving voice to nostalgia.

YOUR TURN

The point of the exercise set here is clear: to search inside yourself for the memory of a very traditional dish, and then to emphasize those aspects that make it old-fashioned. Nonetheless, the execution isn't as easy as it sounds. Carefully examine each element of the dish to make sure you haven't unwittingly modernized it. Some dishes you may wish to avoid. For example, a traditional crème anglaise of the sort Escoffier used to make didn't contain the eight egg yolks per quart of milk that are customary today, but sixteen! No one can eat something this rich any more!

VARIATIONS

IN THEORY

Variations of a certain ingredient—served two ways, three ways, even four ways—are very popular today. The idea of presenting several versions of a dish is hardly new, however. Which raises the question: why it is back in fashion today?

IN PRACTICE

My menus first featured variations of this sort—*"déclinaisons"* I called them—in 1982. It occurred to me that since everyone was eating foie gras, a different approach was called for: a traditional, familiar, acceptable version, but also a more modern version. The current vogue for offering several versions of a dish has made people forget how revolutionary this idea seemed at the time.

DUCK FOIE GRAS TWO WAYS: COLD, POACHED PLAIN, AND SERVED ON A BED OF FRUITS AND NUTS; AND HOT, GLAZED WITH BLACK CURRANT BRANDY AND ENGLISH CHERRIES

In these variations on a theme, which I served more than twenty years ago, the first foie gras was poached in a terrine with no seasoning, allowed to cool, then placed on a bed of apple and quince mixed with some crunchy granola, green apple, walnuts, white grapes, and dried apricots— all of it thickened with a creamy yogurt.

The second foie gras was served hot, glazed with black currant brandy. At the time I was able to get these extraordinary wild cassis berries, hand-picked and marinated in clear fruit brandy. After six months the brandy took on a marvelous flavor, which went perfectly with tart English cherries. Balancing the two required extremely precise control, however, since the delicate sweet-sour flavor of the cherries is lost if it veers too far off in one direction or the other.

Beneath the foie gras I used to put red cabbage that had been stewed for a long time with a bit of fat, some cassis, some grenadine, and some red Syrah wine (whose slight acidity prevents the cabbage from breaking down during cooking). At the time I used to erect the foie gras and cabbage into a scaffolding almost six inches high. My cooks hated this dish because it was almost impossible to keep it from falling apart!

YOUR TURN

Foie gras is an expensive product to experiment with. Try using cheaper ingredients. In the preceding chapter we practiced with green beans. Let's try carrots this time. What variations can you propose?

INCOHERENCE IN THE KITCHEN

IN THEORY

Here we toy with Aristotle's idea that the plausible impossibility should be preferred to the possible implausibility. Nonetheless, incoherence in cooking is a risky proposition, since unrestrained license is apt to lead to inedible dishes! The first task set for the cook is one of the most difficult imaginable: combining whiting and pigeon. The second recipe will make you understand why peas are meant to be small.

IN PRACTICE

I love conger eel, but I've found that most people who dine at my restaurant don't agree, finding it oily and revolting. How, then, can I coax them into sharing my own liking for it? I decided to use conger eel in a dish that can't be ordered separately, only as part of a fixed menu. That way it is something I offer to my guests, not something they request:

my guests place their trust in me, and I can try to make them change their minds.

By now it should be clear that, as far as I'm concerned, the product counts for nothing: the only thing that matters is the effort that the cook puts into setting the scene, in terms of flavor. A while ago I had the idea of making a conger eel sponge cake. An utterly incoherent idea, everyone thought—but in the end it worked! The same goes for certain unusual surf-and-turf combinations: pigeon with scallops, red tuna with duck, the fleshy part of the cuttlefish with beef, whiting with pigeon, and so on. All these apparently incoherent pairings constitute a challenge to the cook's ingenuity.

OVEN-BAKED WHITING AND ROAST PIGEON

Consider, for example, the whiting-pigeon problem. The whiting needs to be cooked beforehand in the oven, with a bit of olive oil and lemon, so that the fish begins to render its juices. Let it cool, then remove the skin and separate the flesh from the bones, arranging the pieces in shallow bowls. Next, roast the pigeon in the classical manner; remove the breast fillets once it has cooled, and cut them into long, thin slices. Then season the cooking juices of the whiting with mustard and horseradish or wasabi, and make an emulsion by whisking in some oil. Finally, I would recommend placing the slices of pigeon on the whiting and the emulsified sauce over the pigeon, together with a brunoise of celery, carrots, and a few red currants.

Mind you, I haven't actually made this dish, but I'm going to try it: I'm fairly sure that this way of attacking the problem will satisfy me—for a day or two.

GIANT PEAS IN A POD

A giant pea? Is it plausible but impossible? Or possible but implausible? From the culinary point of view, at least, it isn't impossible to make: imagine a green sphere, made from a purée of peas thickened with almond powder or bread crumbs, colored a deeper green with parsley extract, and held together by glazing it with a creamy egg yolk—the result of cooking an egg whole in its shell in the oven at 67°C (almost 153°F) for about an hour.

To improve upon this, the incoherence would have to be pushed to its logical extreme by putting this pea along with others in a pod—a fake pod, as giant and fake as the peas themselves. It could be made from a purée of dried peas with flour and egg white, or else by using a green tuile; the stem could be reproduced by means of a suitably sculpted stalk of celery. The pod would be open, and you'd put the giant peas inside.

One might also imagine a dish of peas à la française, only inside out: instead of serving the peas with cubes of bacon, diced onion, and a julienne of lettuce, you could make a giant pea with all these ingredients inside and serve it with a sauce. Done just right, this could be a stunning dish.

And if we've gone this far, why not go even further? Why not a giant pea with mint? Or a giant pea coated with bread crumbs and truffles?

YOUR TURN

Reconciling irreconcilables requires a lot of thought and hard work. To get the hang of it, begin by trying to combine carp and rabbit, and then move on to the two ingredients you most dislike. Keep in mind that nothing obliges you to use large quantities—a little bit of each ingredient is enough. If you're feeling really brave, come up with an idea for a dish that strikes you as a culinary impossibility, and then actually try to make it!

PART THREE

BEAUTY IN THE MIDDLE AGES

TEN

THE PATH TO THE MYSTICAL GOOD

Instinctive cooking or intellectual cuisine? The question is no less pertinent in the case of culinary art than of music or painting, and the answer is obvious: a work must be pleasing, above all, but there can be no
art in making the same choucroute over and over again, any more than
in singing "Frère Jacques" over and over again. Poets and philosophers
in the West who came after Plato and Aristotle pursued this theme, while
distorting their thought. Horace was the first to insist that art must teach
something, that it be didactic. Later, others argued that imitation becomes
enriched by the imagination. With the gradual adoption of a Christian
conception of art, in late antiquity, philosophers came to hold that beauty
must incorporate the idea of God. Thus was born allegory, which systematized the symbolic correspondences between art and Christian ideals,
and gave a human face to abstract ideas and moral notions.

BRINGING FORTH IDEAS FROM MATTER

Denis, at home, has finished working. Papers are scattered all over his desk and on the floor, along with open books. He telephones Jean.

DENIS   Hello, Jean? Did you say you had a friend who's a police inspector?

JEAN   Yes, Jérôme Belmont. An old childhood friend. Why?

DENIS   Because I'm fed up with coincidences that aren't coincidences, and so-called magical influences, thefts, accidents. It all started with that book that Hélène brought back from Geneviève's shop. I don't understand who or what's behind all of this—and, what's more, I don't see what's going to stop these things from happening unless we do something. I asked Geneviève if she knew the person who handed the book to Hélène, but she has no idea.

JEAN   You're imagining things. I know the burglary set your nerves on edge, but—

DENIS   What about the attempted theft outside the Sorbonne, and then Hélène's accident—you think I'm imagining all that?

JEAN   What accident?

DENIS   The day before yesterday, in front of Hélène's apartment. A car crashed into hers and two men got out. Pretending to help her get out of her car, they took her bag and ran off, toward another car that was waiting for them. Frayed nerves?

JEAN   But . . . I didn't know. Is she all right?

DENIS   She wasn't hurt, but she's shaken. The only piece of luck, if you can call it that, is that her wallet was recovered a few streets away. She's gotten everything back, in fact—everything except that book on the quintessential art of cooking. Thieves who don't take your money: you're not going to convince me there isn't something strange going on here.

JEAN   Listen, you mustn't worry. In any case, if this worthless book is what they're interested in, now they've got it, and that will be the end of your troubles.

DENIS   Maybe not! In any case I don't want this business to continue. Can your friend Jérôme help?

JEAN   Let me give him a call. I'll get back to you right away.

One hour later.

JEAN   Hello, Denis? Jérôme isn't there. Away on business for a week. I left a message for him.

DENIS   Thanks. In the meantime I've suggested to Cécile that we go to Burgundy to buy some wine. We'll take my car, get some fresh air, it'll do her good. Oh, by the way, Hélène will be coming with us. Want to come along?

JEAN   No, thanks. I've already volunteered once. Besides, I find all her historical and artistic knowledge a bit irritating. When I'm eating, I want to eat—it really doesn't matter to me which idea governs the arrangement of the dish!

DENIS   You don't really mean that. What about our discussion about art and craft?

JEAN   Look, I simply can't. I've got a ton of things to do this weekend. And, besides, I'm putting on weight. I've got to get some exercise.

DENIS   Well, that's your bad luck. I'll tell you all about it when we get back.

A few days later. Hélène, Denis, and Cécile are visiting the Abbey of Cluny.

HÉLÈNE   I'm so happy you were willing to drive a little further. What a wonderful abbey this is! And just think: the stones we're standing on were here when the monastic movement of spirituality, culture, and art first began to spread throughout Christendom. In the early twelfth century, the Cluniac order numbered more than a thousand monasteries in France and elsewhere in Europe. Just look how beautiful it is!

DENIS   Jean will be sorry he didn't come along.

HÉLÈNE   He didn't want to come? Jean, who's always game for everything? (*A moment's silence*) You can see the hills of the Mâconnais today and—oh, I see the library is open. Will you excuse me for a moment?

CÉCILE   I'll go with you. I need somewhere quiet to write down a few ideas for recipes.

DENIS   Me, too—I've got a paper I'm late writing up . . . My, what a magnificent library!

HÉLÈNE   Everything having to do with the art of the first millennium of the Christian era is here. What treasures! When I stop to think that I was robbed of a miserable little book that's worth nothing—whereas these books are worth a fortune!

DENIS   You know my view: for a few Euros you can buy a paperback edition of Aristotle's *Poetics,* which contains a wealth of intelligence, but you have to spend thousands of times more than that for a car that will last only a few years.

They walk through the stacks, admiring the collection.

CÉCILE   That's odd. What are these loose pages doing here on this shelf? (*She picks them up.*) Remarks on art, it looks like. *"From art proceed the things of which the form is in the soul of the artist."*[36] Aristotle again. Not an easy sentence—especially when my darling hasn't made a detailed analysis of it for me!

HÉLÈNE   It's not unusual to find citations to Aristotle in medieval texts:

he remained the great authority throughout the Middle Ages, and his ideas about beauty continued to be developed.

CÉCILE   Cooks are still searching for what's good today!

DENIS   That gives me an idea. My old friend Jean Largeault, the philosopher, says that he loves bad books because they put him in mind of what he dislikes, which in turn enables him to understand what he likes and why. Perhaps you ought to search instead for the bad in cooking. Yes, I'm perfectly serious: you should ask yourself what makes a dish bad.

CÉCILE   A dish is bad when you don't understand it. Sometimes I make a dish that satisfies me, but my customers can't make any sense of it. They don't know how to talk about it; they can't make up their minds whether it's good or bad. Now that I think about it, though, maybe it's not a question of understanding. My customers don't actually say "I don't like it" or "I don't understand what I'm eating"—they say "I don't know *what* I'm eating." And yet the dish makes perfect sense to me.

   Of course, there have been times when I've had a rather heavy hand, when I haven't been as subtle as I should've been, especially with unfamiliar combinations of ingredients. Chocolate and lavender, for example, don't go together at all well when you smell the lavender. But when you infuse lavender for a very short time in some cream, which is reassuring—

HÉLÈNE   The cream, you mean?

CÉCILE   Yes, when it's soft—not a cream with fermenting agents. Whipping cream, for example. So when I make a chocolate cream icing with infused lavender and a good-quality chocolate that's not too heavy, I get the subtlety I'm aiming for. When I infuse lavender for too long, on the other hand, the result is very bad—I suppose because in our food culture we're not used to encountering chocolate and lavender together, so that anything more than a mild hint of lavender seems unpleasant, even overwhelming.

In any case, this is what I do whenever I introduce a new combination. A friend of mine, the Alsatian pastry chef Christof Felder, does the same thing with his desserts: using a gentle, reassuring product as a base, he achieves complexity by adding only two ingredients to it.

Say, these pages are bizarre! The quotation from Aristotle is followed by this remark: *"Horace* sought the* utile dulcis; *that is, he sought to unite the useful with the agreeable."* It appears in the same form as in the book that was stolen from you—maxims accompanied by historical notes. Here, for example—

HÉLÈNE   Show me—why, it's the same writing!

CÉCILE   You mean—

HÉLÈNE (*taking the pages from Cécile to examine them more closely*)   Yes, it's the same handwriting as in *The Quintessential Art*. Everything is there, even the recipes and commentary. Incredible!

What comes next, I wonder? A quotation from Saint Paul's[†] first letter

---

*HORACE (Quintus Horatius Flaccus; Venusia, 65–Rome, 8 B.C.E.): Latin poet, friend of the poet Virgil and of the wealthy aristocrat Maecenas, protégé of the emperor Augustus. He left a poetry that was at once familial, national, and religious, marked by an Epicurean morality and centered on the search for natural and necessary pleasures, whose ultimate aim was *ataraxia* (absolute serenity of the soul). Horace's work was upheld as a model of balance and moderation by Renaissance humanists and later by French writers of the classical period.

†PAUL (Tarsus, 5~15–Rome, 62~67 C.E.): A fervent Pharisee, known until his conversion by the Hebrew name of Saul, whose vision of Christ on the road to Damascus led him to become an apostle of the new sect. His missionary activity took him to Cyprus, Asia Minor, Macedonia, and Greece, where he established churches in the major cities. In 58, Paul was arrested and brought before the imperial tribunal in Rome. Tradition has ascribed to Paul authorship of fourteen letters, the authenticity of some of which is contested.

to the Corinthians: Videmus nunc per speculum in aenigmate, tunc autem facie ad faciem.

CÉCILE   Which means?

HÉLÈNE   Literally, that now we see in a mirror, in darkness, but then we will see face to face. The commentary reads: *"This is Plato's cave, but it is also the foundation for the symbolic-allegorical view of the universe in the Middle Ages. No one can understand medieval aesthetics without this key."* And then, as usual, there's a historical note on Paul.

That's strange—there's a break in the text. Then it continues with this: *"According to the neo-Pythagorean philosopher Apollonius of Tyana (Tyana, early 1st century C.E.-Ephesus, 97), 'imitation represents what it sees, the imagination what it does not see.'* [37] *With time, the aestheticism of the ancient Greeks faded."*

CÉCILE   That's a good idea.

DENIS   What? That the aestheticism of the ancient Greeks should have faded?

CÉCILE   No, the difference between imitation and imagination. Lately, I've been trying to create new dishes by imagining rather than imitating; the notion that the imagination pictures what it doesn't see is a help.

DENIS   Good for you, darling. Artists need all the help they can get. I've said a thousand times that your life is harder than mine. Nothing in the world could make me trade my life of reason for yours. I'll take intelligence over sensibility any day—

HÉLÈNE   Shall I continue reading? The text quotes Plotinus:* *"Art must*

*PLOTINUS (Lycopolis [today Asyut, Egypt] *ca* 205–Campania, 270): Greek philosopher, founder of a school at Rome whose teachings represented a significant development of Platonist doctrine. Plotinus's works, published some thirty years after his

make the idea rise up out of matter."[38] With this commentary: *"In the third century, Plotinus sought to go beyond the concept of imitation upheld by Plato and Aristotle, and advanced the concept of emanation: a material object is beautiful 'insofar as it participates in the thought that flows from the divine.'*[39] *What does that mean? The beautiful, Plotinus says, consists in a particular relationship to the One, or Good—God, if you like. Invoking the divine was a logical step for anyone, pagan or Christian, who believed that the world could not be explained in human terms."*

DENIS   That's a difficult passage.

CÉCILE   In cases like this I don't always try to understand exactly what is being said; instead I try to get the gist of it and draw culinary inspiration from that. Let's take it one bit at a time: *"Art must make the idea rise up out of matter."* That opens up a whole range of possibilities. For example, one could interpret it in the manner of Curnonsky: art must cause a roasted chicken, which is matter, to give the person who is eating it the idea of the roasted chicken. Hmmm, that doesn't seem very promising. How about this: from a simple roasted chicken, which is matter, culinary art must bring forth ideas?

HÉLÈNE   The idea, you mean—but this is not necessarily the same as *the* flavor of a roasted chicken. It could be a flavor that's associated with particular memories.

CÉCILE   I don't follow.

HÉLÈNE   For example, imagine that the roasted chicken makes you think of Sunday dinner after mass, the family gathered around the table—well, culinary art must make you think of all that while eating a roasted chicken.

---

death by his disciple Porphyry under the title *Enneads*, exerted considerable influence on the Fathers of the early Church, particularly Augustine.

CÉCILE   Perhaps so.

HÉLÈNE   Then there's this bit: *"Plotinus sought to go beyond the concept of imitation upheld by Plato and Aristotle, and advanced the concept of emanation."*

CÉCILE   I like this rather more.

DENIS   Which just goes to show that small mouthfuls are better than big ones, by the way. The passage from Plotinus was indigestible, but cut up into small pieces it's fine.

CÉCILE   When we eat we cut up our food for the same reason, so that we won't choke. These individual sentences are like appetizers in a way, dainty morsels. Even so, they're not as simple as you seem to suppose. This concept of emanation, for example—when you stop and think about it, it's hard to work out what it means.

HÉLÈNE   Remember, Plotinus says a material object is beautiful *"insofar as it participates in the thought that flows from the divine."*

CÉCILE   How am I supposed to put the divine to use in my cooking?

DENIS   By being yourself, darling.

HÉLÈNE   Listen, you lovebirds, if I'm getting in the way ·

CÉCILE   No, please continue reading.

HÉLÈNE   Now we come to Saint Augustine.* There's a quotation. Shall we try our luck again at transposing it?

---

*AUGUSTINE (Aurelius Augustinus; Thagaste [today Soug Ahras, Algeria], 354–Hippo, 430): theologian, Father of the early Church. Born in Roman Africa to a pagan father and a Christian mother (Saint Monica), he followed the teachings of the Persian prophet Mani for many years. A teacher of rhetoric, he converted to Christianity under the influence of Ambrose, the bishop of Milan, and later became bishop of Hippo. Apart from the *Letters,* some of which amount to treatises, Augustine's principal works

DENIS   Go ahead, I'm ready.

HÉLÈNE   Saint Augustine asked *"whether things are beautiful because they give pleasure, or give pleasure because they are beautiful."*[40]

DENIS   Transposing we get: Are dishes good because they bring pleasure, or do they bring pleasure because they are good?

CÉCILE   I would say that we call good that which brings pleasure. After all, the good is a relative concept: there's no arguing about taste or colors, as we all know!

DENIS   Listen to you—an amateur philosopher daring to decide just like that a question that perplexed a thinker of Saint Augustine's stature!

HÉLÈNE (*giving the pages back to Cécile*)   Say what you like—if it's art we're talking about, who's the artist here? The philosopher?

CÉCILE   There's another quote, this one from Saint Thomas Aquinas: *"There are three requirements for beauty. Firstly, integrity or perfection— for if something is impaired it is ugly. Then there is due proportion or consonance. And also clarity: whence things that are brightly coloured are called beautiful."*[41]

DENIS   That harks back to Aristotle. Recall his requirements concerning the general idea of a work, its coherence, the plausible and the necessary, and so on. Integrity and accomplishment are a part of that. What is new is this notion of suitable proportions. (*He looks over Cécile's shoulder.*) And look, there's another quote: *"This is why beauty is a matter of right proportion, for the senses delight in rightly proportioned things as similar to themselves. . . ."*[42]

---

are *The City of God* and the *Confessions*. His influence on the theology of the Catholic Church has been unrivaled.

HÉLÈNE   And, finally, the insistence on dazzling clarity: things are beautiful because they have brilliant colors.

CÉCILE   I'll need some time to think about all this. What shall I do, copy these pages—or take them with me?

DENIS   What, take them with you?

CÉCILE   Well, why not? They probably don't belong to the library, since they come from *The Quintessential Art.*

HÉLÈNE (*going to speak with the librarian*)   Excuse me, sir, we found these loose pages lying on the shelf over there—they don't belong to the library? You're sure? And we can take them? (*To Cécile*) Right you are. They're yours to keep.

CÉCILE   Don't worry, Denis—if Hélène hadn't asked, I would have! One would almost think you'd suspect me of being capable of serving meat or fish that isn't fresh, of putting leftovers on the menu or inflating check totals. Such trust, after ten years of marriage!

DENIS   No, it's just that you made up your mind so quickly. I was surprised, you see.

CÉCILE   Nonsense. You don't have much respect for me, do you?

DENIS   Darling—

CÉCILE   Don't be silly—I'm just teasing! But do help me to understand what that last quote means: *"This is why beauty is a matter of right proportion, for the senses delight in rightly proportioned things as similar to themselves."*

DENIS   Well, think about numbers, for example.

CÉCILE   But Augustine is talking about proportions, not numbers.

DENIS   They're related. Suppose a dish has got two of a certain ingredient, say two turnips, and five of another, say five fillets of fish. They stand to each other in the relation of 2/5, which is a proportion.

CÉCILE   True enough. What worries me about this aesthetic of numbers and proportions, you see, is that I'm afraid I'd be the only one who perceives it.

DENIS   Perhaps not. In laying out text on a page, for example, when a title runs over onto the next line, typographic designers break the title up so that the second line is longer than the first. In this way one avoids giving the reader the impression that the title is unbalanced, falling off too much to the right. No reader consciously notices this, but the balancing effect is nonetheless registered to one degree or another. Surely the same thing would occur with your "proportional" dishes. Moreover, I would be very surprised if this concern with proportion hadn't been handed down by culinary tradition.

CÉCILE   Let me think about this some more. As far as colors are concerned, it seems a little arbitrary: it doesn't necessarily follow that everything that's brilliantly colored is good; the most you can say is that color is a sign of freshness—

DENIS   It all depends on what "brilliantly" means. I understand what is meant by the saturation, or intensity, of a color, its various shades, and so forth; but I don't know what brilliance refers to here. It's an obscure passage. This time it's my turn to reflect.

CÉCILE   Good! Let's see—the text goes on next to speak of Macrobius. Who's that?

HÉLÈNE   Isn't there a note in the pages somewhere? That's surprising. As it happens, I lectured on Macrobius last month. He was a Latin writer who lived around 400 C.E. His works include the *Saturnalia,* a compilation of the knowledge of his time.

CÉCILE   Only one little bit of that knowledge is retained here: "Ideo physici mundum magnum hominem et hominum brevem mundum esse dixerunt." What does that mean?

HÉLÈNE   That the world is man writ large and man is the world writ small.[43] This is the basis for the symbolic correspondences that were later systematized by means of allegory. The aesthetic theories of the Middle Ages demanded that works be interpreted according to this principle. In other words, those works in which correspondences with the cosmos were found were considered beautiful.

CÉCILE   I seem to recall a similar idea in Japanese cooking—a sort of culinary interpretation of miniature gardens. Well then, we move on next to Boethius.

DENIS   Darling, if we go on like this we'll still be here tomorrow. Look, the sun's going down. We've got to get on the road.

CÉCILE   All right, this will be the last one. The text says: *"It was the politician, philosopher, and poet Boethius (ca 480–524) who bequeathed to the Middle Ages the Pythagorean theory of proportions, a tradition that naturally led to a notion of unity, of balance. Thus the architects of the great Gothic cathedrals made use of what is called the golden ratio."* Denis, the golden ratio?

HÉLÈNE   Ah, that's too big a subject to go into today. Why don't both of you come instead to my next lecture at the Sorbonne. Cécile, you'll find out what you want to know about the golden ratio, and Denis can fill in the mathematical details for you. Afterward we can have a drink. How does that sound?

A RECIPE CONSTRUCTED AROUND AN UNUSUAL INGREDIENT

IN THEORY

Classical cuisine frequently made use of unusual products: traders bought spices from distant lands, and the great French chefs often introduced foods that they had brought back from their own travels. This aspect of French gastronomic tradition (the kitchen and the table are, after all, among those things that do not ruin culture—indeed *Le Cuisinier gascon*, published in 1740, was probably written by Louis Auguste de Bourbon) conceals one of the essential reasons for the vitality of French cooking. Where tradition urges modernity forward, there is no reason to wish to put an end to it!

IN PRACTICE

Here it's not a question of using an unusual product gratuitously, just for fun—the unusual product cannot be avoided, because it leads us to unexplored territories of flavor.

ENDIVES, MOLLUSKS, SEA-WATER BEER FOAM, ROASTED PEACHES WITH VERBENA SYRUP AND BEER ICE CREAM

Beer made from sea water is one of those novelties that makes the cook's day: it's so different from anything one has ever tasted! It encourages the cook to be creative.

In France, this beer is made with water brought back by only two ships that are authorized to take water from the ocean for human consumption. I serve it with endives, mollusks, roasted peaches, and verbena syrup. The sea-water beer is put in a seltzer bottle, or soda siphon, and at the last moment expanded to produce a foam. An ice cream made from the same beer completes the presentation.

There is no substitute for sea-water beer in this case. On the one hand, it supplies the inspiration for the dish: not only is the slightly heavy smoothness of the peaches brought out by the bitterness of the beer; its iodized quality prevents the dish from being confined to the classical range of flavors as well. And, on the other hand, it goes together with the other ingredients: the slightly smoky, roasted bitterness of any other beer would give too harsh a result.

Guinness stout, for example, goes well with fowl and game, but not with peaches, unless you were to add some raw ham in order to accentuate their rather dense, rural, uncomplicated quality. But in a dish made with Guinness, the peaches would become an incidental element, rather than the focus of attention, as they are with sea-water beer.

YOUR TURN

Take advantage of your own travels and explorations in specialty food markets and shops. Pick out the most unusual ingredient you can find and try to think of a way to cook it. One possibility: begin by identifying a classical recipe in which the ingredient could play a role, by virtue of one of its specific characteristics.

A RECIPE THAT CONJURES UP
AN IDEA OUT OF MATTER

IN THEORY

One of the hardest things in cooking is the art of suggestion, which is to say bringing forth an idea from the assembled ingredients. In the hands of a great artist, the idea that is brought forth has nothing to do with them—for example, when the idea of springtime suddenly appears from products that are not associated with that season, or when a dish sets you to thinking of abstractions such as transparency, happiness, and so on.

IN PRACTICE
AN ENRICHED PURÉE OF POTATOES
WITH BRAISED CARDOONS IN A GREEN SAUCE

The idea for this potato dish came from a roasted chicken. Just thinking about a really plump roasted chicken is a wonderful thing: you imagine smelling it, biting into the crispy skin, and chewing the white meat and the thighs while the fatty juices flood your mouth. I wanted to begin by simply showing such a beautifully roasted chicken to my guests, so that they would have an idea what it was like. Then it was time to get to work.

Back in the kitchen, the chicken was cut up and treated in two ways. The breasts and wings were deboned and cooked with cinchona (Peruvian bark), which gives the juices a green color. The thighs were also deboned, but cut up into pieces and served *en parmentier* instead: boiled potatoes were coarsely mashed and combined with a thick dice of foie gras along with the chicken pieces and the juices of the roasted chicken; this mixture was then browned with a topping of bread crumbs and herbs.

In this way the roasted chicken is turned away from one's initial, intuitive idea of it and turned into something else. A simple roasted chicken is a fine idea, but it needs to be refined, because in reality the juices run all over the plate. Here, to the contrary, everything is carefully constructed, and the potatoes substitute for the bread you would use to wipe the plate with at home.

Naturally, each of the ingredients is important. For example, the potatoes should be fairly new, of the Pompadour variety, with a delicate flesh and a lovely cream color, so that they don't fall apart after cooking.

The cardoons, which I've not yet mentioned, must be at once fibrous and tasty. In any case they can't be replaced by fennel, which would be too Mediterranean a touch for a dish that itself isn't Mediterranean: *gratin de cardon*, for example, is a typically Lyonnais dish.

As for the green juices, their freshness calls to mind a chicken running through the grass. No, I'm just kidding. There are some combinations I can't seem to explain. I can't explain the reason for these juices, any more than I can justify one day having had the idea of roasting some huge 25-year-old oysters (each weighing about two pounds) in goose fat! First I removed the oysters from their shells, which were heated and the oysters then put back inside; next I put them in the oven and cooked them in the fat for a short while; and then finally I brought the oysters out into the dining room, where the steaming goose fat was poured over them. The oysters were then removed from the shells again and placed on a fondue of cabbage and radicchio, with an oyster cream sauce.

This preparation was a sidelight to the main dish, which was composed of a small slice of John Dory that had been "frightened"—that is, sautéed for a few seconds in spicy butter—and served with a large grilled scallop, Guernica peppers, sea-urchin aspic, Hawaiian red salt, diced turnip with Campari, and, last but not least, slices of toasted bread sprinkled with melted butter and lemon. All this was presented on fine red porcelain plates. The oysters were brought out first, followed by the John Dory, and the diners were invited to season their fish with the red salt, which came in a little spoon.

The overall effect of the dish, however, served only to highlight the steaming goose fat, which lent the scene a brutal, violent aspect, further emphasized by the monstrous size of the oysters themselves. And so an idea was made to rise up out of matter. . . .

YOUR TURN

Before plunging in, a word of advice: write down your ideas first, and don't worry if they fill up whole pages. And don't start out by trying to suggest an abstract idea right away: this is the most difficult thing of all. Try first to come up with ideas related to a set of basic ingredients—using red objects to suggest the idea of redness, for example, while at the same time making something edible, is already difficult enough!

ELEVEN

OF COOKING AND CATHEDRALS

Numerology is the tendency to search for numbers everywhere—even where they aren't to be found. Many numbers display interesting mathematical properties, of course, notably the number pi (the ratio of the circumference of a circle to its diameter) and the golden ratio (also called the golden section or the divine proportion), which was used in the construction of the great Gothic cathedrals during the Middle Ages. Despite the undeniable fascination of the golden ratio, its presence in a work of art cannot be regarded as a condition of beauty.

FIBONACCI'S RABBITS

A lecture hall at the Sorbonne. Denis and Cécile are seated in the first row, on the left. Hélène is finishing her lecture.

HÉLÈNE   The greatest mathematician of the Middle Ages was Leonardo of Pisa (*ca* 1175–*ca* 1250), better known by the name of Fibonacci (from the Latin *filius bonacci,* meaning "son of Bonaccio"). His father was an Italian consul in Algeria, in the city of Bougie, where Fibonacci studied with an Arab mathematician. Recall that Greek mathematical learning had been preserved by Islamic scholars, and was retransmitted to Europe only toward the end of the Middle Ages.

Owing to his dual education, Fibonacci had the good fortune of being able to compare the Roman numerical system, still current at the time in the West, with Arabic notation, which made use of ten figures whose value was determined by their position (first place for ones, second for tens, third for hundreds, and so on) in addition to zero.

This system seemed clearly superior to Fibonacci, who employed it in a treatise on arithmetic and algebra entitled *Liber abaci,* or Book of the Abacus (1202). This work has come down to us thanks only to the nineteenth-century French number theorist Édouard Lucas, author of a book on mathematical games that associated Fibonacci's name with a series of numbers occurring in a trivial problem in the *Liber abaci.*

The problem is as follows: Suppose that a couple of adult rabbits are placed in a pen. Suppose further that two young rabbits, one male and one female, are born two months after the birth of their parents, and again that two young rabbits are born of the same parents a month later, and so on each month thereafter. Make the same assumption for each pair of young rabbits: they produce two offspring every month after reaching the age of two months. Supposing that no rabbit dies, how many pairs will there be at the end of a year?

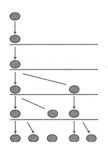

After the first month, there will be one pair. After the second month, one pair. After the third month, one pair of parents and one pair of offspring. After the fourth month, one pair of parents, one pair of offspring born the month before, and two newborn rabbits. Look at this figure. You see that the number of pairs of rabbits grows in the following sequence: 1, 1, 2, 3, 5, 8, 13 . . . Note that each number is the sum of the two preceding numbers. This series (1, 1, 2, 3, 5, 8, 13, 21, 34, 55, 89 . . .) is the Fibonacci series.

One of the most remarkable properties of the Fibonacci series is that the ratio of any number in the series to the one preceding it oscillates around a value slightly larger than 1.6: $1/1 = 1$, $2/1 = 0.5$, $3/2 = 1.5$, $5/3 = 1.666 . . .$, $8/5 = 1.6$, $13/8 = 1.625$, $21/13 = 1.61538 . . .$, $34/21 = 1.61904$, and so on. Carried out indefinitely, these divisions would converge upon 1.618033989 . . . ; this value is called the golden ratio. It is an irrational number, which means that it cannot be written as simple fraction. It is precisely equal to $(1 + \sqrt{5})/2$.

The occurrence of the golden ratio and of the Fibonacci series in the growth of plants and animals has been very extensively studied. The most striking manifestation of Fibonacci numbers in the plant kingdom is the spiral arrangement of seeds in the inflorescence of certain varieties of sunflower. These flowers exhibit two sets of spirals. The spirals of one set move in a clockwise direction, and those of the other set in a counter-clockwise direction. The numbers of spirals in the two sets are not the same: they lie between consecutive numbers of the Fibonacci series. Thus sunflowers of average size have between 34 and 55 spirals, whereas giant sunflowers may have as many as 89—even 144—spirals.[44]

Because the golden ratio is found in a great many natural phenomena, some authors have argued that it must play an essential role in poetry and music. Fibonacci series are claimed to have been deliberately employed by Virgil* and other Latin poets in composing their works, and

---

*VIRGIL (Andes [today Pietole, near Mantua], *ca* 70–Brundisium [Brindisi], 19 B.C.E.): Latin poet who composed the *Bucolics*, then settled at Rome where he published the *Georgics*. Later he undertook a great national epic, the *Aeneid*, left unfinished at his death.

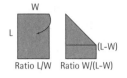

W

L

(L-W)

Ratio L/W   Ratio W/(L-W)

historians of art have detected its use in architecture and painting.[45]

If you want to have a geometric idea of the golden ratio, take a rectangular piece of paper, the length of which may be said to be a number L and the width another number W. When the length is divided by the width one obtains a third number $X = L/W$, which is greater than 1. How many times does W go into L? At least once, since L is greater than W.

Look at this series of rectangles. In the case of the very elongated rectangle on the left, L is far greater than W, and the ratio X is a very large

number. By contrast, in the case of a square, which exhibits no elongation whatever, the quotient of one side divided by the other is equal to exactly 1. From these different rectangles you can see that the ratio of length to width falls between infinity and 1.

The golden ratio is the relation expressed by a quite particular rectangle. Take the rectangular piece of paper above and fold back the upper right-hand corner along the opposite side: you obtain a right isosceles triangle and, below this, a new rectangle, less elongated than the one you started with. In this case the sides have the values W (the width of the initial rectangle) and L–W (the length of the initial rectangle less its width).

For the new rectangle, let's once again calculate the quotient of the length divided by the width. We come up with another number Y. Compare X and Y. Generally they are different—except in the case of very particular rectangles, where X and Y are equal to 1.618033989 . . . , which of course is the golden ratio.

Like the number pi, which is equal to the area of any circle divided by the square of its radius (or, what comes to the same thing, the circumference divided by the diameter), the golden ratio has long fascinated mathematicians and number lovers. To my mind, those who believe that the golden ratio constitutes an absolute criterion of beauty are like moths that immolate themselves in the flame of a candle. Still today, however, stone masons, cabinetmakers, musicians, sculptors, and painters make use of this ratio, carrying on a tradition that goes back at least as far as Pythagoras. *With a wink at Cécile, Hélène continues.*

Finally, we may dispose of an idea that is common in restaurant kitchens today, namely that eggs display the perfection of the golden ratio. Using measurements that I have made myself, together with ones carried out by specialists at the INRA station in Nouzilly, I have calculated the result of dividing the length by the diameter for various eggs: 1.39, 1.36, 1.379, 1.4, 1.376, 1.402, 1.265, 1.273, and so on. No golden ratio to be found in this list!

Thank you for your attention. See you next week.

The students leave the lecture hall, talking among themselves. Hélène gathers up her notes and leaves with Denis and Cécile. Passing through the gates of the university, they go on to a café on the Place de la Sorbonne.

DENIS   Incorporating the golden ratio in cooking is simple. You could make a cake, for example, in the shape of an ellipse, with the golden ratio expressing the relation between the long and short axes. Or a square cake with a chocolate fondant icing, where the relation between the cake's thickness and the length of its side is expressed by the golden ratio, with a leaf of gold being applied to the icing on top. Other possibilities could easily be imagined: a rectangular layer cake, for instance, whose width and length are in golden proportion to one another, with one of these two dimensions being in golden proportion to the thickness of the cake as a whole and the other dimension being in golden proportion to the thickness of one of the cake's layers.

CÉCILE   But the flavor? It's the flavor that matters! How about using a quantity of salt, measured in grams, that's 1.6 times greater than the amount of pepper, measured in tenths of grams? Or making the volume of a raspberry purée icing on a cake equal to the product of the golden ratio and the area?

HÉLÈNE   There are any number of possibilities—and with enough patience you'd probably end up with something good. But be careful: as I said in my lecture, whole generations of people have wasted their lives playing with the golden ratio.

CÉCILE   I can hear my friend Pierre Gagnaire telling me that I'm talking nonsense, that numbers can't form the basis for true art. Only a very gifted cook who's truly in love with the golden ratio, and convinced of its creative importance, could make genuinely artistic use of it. The rest of us are better off exploring other aesthetic ideas.

A RECIPE APPLYING THE GOLDEN RATIO

IN THEORY

Just for fun, let's pretend that a dish will be good if the golden ratio is found in it. But since no one can place two flavors in a numerical relation to each other, the only option available to the cook is to apply the golden ratio to the form, or physical shape, of the dish. Here's an example.

IN PRACTICE

The golden ratio in relation to flavor? For the idea to have any real culinary meaning, you would first have somehow to quantify flavors, which has not yet been done, except in a purely subjective way as, for example, when tasters are asked to register the intensity of a given flavor by moving a cursor across a scale. A recipe can be based on the golden ratio only superficially: the "divine proportion" can be exhibited only by the appearance of the dish, not its flavor.

PRESSED CRABMEAT AND CABBAGE

I begin by immersing a crab in ice water, then putting it into salted boiling water. Next, the meat is meticulously extracted. My cooks use ultraviolet lamps to pick through the meat, or otherwise perform a series of inspections at right angles to make sure that no shell fragments can be found in it. At my restaurant on the Rue Balzac in Paris the latter method is employed: one cook extracts the meat from the shell and throws it onto a metal plate so that you can hear if any part of the shell remains attached. Then a second cook immediately rotates the plate by 90' and picks through the meat with a knife, millimeter by millimeter, in search of the least shell fragment. A third cook turns the plate another 90' and repeats the same operation. Every culinary operation in my restaurants is performed with the same precision. I do not tolerate the slightest error.

The cabbage is boiled in heavily salted water. Once it is cooked, the ribs of the individual leaves are cut out and discarded, and the remaining soft part is finely chopped and mixed with the crabmeat, which is then moistened with olive oil.

To obtain a dish incorporating the golden ratio, you could press the mixture of crabmeat and cabbage into a mold whose length is 1.6 times the width, and whose width is 1.6 times its height. (The golden ratio is equal to 1.618033989 ... , but the decimals are imperceptible; we need not take them into account any more than did the builders of the cathedrals, who did not have the means to do so.) On top, put a strip of gelatinized mayonnaise whose width is equal to the thickness of the crabmeat-cabbage mixture and whose thickness is less than that of the mixture by a proportion of 1:1.6. If we're going to play around with this number, we might as well be serious about it!

To make the mayonnaise, begin by infusing *kombawa* (a small green lemon from the western shores of the Indian Ocean) in water with a bit of lemon or vinegar; next put a leaf of gelatin in the heated infusion and whisk in some oil, drop by drop. Just when the resulting emulsion begins to cool, place it on the crabmeat-cabbage mixture so that it gels.

Alternatively, one might make a mixture of pears, celery, fennel, and caraway. As I say, while the golden ratio can reside in the form of the dish, the idea of somehow embedding it in a combination of ingredients is meaningless: numbers have no gustatory existence. Truth, or at least *my* truth, resides only in flavors!

YOUR TURN

Play with different ways of incorporating the golden ratio in the presentation of a dish, using its width, length, thickness, diameter, or height, or its arrangement on a plate, or the number of its elements, or the quantities of salt and pepper to be added, or the weight of the fish or meat, or what have you. The essential thing is that you make something that's good to eat. Will your guests be able to recognize the presence of the golden ratio without your telling them?

TWELVE

BOETHIUS AND THE BRAIN

We recognize geometric forms because our brain has been shaped by millions of years of evolution: without the capacity to recognize predator or prey, neither survival nor reproduction nor descent with variation would be possible. Similarly, we must be able to recognize tastes, whether the sweetness of energy-giving berries or the bitterness of poisonous vegetables.

There is a certain tradition in cooking that reinforces flavor by visual appearance, but a culinary art that seeks to free itself from outmoded rules may also wish to avoid such redundancies.

And what are we to make, today, of the medieval view that gluttony is acceptable so long as the idea of God is present?

PROPORTIONS

Jean, Hélène, Cécile, and Denis are in a small Vietnamese restaurant in Paris.

JEAN   What an extraordinary place! I don't think I've ever had a phô like that!

CÉCILE   Hélène, you were right to suggest we come here.

JEAN   Hélène? I thought it was you, Denis, who—

CÉCILE   Did you notice how well balanced all the ingredients of the phô were? For once, the cilantro didn't crowd out everything else. I'm sure there was a little coconut milk to soften it—

HÉLÈNE   And some ginger?

JEAN   Yes, ginger. Bravo! You really have to search for it before you sense its presence. All the proportions are just right. Do you know the chef? I must have a word with him before we leave.

HÉLÈNE   With her, actually. She's not a professional cook—these are dishes she's always made for her family at home.

JEAN   Incredible. An unrecognized genius.

HÉLÈNE   You don't know this place? You told me that you knew every restaurant in Paris.

JEAN   Well, almost every one—

HÉLÈNE   It must be very difficult, your work. How can you—

A waiter appears with a large envelope.

WAITER   A gentleman asked me to give this to you.

JEAN   To me?

WAITER   I'm not sure. He only said that he was in a hurry and that it was for your table.

JEAN   Let's see. There are a few written pages here. This one begins:

"Boethius:* Amica et similitudo, dissimilitudo odiosa atque contraria: *We love similarity, but hate and resent dissimilarity.*"[46]

HÉLÈNE   Show me—but this is another fragment from *The Quintessential Art*. And it follows on exactly from what we found at Cluny! (*She calls the waiter.*) Excuse me, sir. This person who gave you the envelope, what did he look like?

WAITER   I didn't get a very good look at him. Rather tall, not too young. Nothing in particular that I recall—except, perhaps, something about his eyes. He seemed to be enjoying himself. Well, no, not exactly: there was some—how does one say in French?—some mischieviosity about him.

JEAN   Something mischievous?

WAITER   Yes. I'm sorry, I didn't look at him very closely.

HÉLÈNE   Thank you, sir. (*To the others*) He sounds like the same man who was at the bookshop. Why does he keep on giving us these documents? They'll only bring us more problems. I've had more than my fill. Jean, would you mind taking over for me?

JEAN   How thoughtful of you. You want me to deal with all of this?

HÉLÈNE   I don't mean it that way. But you're a smart guy—and no one would dare to attack someone your size.

CÉCILE   Repeat the line from Boethius, would you?

JEAN   He says that man is made according to the measure of the world.

CÉCILE   Yes, but what mainly interests me is what he goes on to say next. Show me the page? Ah, yes, here it is: *"the manifestation of a sim-*

---

*BOETHIUS (Anicius Manlius Severinus Boethius; Rome, *ca* 480–Pavia, 524): Latin philosopher, advisor to Theodoric the Great, and author of *On the Consolation of Philosophy*.

ilarity between man and the world is the source of beauty." Hmmm. That's rather like what Macrobius was saying, but I don't know how to use it in cooking.

DENIS   You know, in a strange way it puts me in mind of modern neurobiological research, which treats the brain as a sort of machine for recognizing shapes and patterns. It turns out, you see, that the brain is pleased when it encounters things that it knows.

JEAN   What do you mean?

DENIS   For example, even though the stars seem to be almost randomly distributed in the night sky, our brain manages to distinguish shapes: a pot, a W, a cross, and so on. In other words, it recognizes visual patterns— geometrical shapes, if you like—that we call constellations: the Big Dipper, Cassiopeia, and so on. And recognizing geometrical shapes in the world around us is important for our survival: we need to be able to recognize the shape of a lion that wants to devour us or, by contrast, the shape of a rabbit that we want to eat. Pattern recognition is biologically important.

It's the same with sounds: when someone sings the melody of a children's song like "Frère Jacques," you recognize its musical form at once. Here again, pattern recognition is an important element of survival: if a lion is hidden from sight, but we hear it roar, we can run to safety; conversely, if we hear a hen cackle, we can chase it down for food. In this case the recognition is auditory rather than visual.

The same is true for smells and tastes as well. Take, for example, a wine that has an aroma of sweet green pepper. There was never any green pepper in the wine, nor does the grape from which the wine was made have any botanical relationship with a sweet pepper; indeed, their odorant molecules may be entirely different. And yet our brain, when it receives information from our gustatory apparatus, recognizes the smell of green pepper.

We perceive with our senses, and our brain then sorts through the sensory data that reaches it. This is why the autostereograms that you were talking about the other day are so intriguing. It's also why, Cécile, your teachers told you that flavors shouldn't be so intense that they're instantly recognized. Looking at an autostereogram, first you see nothing but a jumble of shapes. Yet a three-dimensional pattern is hidden inside. Meanwhile your brain is busy processing the information it's receiving. All of a sudden it finds a solution: you detect a correspondence between something you perceive and something you know. This produces pleasure, as Boethius said— in the case of cooking, because the brain has to work for an extended period before it finds a solution to the culinary enigma with which it is presented.

HÉLÈNE   One finds something similar in painting and music as well. For example, painters and photographers know that a work must have a foreground and a background.

CÉCILE   It's the same in cooking: one flavor must be in the foreground and others in the background. This gives depth to the dish, not only with regard to the intensity of the flavors, but also for the sequence in which they are perceived.

JEAN   You mean their length in the mouth?

CÉCILE   Yes. I often try to structure dishes in such a way that one flavor comes before or after another. I also look for ways to make particular sensations last longer. In composing a dish, you need to know that the diner will smell what is above first and what is below last. In the dishes made to fit on a spoon that are fashionable at the moment, you smell the ingredients that are at the tip of the spoon first, and the ones that are near the neck last—and yet all of them arrive in the mouth at the same time.

There are plenty of other tricks. For example, wrap a large asparagus and a sprig of basil in a sheet of rice paper, cook it until the paper is crispy, and then pour a generous amount of olive oil over it. When you bite into the asparagus, you first perceive the fattiness of the oil that coats it; only later, when you chew the asparagus, do you register a sensation of moistness. It's refreshing, because you've delayed the perception of the liquid in the asparagus. By contrast, when you eat a mayonnaise-based sauce, you first perceive the aqueous phase, but your mouth is then coated with the oily phase, which lengthens the sensation. All these particular properties are so many notes that cooks play on the culinary piano.

DENIS   In the case of a mayonnaise, what's still more interesting is that you perceive both the odorant and sapid molecules that are in each phase.

HÉLÈNE   Which means?

DENIS   Mayonnaise is an emulsion. This means that the whisk has broken up the oil into small droplets, which at the same time are dispersed in the water contained in the egg yolk and the vinegar. You can taste the aqueous phase—the water—because along with the water molecules there are water-soluble molecules that give it a smell and a flavor. The oil, on the other hand, contains different molecules that aren't soluble in water.

Besides, now I come to think of it, Cécile, did you know that you can delay the release of the molecules present in a particular phase?

CÉCILE   How?

DENIS   By using chemical forces to bind the molecules to one another. Take, for example, the fact that sauces thickened with flour have less flavor. This is because the flour molecules bind themselves to the odorant molecules—

JEAN   Hold on, we're getting too far away from the text. Next comes a reference to Alcuin of York:* *"In his* De Rhetorica, *Alcuin holds that anything that is not indispensable to the development of a subject must be*

---

*ALCUIN (Albinus Flaccus Alcuinus; York, *ca* 732–Tours, 804): English scholar and ecclesiastic, Alcuin became head of the Palatine school founded by Charlemagne at Aachen and played a leading role in the Carolingian renaissance.

stripped away. In cooking, this principle requires the elimination of every-thing that is superfluous."[47]

CÉCILE   Think of the sprig of parsley placed on top of a piece of fish, or the mint leaf on a sorbet: these are annoying and superfluous touches—annoying because you have to push them aside before eating the fish or the sorbet. And then, it's all a bit too conventional. A bit silly. A simple-minded and inexpensive way of making something pretty to look at—

JEAN   That's true for communication in general. Communication is a question of telling a story, and telling a story makes the listener travel along a road. Every wrong turn leads away from the destination. Obviously it's not forbidden to wander about every now and then, or to dawdle along the way, but in the end if all you do is dawdle you never get there.

HÉLÈNE   All this can be found in Aristotle, by the way. And it really ought to be of practical value to Cécile—conceiving of a dish as a road that diners travel, and guiding them to their destination. This applies as much to the presentation of the dish as to its flavors.

CÉCILE   The flavors—that's the hardest thing. It's quite true that for a series—

JEAN   Wait, our book has this to say about the medieval conception of beauty: *"Just as there were infinite ways of being, so there were infinite ways of making things in accordance with proportion."*[48]

CÉCILE   Fortunately so—otherwise art would be very monotonous indeed. Now that I come to think of it, though, what I said a moment ago about getting rid of the parsley and the mint may not always be right. Sometimes their presence can be justified. In one kitchen I worked in, for example, the chef insisted on "announcing" the flavor of his dishes. If a dish has the flavor of mint, then the mint must be visible. In this case, using a mint leaf is perfectly defensible.

JEAN   Maybe so—but if, for everything we assert, we then assert its opposite, we won't get very far. Let's go on. *"Alcuin recognized that it is easier to feel love for 'beautiful creatures, sweet scents, and lovely sounds' and so on, than to love God; nonetheless, insofar as we admire these things with the firm intention of better loving God, we are not prohibited from indulging our penchant for* amor ornamenti, *for the sumptuous decoration of churches, for song and fine music."*[49]

Marvelous! A rehabilitation of the supposed sin of gluttony. If we appreciate the beauties of life, particularly works of art, with the intention of better loving God, then we can let ourselves go and enjoy fine cooking! This sort of argument suits me very well: the next time I eat a *truffe en croûte,* I'm sure I shall feel very grateful to him who has given us such delights. It calls to mind the wonderful words of Saint Vincent de Paul: "One must take care of the body so that the soul can be happy in it."

But to return to the subject of communication. We were all taught that in reading a text we must ask ourselves what it means, what it says, what it makes us think it means, and so forth. Cécile, don't you think that dishes could be conceived in a similar manner, so that diners ask themselves the same questions?

CÉCILE   That's getting rather intellectual!

DENIS   Well, why not—if it's one of the thousand roads that lead us to the good—

HÉLÈNE   It seems to me that we've passed a little too quickly over a crucial difference between Plato and Aristotle. With Plato we have idealism: one assumes the existence of the Good, with a capital *G*—a Good in and of itself, absolute, ideal. With Aristotle, on the other hand, we have realism: something is good, with a small *g.* Surely this difference in point of view leads to different attitudes toward cooking? There are those who devote themselves to finding just the right flavor, and others who would rather search for a multitude of flavors, who would rather—what do you think, Jean?

DENIS   I think that it's late. We must be on our way. Cécile, my darling, I've got to get up early tomorrow.

———

WHEN THE FLAVOR IS ANNOUNCED BY A VISIBLE INGREDIENT

IN THEORY

There are more subtle ways to announce a flavor than garnishing a dish containing mint with a mint leaf. One can choose to emphasize a particular ingredient (as we saw in chapter 8 with the recipe featuring the button mushroom), or to confound expectations. Here we consider the element of surprise.

IN PRACTICE
CALF'S HEAD, BEEF, AND MOLLUSK TARTARE

To make this dish I use only the scalp of the calf's head (not the tongue). The scalp is dressed, soaked in cold water, and then blanched in boiling water. This yields a substance that has an interesting consistency, a little rubbery, but not too much so.

The beef must be cut with a knife in order to obtain large pieces of meat that retain all their juices. Make sure to use a knife that has been perfectly sharpened, not a cleaver or a dull knife that tears the meat instead of cutting it cleanly.

The mollusks also have a rubbery quality: you can use cooked whelks, raw dog cockles, raw Spanish mussels, or raw scallops.

In deciding how to combine these ingredients, I finally settled on the following proportions: 40 percent beef, 20 percent calf's head, 40 percent mollusks. For some reason I can't explain, these proportions make the dish legible, that is, they allow each element to be properly appreciated.

The mixture is seasoned in the classical manner, with red pepper, olive oil, a dash of vinegar or tartaric acid, capers, fresh herbs, mustard, and a drop of water or beer. This addition of liquid is important in order to make the mixture slightly gooey (there's no need to add an egg yolk since the proteins are already there). This way the elements of the tartare ring out, one by one, each one declaring its own identity. The succession of flavors makes for a richer story.

To call this a tartare may seem misleading, since tartares are usually made with beef, but there's no reason why they can't contain other things as well. The idea of taking liberties with a familiar composition is one that I find very interesting. My customers often find it disconcerting, however. "I don't know what I'm eating," some of them say. This isn't quite right: they know what they're eating, but their usual points of reference are no longer there. The confusion is deliberate on my part. I don't cook in the traditional way; I don't play Bach or Mozart. In cooking as in music, there is a place for modern art.

YOUR TURN

There are a thousand ways to fool your guests. The simplest way, as we saw in chapter 5, is to give a dish a different color than the one it normally has. Begin by making a fruit jelly with beets rather than black currants, for example. Then go on to play with the dish the jelly is meant to accompany. Your experiment will have succeeded if your guests ask you, "What is it exactly that we're eating?"

A DIVINELY SUMPTUOUS RECIPE

IN THEORY

Nothing is too beautiful when divinity is involved! Think of the sumptuously gilded and decorated altars that are found in certain churches in Europe and South America. Is cooking capable of raising its own monuments to the glory of God? What would a sumptuous flavor taste like?

IN PRACTICE
COFFEE AND LOBSTER SABAYONS

A beautiful piece of beef can be sumptuous—but only to the eye. Here it's the sumptuousness of the flavor that we're concerned with.

One finds it in sabayons—surprisingly, perhaps, since sabayons may be either soft or sumptuous, depending on the ingredients. Lobster and coffee beans will each yield the sumptuousness we're looking for.

The recipe for a lobster sabayon is simple: you whisk egg yolk with lobster juice—a lovely juice without any burned or bitter taste, clear, with a fine purplish red color. You heat the mixture gently, having added a dash of starch to prevent lumps from forming, while whisking vigorously. Gradually the preparation foams and increases in volume. Remove it from the heat when the foam is thick but very smooth, and continue whisking while it cools. The sabayon obtained in this way has a powerful flavor. And because the flavor is enriched by the foam, it is sumptuous as well.

The recipe for coffee sabayon is the same, except that sugar is added to the egg yolk and the lobster juice is replaced by coffee. The sweetened coffee, with its bitterness doubly enveloped by the sugar and the foam, lends the sabayon a quite wonderful sumptuousness.

YOUR TURN

I leave it to you to produce your own vision of sumptuousness. Consider using salty and sweet ingredients. Is a foam always necessary? Can you manage to do without egg yolk or cream? The game can be made still more difficult. For example, can you achieve a sumptuous result without using fats or starches?

A GENTLE RECIPE

IN THEORY

Creating a sumptuous dish raises questions that may point in another direction. Consider the problem of making a soft, or gentle, dish. It doesn't necessarily have to be something sweet, though the recipe that follows is sweet. The main thing that becomes clear is that there's an essential difference in cooking between sumptuousness and gentleness.

IN PRACTICE
VANILLA, RUM, AND SAUTERNES SABAYONS

Sabayons, when they are made with lobster juice or coffee, are sumptuous; but when they are made with vanilla, rum, or Sauternes, they become rather gentle, though I don't quite know why. Perhaps because they don't really work with vanilla alone, or rum alone, or Sauternes alone: to make them work, you need to add something, which turns them away from sumptuousness toward another, softer register.

For example, if you make a sabayon with rum or a mixture of rum and a light syrup, you get a delicious result that I like to serve, in small quantities, with mangos. Nonetheless, this combination is a bit listless, even slightly disagreeable. It needs to be accompanied by a salad of fresh herbs, such as cilantro and tarragon, with strips of angelica and diced pineapple.

Yes, this is a dessert, despite the tarragon and cilantro: these two ingredients are there only to liven things up—and, because of the intensity of their flavor, only in tiny amounts!

YOUR TURN

Keep in mind that making something gentle doesn't necessarily mean it has to be a dessert. The questions posed in connection with sumptuousness, at the end of the preceding recipe, remain of interest here: can a gentle dish be made without fats and starches? Can it be made in both sweet and salty versions? Here's a hint: think about using a gelatinous stock, which has a lovely smoothness to it when it is properly made.

THIRTEEN

THOMAS AQUINAS
AND THE GREEN OF THE GRASS

In medieval Europe, the Church dominated intellectual life and God was necessarily at the center of aesthetic debates. Those things were considered beautiful that had pure colors, particularly green for its identification with spring, which symbolized the renewal of life associated with the resurrection of Jesus Christ. Art was identified with making, which is to say achieving a certain result by means of technical skill. Thus a work of art was said to be beautiful if it corresponded to the end in view. In cooking, the technique of making "extracts" is a form of distillation that leads us back to some of the main concerns of medieval aesthetics.

OF COLORS AND SECRET KNOWLEDGE

In a bistro. Denis is at the bar with Jean and his friend, the police inspector Jérôme Belmont.

JÉRÔME BELMONT   Your story is rather unusual. Someone puts a manuscript book in your hands and then takes it away from you. Thefts, accidents, an attack. Have you filed a complaint?

DENIS   Serially, yes. I mean: yes, for the burglary, yes, for the attack, and so on, but these are separate complaints, whereas everything suggests that it was this stolen document that was the cause of—

JEAN   A romantic! I told you, Jérôme.

JÉRÔME   This whole business is strange, no question, but that by itself doesn't warrant an official inquiry. These are only small events—small by comparison with a murder, that is, which automatically triggers police investigation. My advice is to be careful. And I believe that your troubles may be over, now that the book has been stolen from you.

DENIS   Yes, but additional pages have been given to us that seem to belong to the same book, and—

JÉRÔME   May I have a look?

JEAN   Of course. I've brought you the pages we were given last night. Hélène wanted to take them with her, but I thought it would be better if I kept them in my possession.

JÉRÔME   Hélène, is that the stuck-up woman you've been seeing?

JEAN   She's not stuck up. She's a wonderful girl.

DENIS   But I thought you said—

JEAN   Well, yes, but a woman's moods are changeable. And it's true that she knows a huge amount—and she's very pretty!

JÉRÔME   Look, Jean, I'm not here to talk about your love life. Have you noticed anything unusual in these pages?

JEAN   No, not at least up to this point here, where we stopped reading. Further on perhaps?

.JÉRÔME   Let's see. (*Begins to read*)

Culinary art must create an aesthetic for itself. Not a visual aesthetic, but a gustatory aesthetic. In cooking, the beautiful is the good. One method consists in identifying aesthetic ideas agreed to hold for the other arts—painting, music, poetry—and to imagine how they could be transposed to cooking. Naturally these are not to be adopted as rules, but as ideas that may serve to stimulate the thinking of culinary artists.

What need do artists have for theory? Isn't the sense of beauty that resides inside them sufficient to guide them along the road of artistic invention? The experience of the other arts throughout history has shown, to the contrary, that artists have not shrunk from trying to understand the inner mechanisms of their creativity.

In the Middle Ages, in Europe, the Church ruled intellectual life. God was necessarily at the center of philosophical discussion, and therefore of aesthetic discussion as well, since aesthetics is a branch of philosophy and since philosophy, as it was understood at that time, was a Christian philosophy. No less than other thinkers, theoreticians of art sought to justify pagan ideas by reference to the Scriptures.

For religious reasons, people in the Middle Ages wanted to believe that they were simply doing what had been done before. Innovation was not acknowledged—rather as though art did not exist, and only craft was permitted.

Medieval artists nonetheless benefited from a strong belief in God and the existence of a heavenly world: while they had no difficulty in accepting the idea that our senses perceive only the terrestrial world, their aesthetic curiosity extended to a domain of beauty that was not accessible to the senses.[50] This led them, altogether naturally, to revise old meanings and elaborate new ideas. Thus, for example, the word "form," which in the twelfth century signified that which is visible, gradually came to refer to what is hidden behind things.

Form in cooking? Naturally, there are geometrical shapes: a doughnut has the form of a torus, a soufflé has a cylindrical shape, and so on. Nonetheless the word "form" can also denote nongeo-metrical shapes. Just as the melody of a song such as "Frère Jacques" traces a path that gives it a distinctive musical form, so one can recognize gustatory forms. For example, when we eat a peach Melba, we perceive the juxtaposition of the softness of the fruit with the iciness of the ice cream, the contrast between the cold of the ice cream and the relative warmth of the raspberry sauce, the song of the raspberry and the flavor of the peach, and so forth.

If the Middle Ages innovated with regard to the concept of form, it may nonetheless be wondered whether Christians had the right to take pleasure in beauty. Since everything that was not in praise of God (beginning with sexual pleasure and the delights of the table) was considered reprehensible by Church doctrine, other sources of justification had to be found.

Interesting, but no clue so far as I can see.

JEAN   There may be something further on.

JÉRÔME   There's a sort of note:

According to Thomas Aquinas,* in the Summa Theologiae *(1266– 1272), those things that are brightly colored we call beautiful.[51] The color green was especially valued, for it symbolized springtime and the revival of life associated with the resurrection of Christ. The taste for brilliant colors also had a further religious justification, deriving from the conception of God as the infinite sum of all perfection, and*

---

*THOMAS AQUINAS (Tommaso d'Aquino; Roccasecca, Kingdom of Naples, 1224 *or* 1225– Fossanova, 1274): Italian theologian and member of the Dominican order who taught mainly in Paris, where he had studied under Albertus Magnus and discovered the work of Aristotle. The main part of Thomist teaching is found in the *Summa Theologiae*, which sought to restore the autonomy of nature and reason in a manner consistent with Christian faith. Thomas Aquinas was canonized in 1323.

therefore of all colors of light. These ideas lent themselves to a cer-
tain quite colorful style of cuisine, achieved through the use of saf-
fron, for example. Might this also have been the origin of spinach
extract?

JÉRÔME   What's spinach extract?

DENIS   Cécile makes it sometimes. It's an almost alchemical preparation. You either grind in a mortar or finely chop a handful of spinach
that has been stemmed and washed and then mixed with a little tarragon
and chervil; next you put the chopped herbs in a towel and wring out
the juice into a bowl. If you heat this juice very gently you will see that
the juice from the herbs decomposes: one part "coagulates" and floats on
top, while the other is clarified; the green, coagulated part is what you
use to color foods with—a very lovely shade of green, it's true.

A while ago I had what I thought was a brilliant idea. Since chlorophyll is what you recover by means of this procedure, I suggested to Cécile that she make a grass extract, using the grass you find in a lawn. But
then I realized that a lawn is liable to have any number of weeds in it as
well, some of which may be toxic! This goes to show that tradition, in
commanding us to faithfully follow classic recipes, may serve to protect
us from our wilder impulses. On the other hand, the modern food addi-
tive E 410 is pure chlorophyll, much better prepared than spinach extract,
much purer—which proves that innovation, when it's properly tested, is
superior to tradition.

JÉRÔME   So it turns out you're the real source of harm in all of this!
All right, let's go on:

Art, artisan, artist—all these notions were debated in the Middle Ages.
In medieval Latin, the word ars signified "technique." For Aquinas,
a work of art was beautiful if it was functional, that is, if its form
was congruent with its purpose: "Every craftsman aims to produce
the best work that he can, not in a simple manner, but by reference

to the end."[52] *Elsewhere he adds that art (ars) is associated with making (facere): "Ars est recta ratio factibilium" (Art is the right conception of that which is to be made).*[53]

Aquinas was not alone in confusing the theory of art with the theory of trades. The English theologian John of Salisbury (ca 1120–1180) defined method as "an efficient plan, which avoids nature's wastefulness, and straightens out her circuitous wanderings, so that we may more correctly and easily accomplish what we are to do."[54] *Indeed, according to Cassiodorus, ars was so called because it constrains.*[55]

JEAN   Say, Denis, that's something that Cécile should keep in mind when she's run out of ideas—imposing constraints. She could restrict the number of ingredients in a dish to a certain number, say two: crab and turnip, for example; or orange and monkfish; or foie gras and crayfish—

JÉRÔME   This mention of artisans and trades gives me an idea. Certain trades have a whole mystique about them. For example, the guild network known as the Compagnonnage* claims to be the heir to a forgot-

---

*In France during the Middle Ages, in reaction to the old system of corporations, artisans formed a network of guilds that gave members (known as *compagnons*, or "companions") a certain liberty of movement in accepting employment, depending on their qualifications, and permitted them to escape the domination of abusive masters. This system of fraternal trade associations, known as the Compagnonnage, later came to be divided into several opposing movements, some of them religious in orientation, which gave rise to the chapters that survive still today.

The ultimate origins of the Compagnonnage are unknown, though it is believed to have grown out of the *collegia* in which the building trades were organized in ancient Rome. Under the name *Devoir*, the existence of the Compagnonnage is attested during the period when the great Gothic cathedrals were built in France. It acted as guardian of the professional secrets of the various trades and, in order to protect employment, limited their transmission to those who were judged worthy of possessing them, while also giving members moral instruction in the form of symbolic knowledge. Additionally, it developed a scheme of mutual assistance based on the notion of solidarity.

ten tradition, the guardian of a body of knowledge whose secrets it transmits only to a select few. What's more, the Compagnons observe rites of a sort. Could this be a clue?

DENIS   Yes, it could—after all, the Pythagoreans used to kill anyone who revealed the secrets of numbers.

JEAN   That's going too far! I have friends who are Compagnons, and they're good hard-working people, not assassins!

JÉRÔME   Let's go on:

Medieval scholars distinguished between the useful or menial arts, which are technical in character, and the liberal arts. An artist in the Middle Ages was a person who studied the liberal arts, which were seven in number and divided into the quadrivium (composed of arithmetic, geometry, astronomy, and music) and the trivium (grammar, rhetoric, and logic). This last field of study was the cornerstone of the trivium: it assumed a sound training in grammar and consisted in trying to separate truth from falsity through the analysis of the words of statements, or propositions.

The thirteenth century witnessed a revival of interest in art and beauty. "In any learning that results from human activity," Aquinas held, "no other meaning can be given, strictly speaking, than the literal meaning."[56] Here the word "literal" means that which is intended by the author. This doctrine spelled the end of allegorism: observation once again became possible. By making room for the natural universe, Aquinas permitted artists to observe the world instead of

---

The title of Compagnon was awarded to a worker who, having fulfilled his contract of paid apprenticeship, had undertaken a tour of France and created a masterpiece. In the sixteenth century, as a consequence of the upheavals of the Reformation, the Compagnonnage underwent a schism that led to rivalry among regional chapters and struggles for territorial control. The many symbols of the Compagnonnage later adopted by Freemasonry are proof of their common legendary origins.

representing it in accordance with a priori principles of mankind's relationship to God. For Aquinas, what was beautiful deserved to be recognized on its own account. Already, in the Treatise on Good and Evil *(1228), the theologian William of Auvergne had argued that sensible beauty is "that which pleases him who looks at it."*[57]

The document ends here. I see nothing more to enlighten us, beyond the clue I mentioned of secret knowledge—a circle of initiates. Listen, you've got my phone number. Give me a call if anything new develops, okay?

PLAYING WITH BRILLIANT COLORS

IN THEORY

A dish with brilliant colors that evokes the idea of God? It's easy enough if one uses spices. Yellow can be obtained by using saffron, for example. Green? Cooks use spinach extract. Blue? This is more difficult, because bright shades of blue, such as turquoise, are seldom found in foods. There is a well-known food coloring called brilliant blue, but it repels most people. Orange? One mixes red and yellow. And so on. Long live colorful cooking!

IN PRACTICE
HELL

The name for this dessert is Hervé's, not mine—he sees it as a vision of hell, because it sets an almost sulfurous yellow next to a deep red and an opaque black.

It's a powerful dessert, yet at the same time a very typical one. Most people like it, but not everyone. So much the better: the fact that it leaves no one indifferent is proof of its artistic success as far as I'm concerned. I recently included it in the menu for a dinner given by a company for some clients. The chief executive officer, a man of North African descent, was outraged that I dared to propose such a thing. By the time I came out to serve it, he had managed to make everyone at his table share his disgust. Afterward he confessed to me that the dessert reminded him of an incident in his private life (it was the saffron that aroused his anger). But isn't this one of the purposes of art—to stir the emotions?

In this dessert, there is an orangish-yellow ice cream that owes its color to the infusion of saffron in boiling milk. This milk is then added to egg yolks that have been whisked with sugar to make a crème anglaise. The custard sauce is then cooked, and crème fraîche incorporated at the end to make a very smooth, creamy ice cream without any specks.

The fire for this inferno is obtained from sweet red peppers and hot red peppers. Here (as with so many other things in cooking) everything depends on intuition: from experience I know that cooks who execute this dish in my restaurants succeed only if they have a genuine feel for cooking. It's not a question of mechanically following a recipe, but of having the right touch.

First, contrary to normal culinary practice, it's very important not to remove the skin of the peppers prior to cutting them into rather large pieces. You then sprinkle the chopped peppers with sugar (not too much) and add slices of lemon, a little saffron (again, not too much—the color must be very carefully judged), and a little water, then heat the mixture in a covered pan. Knowing when the peppers are cooked is a matter of instinct: there comes a moment when they are completely wilted, but not yet saturated with sugar; too much sugar causes them to lose their distinctively slight bitterness. The skin nonetheless must be crystallized, so that it has an elegant wrinkle to it. In the mouth, then, you taste the destructured flesh of the peppers, on the one hand, and the crispy skin on the other.

Olives are then combined with the ice cream and the peppers to complete the dish. You take black olives, pit them and cook them rapidly in boiling water to eliminate the salt; next, drain the blanched olives and dry them in the oven, leaving the door ajar, at 120°C (about 250°F) for 20 minutes. You then mix them with a syrup made with two cups of water, a pound of sugar, and a third of a pound of invert sugar (a product obtained by the slow reduction of sugar syrup, which hydrolyzes the sucrose into glucose and fructose) in order to prevent crystallization. Cook the mixture at 180°C (about 350°F) to caramelize the syrup and then finish the cooking at 100°C (212°F) to let it dry and harden. Finally, chop the olives into small crunchy pieces. This must be done at once in order to prevent a rancid taste from developing.

Recently I've changed this last element slightly, mixing green olives with the black olives. The green olives are treated the same way, except that they are cut into strips before being blanched in boiling water. This way they are purged of their salt more quickly and you don't run the risk of winding up with a sort of olive soup.

The artistic idea behind this recipe? Whether there is art in a well-executed piece of work is a matter for others to decide, not the person who made it. Cooking is like music and literature in this respect: there are those who call themselves artists (rather pretentiously, in my view) and others who are considered artists because they have succeeded in arousing the emotions. In a certain sense, art is something that is always discovered afterward: the work itself is more like a piece of craftsmanship to begin with; later it is acclaimed by those who hear it or read it or taste it, and declared to be art by them.

However this may be, some may yet wonder what led me to combine saffron, peppers, and olives. Two years ago I created another dessert, composed mainly of red peppers and wild strawberries; they worked well together, because I had observed that the bitterness of the red pepper, instead of interfering with the flavor of the wild strawberries, complemented it. This was my first attempt at highlighting red peppers in a dessert.

Then I refined the idea: when tomatoes came in season, I combined the red peppers with some fresh tomato pulp and some crystallized fennel. The dish became more anecdotal, more far-fetched. Why? The sweet red pepper has a hard texture, like many products, and doesn't naturally lend itself to a dessert. But I wanted to use it to make yet another dessert, because I had a feeling it was possible. The question was: how can I tell a story by combining the pepper with a new set of ingredients? Or rather: how can I tell an even more beautiful story than the one of the peppers and wild strawberries? The answer was that the red peppers had to be distorted, prepared in a new way—in this case, with saffron and olives. During the same period, as it happened, I was tinkering with saffron, which is an interesting ingredient, but not one that is often diverted from its usual uses. In the event, this dual diversion worked well.

It may seem that none of this amounted to very much, but in cooking "not much" sometimes does a lot. One day, for example, I asked two of my pastry cooks each to make a fruit salad. One was a workman-like job in the style of the 1950s: it had all the necessary ingredients, vanilla, syrup, and so on. It was good, but not as good as the other one, which had been rid of the accumulated dross of centuries of artisanal cooking; it was more expressive, with a true fruit flavor that wasn't encrusted with layers of tradition. You have to throw a spoke in the wheels of habit to keep it from rolling on.

YOUR TURN

In the Cathedral of Sainte Cécile at Albi, in southern France, there are superb pictorial representations of heaven and hell. Here, Pierre has treated the idea of hell with a certain playful irreverence. There remains the question of heaven: can you manage to devise a culinary image of it?

THE GREEN OF HOPE

IN THEORY

To create a dish in green tones, one that evokes renewal and hope, shouldn't be difficult—so long as you guard against a phenomenon with which cooks are well familiar: green beans, when they are overcooked, turn an olive shade of brown, as do broccoli, Brussels sprouts, and the like. Unless you restrict yourself to raw green vegetables, then, a tried and tested culinary technique is needed to give a nice deep green.

IN PRACTICE

LETTUCE STUFFED WITH BEEF MARROW AND FINES HERBES, GREEN CRAB ESSENCE, SPINACH EXTRACT, AND CRUNCHY SNOW PEAS

The idea behind this recipe is simple: you peel the leaves from a head of lettuce and braise them. It's a classic, traditional idea that allows you to make something very good.

The braised leaves are collected into small piles, in the center of which you place beef marrow that has been sautéed in clarified butter with a dash of lemon juice and a little garlic, bread crumbs, tarragon, parsley, chives, chervil, and some chopped green leaves of a leek. You then tie up the lettuce leaves to form little packets and sauté them in some chilled butter.

The stuffed lettuce is served with a very tasty green crab essence, which is made by cooking down a crab bisque for a long time and, at the end, adding a good amount of butter to the reduced juice.

The spinach extract is prepared using spinach leaves that are first blanched, then strained and cooked in hazelnut butter, which gives them a delicious flavor (and softens their slightly sharp edge).

Finally, the snow peas are cooked al dente: you cut them in strips and cook them in olive oil and clarified butter over low heat in a nonstick pan that has first been rubbed with garlic. You have to add enough water to control the cooking, to slow it down, but not so much that the peas swim in the liquid.

The motivation for this dish? The crab is at the heart of it, because its reduced juice serves the same purpose as a vinaigrette in a salad—it's a punctuation mark that serves to enliven the blandness of the beef marrow. Why the beef marrow then? In one way there's nothing very exciting about it, it's true; but its texture and flavor make it a very interesting ingredient, especially if it's lovingly prepared and served a little on the cool side. The peas bring a crunchiness that offsets the overly soft texture of the marrow, but they don't give the dish its real flavor. Nor does the lettuce.

This is a summer dish: the green is obligatory by virtue of the season, not for any religious reason. The visual aspect of the main elements is obviously important, for it stimulates the appetite—but it would be a mistake to stop there. Hence the importance of garnishing the plate: the stuffed lettuce and snow peas should be placed in the center, with streaks of the crab sauce and spinach extract around it, so that the eye is invited to wander about.

YOUR TURN

Color isn't everything. In considering the various methods for imparting a deep green color to foods, keep in mind that flavor mustn't lag behind. Ultimately, it's the flavor that has to evoke a sense of resurrection and hope. How would you go about achieving this effect?

FOURTEEN

DRAWING EARTH NEARER TO HEAVEN

The artists of the Middle Ages made use of allegory as a means of explicating the supernatural correspondence between material objects and the cosmos, and of discerning in earthly things a reflection of God. They also sought to create works having the proper size and proportion, since it was in accordance with this rule that God created the world.

DIVINE INSPIRATION

Jean and Cécile find Hélène at the entrance to the hall where she is about to give her lecture. Students pass by, talking, without paying any attention to them.

JEAN   Hello, Hélène. Cécile told me about your lecture and I thought I'd come along with her. The last packet of pages we were given contained passages on allegorism, and since that's your topic today—

HÉLÈNE   But I shall be most horribly intimidated! All right, be on your best behavior then! In we go.

At the end of the lecture the students file out of the hall, and Cécile and Jean go out with Hélène for a walk. Not far from the Sorbonne, in the Place Paul-Painlevé, they pass before the Musée de Cluny.

HÉLÈNE   You know, this is really where we should go to see medieval art. If you look at *The Lady and the Unicorn,* an extraordinary set of tapestries, you can plainly see that the medieval distinction between artisans and artists didn't always apply: this is an example of an artisanal production that is nonetheless a great work of art.

And you can also see in these tapestries how the artists of this period—artists in the modern sense of the term—made use of allegory, which is to say a method of placing the physical world in correspondence with the spiritual world; a way of grasping the supernatural connections between material objects and the cosmos, of discerning in worldly things a reflection of God.

In my lecture I forgot to point out a distinction between that which is beautiful in and of itself (the Latin term is *pulcher*) and that which is beautiful as a function of something else (that is, *aptum).* To enjoy things of this world meant wallowing in an earthly mire, and yet certain pleasures were considered to be useful insofar as they helped to raise up the soul toward God.

JEAN   In other words, eating without any thought of higher things was considered sinful, but enjoying dishes that made one think of God was acceptable? If you please, Cécile, your next menu must have brilliant colors, with a mass of details that will make me think of something other than what I'm eating: the cosmos, God—

CÉCILE   But this is exactly what I'm trying my best to do! It seems to me, Hélène, that the distinction you mention is the origin of Brillat-

Savarin's famous aphorism, "Animals feed themselves, men eat; but only wise men know the art of eating." The wise man, or woman, is one who eats spiritually. And the cook, for his or her part, is called upon to ensure that we partake of lofty ideas rather than mere nutriments.

HÉLÈNE   In any case, isn't it still true—that culture is something higher than mere nourishment?

CÉCILE   Yes, but culture alone isn't sufficient. Culture is something you need to think about; if you don't, it passes by unnoticed, like water or a commonplace food. The cook must find a way to produce dishes that speak to the soul *and* the mind—not just in contemplative terms, as it were, as something one likes or dislikes, but in intellectual terms as well.

HÉLÈNE   Or you could stick more closely to the medieval idea by trying to create dishes that make one think of God: the whole religious iconography of the Middle Ages is there for you to exploit, from eating fish on Fridays to breaking bread with one's hands rather than cutting it with a knife. The cook's task is to adapt these references to new culinary purposes.

Keep in mind, too, that a dish that exemplifies Christian aesthetics must exhibit just the right balance and proportion, because it is in keeping with this principle, according to the Wisdom of Solomon, that God created the world: thus all things are ordered "by measure and number and weight."[58] It shouldn't be difficult to apply this idea. By not using too much salt, for example. Or by putting so little tarragon in a tarragon sauce that diners can't identify the sensation at once, rather than bombarding them with a massive dose—this is also a way of suggesting there is something hidden that has to be discovered. Or you could experiment with a "pastel" style—a cuisine all in halftones, without overly pronounced flavors, using sauces that aren't too reduced, that are softened with cream, and so on. Or how about this: you could also go against the medieval idea, subverting it by serving fish every day of the week except Friday, or bread that's been cut rather than broken—

JEAN (*laughing*)   Or you could start believing in God with every fiber of your being—in the hope that he would give you the inspiration needed to bring forth the good. . . .

AN ALLEGORICAL RECIPE

IN THEORY

Is Pierre Gagnaire a believer? If so, of what denomination? The question is indiscreet and, in any case, inappropriate to a work such as this. The task set for him here involves a constraint no less challenging than the twelve syllables of an alexandrine line: to devise a "religious" recipe in the allegorical spirit of the artists of the Middle Ages.

IN PRACTICE
TWO PASTRIES PLUS A SOUFFLÉ WITH CHARTREUSE

I know this may seem a bit facile, but behind the names of the two pastries—*sacristain* and *religieuse*—lies a true monastic dessert, based on Chartreuse, whose religiosity is threefold: first, it is produced by the Carthusian monks; second, it is green, like the hope symbolized by the resurrection of Christ; and third, its flavor also has something religious about it, since it is neither dry like vodka, nor hot like rum, nor woody like Cognac. It has the smooth, suave air of a priest shrouded in incense and cloaked in rich fabrics.

The dessert is composed of three parts, which recall the Holy Trinity:

- The *sacristain* is a flaky pastry sprinkled with powdered sugar. The white-ness of the sugar must be immaculate.
- The *religieuse,* on the other hand, is made from a classic choux pas-try, light yet starchy, filled with Chartreuse-flavored pastry cream.
- The soufflé has the lightness of an angel, airy and ephemeral. It is made with egg yolks, verbena liqueur, and cornstarch. Stiffly beaten egg whites are then carefully folded in, and the whole preparation is cooked in a metal ramekin that has been buttered and sprinkled with sugar.

Hervé's three rules for making a soufflé must not be forgotten. First, be sure to beat the egg whites until they are very stiff, so that on the one hand the steam formed at the bottom of the ramekin during cooking can-not easily escape, and on the other, the steam pushes the soufflé upwards rather than sideways. Second, before cooking, quickly put the ramekin under the broiler in order to get a very smooth, slightly golden surface that will retain the steam formed during cooking and assure a more uni-form expansion. Finally, the soufflé is cooked by heating the ramekin from the bottom (you may wish first to place the ramekin over a flame to make the soufflé rise before putting it in the oven).

YOUR TURN

Let your soul breathe in a bit of the mystical spirit that inspired artists during the Middle Ages. Pray and faith will come: what dish would you propose to offer up to the glory of God?

DISCOVERING SOMETHING HIDDEN

IN THEORY

This is a less difficult exercise than the last, since it follows from the basic idea of a *religieuse:* creating a dish in which there is something hidden waiting to be discovered. Give your imagination free rein. The talented cook will want to go beyond the simple idea of stuffing something with something else.

IN PRACTICE
DUCK BREASTS WITH BARBERRY MOUSSELINE
IN SAKE-FLAVORED BROTH

Stuffing an animal or a bird is always guaranteed to surprise, giving your guests the feeling that you've devoted special thought to them—that you've made their pleasure your responsibility. The idea is hardly new, of course: it was employed to spectacular effect in medieval banquets, where an entire stag was cut open to reveal a roasted wild boar, which was itself stuffed with a goose, which in turn contained small birds.

This technique lends itself to more delicate and subtle treatment as well. Begin, for example, by placing some duck breast fillets on a flat surface and covering them with a shallot-based filling. Then roll up the fillets, coat them with a barberry mousseline, and cook them in pork caul. They should be served in shallow bowls along with a duck broth flavored with sake, whose slight bitterness gives it a sharper edge.

The colors are muted, but the flavors are pure. The quality of the broth justifies stuffing the breast fillets in this manner. It's a little like a pot-au-feu that's been diverted from its usual course, sent off in another direction. Of course, enclosing one ingredient by another has its own culinary raison d'être in this case: the succession of layers serves to prevent the duck meat from coming directly in contact with the broth.

YOUR TURN

As a technical matter, embedding one ingredient inside another is not always easy to do, but the manual labor is less arduous than the intellectual labor that goes into a good recipe. It should be noted that there are lots of ways to form a stuffed piece of meat or fish. For example, put the fillet of meat or fish on top of some plastic food wrap, place a ball of stuffing on top of the fillet in the middle, then enclose the stuffing by joining the long sides of the fillet and pulling one side of the plastic film over the other to form a cylinder.

PASTEL RECIPES

IN THEORY

Everyone is familiar with the use of pastels in painting. The tones are soft, on the verge of being washed out. What I propose calling pastel in cooking has nothing to do with the color of a dish: as always, the essential thing is flavor. Pastel flavors have a gentle subtlety that nonetheless manages to avoid being insipid. A thoroughly delicate kind of cooking, very difficult to pull off.

IN PRACTICE

A LIGHT SOUP OF FROGS' LEGS WITH MUGWORT,
CREAMY SORREL POLENTA, AND DACE MOUSSELINE

Begin by sautéing the frogs' legs in some chilled butter, with pale gray shallots and a very good white wine from Alsace (a Riesling or a Gewürztraminer); work the sauce to a smooth, creamy consistency and add a delicate infusion of mugwort; then grind up the meat of the frogs' legs so that it absorbs the liquid. Push this mixture through a chinois, and thicken the soup with a little butter so that the consistency is a bit less thick than a crème anglaise.

The polenta is made with fresh corn flour and heated in the cooking juices from the frogs' legs. When it has swelled up and acquired a creamy quality, add a little sorrel or watercress to acidify it and in this way combat its blandness. The granular texture of polenta contributes an interesting dimension: you can use it like bread or pasta to mop up sauce on a plate.

The dace mousseline is made in the classical manner by pressing the flesh of this small freshwater fish through a sieve and folding in egg whites and cream. It is cooked in a mold at a low temperature, thus dispensing with the traditional technique for making quenelles, in which the fish mixture is shaped by passing it back and forth between two spoons. After all, why shouldn't we try to devise new shapes?

In the combination proposed here, everything is pastel except the sorrel. The frogs' legs, since they don't have much flavor, force the cook to play softly. Apart from the sorrel, only the note of a dash of juniper berry rises above the choir of muffled voices.

CREAMY CORN WITH SHEEP'S MILK
VELOUTÉ, POPCORN, AND VANILLA CHANTILLY

This recipe blends the tender, sweet, and savory with a bit of dreaming. Even the color contributes to this pastel mood. Nothing assaults the senses, and yet it is by no means an unmemorable dish.

The edge of the corn in this creamy soup is slightly softened by the sheep's milk velouté. The popcorn, though rather flavorless, imparts some chewiness since it is softened in its turn by contact with the cream.

YOUR TURN

Pastels often charm connoisseurs of fine painting. In cooking, however, there's always the risk that shades of flavor may become blurred. If a pastel dish is to avoid being nothing more than an accumulation of gustatory notes, none of them louder than the others, it must be carefully thought through beforehand. Can you manage to come up with an original pastel recipe, one that isn't just a muffled version of a traditional restaurant dish or recipe that you often make at home?

PART FOUR

ARTISTIC CREATIVITY UNBOUND

FIFTEEN

MEDIEVAL RAMIFICATIONS

The Middle Ages lasted nearly a millennium. Conceptions of man's relation to God quite naturally changed over such a long period, with the result that notions of what constituted art were many and varied. Robert
Grosseteste, Albertus Magnus, and Saint Bonaventure each made important contributions to the formation of aesthetic theory. With the optical
researches of Vitellion, a new emphasis came to be placed on the quali-
tative, subjective aspect of sensory experience, the full implications of
which were to be appreciated only much later.

INNER BEAUTY

*After discussing the most recent packet of pages with Cécile and Hélène
on their walk after Hélène's lecture, Jean telephones Inspector Belmont.*

JEAN   Hello, Jérôme? One more thing. You know those pages we showed
you about the Middle Ages? Well, there are more. They arrived in my mail-

box. Apparently I'm the one who's being targeted now. Read it to you?
Sure, but it's rather long. You've got time? Fine, here we go:

> The aesthetic tendencies of the Middle Ages were many and var-
> ied, for new ideas could hardly fail to evolve over such a long period.
> Moreover, the Church did not succeed in blending all these ten-
> dencies into a single movement.
>
> One approach is associated with the English philosopher Robert
> Grosseteste,* who observed: "If everything desires the good and
> the beautiful together, the good and the beautiful are the same."[59]
> What use can be made of this idea in cooking? The cook who con-
> cerns himself solely with the well-being of his guests, who endorses
> principles of healthy diet and nutrition, feeding his guests vegeta-
> bles because they contain fibers and vitamins, for example, might
> suppose that he is communicating beauty. The cook who seasons
> his food with the right amount of salt also makes use of this idea.
> But it would not be of much help to culinary artists, unless it were
> to be interpreted as a kind of constraint, just as the alexandrine (a
> line of twelve syllables) with its caesura (pause in the middle of the
> line) later provided authors such as Victor Hugo with a framework
> for composing poetry.
>
> Another aesthetic current derived from the thinking of the Ger-
> man theologian Albertus Magnus,† who proposed that beauty be
> defined not as a function of the perception that someone has of it,

---

*ROBERT GROSSETESTE (County of Suffolk, *ca* 1170–Lincoln, 1253): English church-
man and philosopher, one of the first chancellors of Oxford University. Noted for his
commentaries on the newly discovered works of Aristotle, many of which he translated from Greek into Latin, Grosseteste was an early proponent of the importance of
experiment in arriving at scientific truth.

†ALBERTUS MAGNUS (Albert the Great; Lauingen, Bavaria, 1200–Cologne, 1280): Dominican theologian and philosopher whose teaching in his native Germany and in Paris
helped make Aristotle's philosophy known in Europe. His students included Thomas
Aquinas.

but as a property of objects. In other words, just as a picture might be considered beautiful by all those who look at it, a dish might be thought good by all those who eat it. But this seems doubtful: cooks have not ceased to observe in the centuries since that opinions about food differ.

On the other hand, Albertus Magnus's theory did lead to one fruitful idea: if one hopes—without, however, being convinced of it—that the good exists, then one will be led to search for it. In much the same vein, the French poet Paul Valéry later remarked that "a true writer is someone who is unhappy with the words he has, and so goes out in search of better ones and finds them." Similarly, couldn't we think of a culinary artist as someone who, failing to achieve the flavor that he wants, looks for something better and finds it?

JÉRÔME   Is there much more?

JEAN   No, not too much. Now we come to the Italian theologian Bona-venture,* born in Bagioreg—sorry, Bag-no-re-gio—in Tuscany, who wrote: *"It will be said of the image of the devil that it is beautiful when it well represents the devil's ugliness, and that, as a result, it is ugly."* [60] The commentary continues:

The opposition between the absence of outward beauty (the tortured bodies of martyrs were ugly) and the presence of inner beauty is an important theme of the Middle Ages. [61]

Think of good and bad in relation to food. Is Munster good? The appearance of this cheese, which is to say its smell, is powerful and

---

*BONAVENTURE (Bagnoregio, 1221–Lyons, 1274): Italian theologian, appointed minister-general of the Franciscans in 1257 and cardinal bishop of Albano in 1273, who served as papal legate to the Council of Lyons. His many works of theology, inspired by the teachings of Saint Augustine, earned him the name "the Seraphic doctor." Bonaventure was canonized following his death.

commonly thought to be "ugly," but its flavor is smoother and thought to be "beautiful." By everyone? Or only by Alsatians?

In this connection, why do we sometimes like what is not a part of our cultural background? How do Japanese react to French cuisine? How do you react to Japanese cuisine?

JÉRÔME   This passage is interesting: it's the first time that the author directly addresses his reader—who, as it happens, is you.

JEAN   Finally, there's this:

During the same period, Vitellion* laid down two principles of interpretation in his treatise De Perspectiva: *the relativity of tastes, which are founded on differing cultural conventions; and the subjective orientation of sensory experience.*[62]

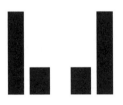

Toward the end of the Middle Ages, aesthetic curiosity began to venture beyond the realm of beauty that was apprehensible by the senses.[63] *"Form," which had referred to that which was visible on the surface, came to denote that which is concealed in the background.*[64] *Keep in mind that the significance of the places of Peter and Paul, to the right and the left of Christ in old mosaics in Rome, used to be a subject of intense debate.*[65] *There is a difference between these configurations. Construct the dish! Unite contraries!*

JÉRÔME   The author continues to address you directly, only now the tone is more personal. We need him to reveal himself a bit more—look,

---

*VITELLION (*also* Witelo; Borek [Lower Silesia], *ca* 1230–?, after 1280): Polish monk and geometer who made notable contributions to optics, summarized in *De Perspectiva* (1270), which developed a Neoplatonic metaphysics and emphasized the psychological aspects of visual perception.

send me a photocopy of all the pages so that I'll have my own record, okay? Everything you've got. And let me know if anything new develops.

A DIVINE EMANATION

IN THEORY

God can be present in a dish because he has been represented allegorically in it: this was the idea behind the recipes in chapters 13 and 14 involving the use of the color green. Nonetheless some dishes do seem to be infused with a sort of divine grace. Why this should be so is hard to say. Aesthetic analysis, still in its infancy in relation to cooking, struggles to explain why we react to certain combinations of flavors in certain ways, though the basic sensory facts are well understood. We need therefore to start with cooking itself, and work our way back to the aesthetic problems it raises.

IN PRACTICE
L'ORIENTALE

The idea for this recipe came to me during a trip to Morocco, during one of those idle moments when I was relaxed and my mind was free to wander. The problem was how to translate this restful moment of inspiration into a dish. It may be in this respect that I am, in my own modest way, a creator: one must try—quickly, at once!—to find a way to break through, to reach a space of freedom. This is why I try to make dishes evoke worlds, colors, feelings: in this case, a composed, carefully constructed vision of the Arab world—"the East"—using saffron, garlic, almond paste, sweet red peppers, white grapes, and so on.

In order to take into account the whole set of constraints of textures, smells, colors, flavors, and tastes, I made a sweet red pepper aspic with red currants and cubed watermelon, set at the edge of a bowl alongside a fillet of pigeon glazed with a kneaded almond paste. The pigeon itself rested on a bed of date paste, and was glazed a second time with its juices, which were sweetened and acidified by the addition of the juice from a bitter orange. The dish was garnished with a large prawn of the kind found off the Algerian coast, a few chickpeas, argan oil, and Nana mint, and served at room temperature.

TRUFFLES WITH SCALLOPS

I don't know why this dish inspired by the East seems divine to me—and still less why I associate it with another dish, involving truffles, which has nothing to do with it.

There is something transcendent about truffles, of course. Once I served them with a delicate scallop mousse, made by grinding the meat of the mollusk and combining it with cream and Manzanilla sherry, and then cooking the mousse at low temperature. On top I arranged a puree of truffles. I made this by sautéing some chopped truffle shavings in butter and deglazing the pan with Port, then adding some chicken stock and Balsamic vinegar, thickening the liquid with just a touch of butter, and cooking the shavings in the oven for ten minutes. At the last moment, just before serving, I sprinkled raw chopped truffles over the dish, with some hand-harvested sea salt and warm potatoes.

What makes a dish like this divine? I don't know. Everything has an earthy smell, a powerful odor of mineral oil and musk, an animal odor. Perhaps it is the ascending movement of these smells, rising up from the ground, that puts me in mind of the divine? Leaving the earth in order to be lifted up . . .

YOUR TURN

We find ourselves plunged back into difficulty. If Pierre himself doesn't know why these dishes make him think of heavenly things, how are we to know? There's only one possibility: like a man whose brains are made of gold, which he racks in search of the least particle of precious metal, we must dig deep to extract our innermost ideas of God—and then go into the kitchen.

SIXTEEN

THE OCCULT INFLUENCE OF ARISTOTLE LIVES ON

One influential medieval tradition, adopted from the ancient Greeks, sought to divide the world and most phenomena into four parts: four regions of the world, four cardinal points, four elements. In chemistry, a revolution occurred with the development of distillation, which produced a fifth element, the "quinte essence." Today we preserve something of this ancient prejudice in the form of the false doctrine of the four tastes. The time has come to combat it, in order to free cooks from an unproductive constraint that stands in the way of creativity. For the same reason, culinary techniques, which to a large extent even today remain medieval, need to be transformed.

THE FOUR ELEMENTS

It is dark outside, the city has fallen quiet. All the lights are turned off in Denis and Cécile's apartment, except in the study. Cécile sits at a table, writing in a notebook.

It's strange: I was the one who was most affected by *The Quintes-sential Art* to begin with, but now I feel removed from it—and re-lieved. New pages continue to appear but only in dribs and drabs, and now they are delivered alternately to Jean and Hélène.

Hélène recently found a page in her bag, which she'd left open next to her at the Bibliothèque Sainte-Geneviève, that began with the words: *"Our culinary culture and traditions are at once precious assets and brakes on innovation."*

"In the Middle Ages," it went on to say, *"an anonymous Carthu-sian monk composed a treatise on music. The ancients, he said, ar-gued in the following way: 'As it is in nature, so it ought to be in art: but nature divides itself in a quadripartite manner. . . . There are four regions of the earth, four elements, four primary qualities, four winds, four conditions of the body, four virtues of the soul and so on.'"* [66]

The next morning, Jean came by to discuss plans for the new restaurant we're opening together. He told me that he'd been jos-tled in the bus on his way here and that afterward, in his pocket, he found a page that elaborated on the idea communicated to Hélène: *"Four regions of the earth, four elements, four primary qualities, four winds, four conditions of the body, four virtues of the soul—and four tastes! Yet we know perfectly well that there are neither four re-gions of the earth, nor four chemical elements, nor four primary qual-ities, nor four tastes. The Middle Ages have to be left behind."*

That evening Jean called Hélène, who read him a new passage that had come to her in the mail, further clarifying the one Jean had received.

It's curious how this unknown person (or persons) goes about transmitting these commentaries on art to us. They seem now to want to draw Jean and Hélène closer together. I don't really know if they'll succeed in this: Hélène is lost in her tales of the past, in her abstractions; and Jean is caught up in the action, the events of the present. You can see they're circling around each other, but will their paths ever coincide? I don't know.

When I told Denis about this business of dividing things into fours, he mentioned Aristotle's theory that all matter is made up of four elements: fire, water, earth, and air. This quadripartite division delayed the development of chemistry until the Swiss physician Theophrastus Bombastus von Hohenheim, better known as Paracelsus (1493–1541), put forth a theory of distillation, which he saw as separating the essential part of a raw material from the dross. This led him to formulate the doctrine of "quintessence," according to which the distilled part constituted a fifth essence, or element.

And that is how, several centuries later, the same idea came to be found in Marin's book, *The Gifts of Comus*, which argued that cooking was a branch of chemistry that aimed at "quintessentializing" sauces! Mainly this meant searching for hidden meanings: to quintessentialize was to distill, but also to extract, reduce—to give flavor, in a sense. All of which reminded me of a long passage from the old book that I had copied down before it was stolen:

In order to bring out the flavors of a dish, there are two main possibilities. The first is that the principal ingredients either have flavor or are capable of acquiring flavor in the course of cooking. In this case, the art of cooking consists largely in choosing products that have the most flavor (in keeping with predefined artistic standards) or that are most likely to possess flavor as a consequence of culinary transformations.

The second possibility, which is often encountered, is that the cook needs to introduce into a given food, whether solid or liquid, a flavor that does not appear in it. One way to do this is by adding spices, but it is not the only one. Cooking is related to other "chemical arts," which have learned how to extract molecules from natural products in order to obtain concentrated solutions or pure liquids—what are called extracts.

Thus, for example, pure liquids may be obtained as a result of pressing: vegetable and animal matter, broken up by the application of pressure, releases its juices. These fluids sometimes separate spontaneously into two phases, one watery and the other oily, each of which dissolves different molecules, with the result that they have different flavors.

Grinding is an operation of the same type as pressing, but the destructuring of the vegetable and animal matter is more thorough.

In order to obtain odorant or sapid molecules in solution, one puts aromatic substances in a liquid, either water or oil. A family of related techniques—maceration, infusion, and decoction—has the purpose of dissolving the various odorant and sapid molecules. Each of these methods yields a different result, essentially because the hotter the solvent (the liquid that dissolves the molecules) and the longer the operation lasts, the more completely the molecules are extracted.

Maceration consists in placing a solid body in a cold liquid for a certain period of time. Examples of this method include fragrant oils (flavored with herbs such as basil) and vinegars (made by introducing a sprig of tarragon, for instance).

Infusion is a procedure well known to drinkers of teas of various kinds: odorant and sapid molecules are extracted with the aid of water that is heated, though not to the point of boiling, lest these molecules escape into the air.

Finally, decoction involves boiling one or more ingredients in a liquid. A broth or stock is a product of decoction, for example.

These three operations can be carried out in oil, water, or alcohol. Obviously, the lower the temperature at which extraction occurs, the fewer odorant and sapid molecules react chemically and the less completely they are denatured. Infusion stands in particularly sharp contrast to decoction. If you compare an infusion made by putting tea leaves in hot water for less than three minutes with a decoction made with the same leaves, you will find that the infusion has a delicate fragrance, whereas in the decoction the smell has been lost and a bitter taste appears.

French cooks have intuitively understood this phenomenon. Indeed, both Escoffier[67] and Madame Saint-Ange[68] advised their readers that pepper must not be left for more than eight minutes in a boiling liquid. One has only to perform a simple experiment in order to confirm this venerable maxim. Divide a quantity of stock into two equal parts and place the pots over identical burners. Put fifteen peppercorns in one of the pots and none in the other; after twenty minutes of cooking, put fifteen peppercorns in the other pot and cook the two stocks for another four minutes. Then taste the two stocks: the one in which the pepper was boiled longer has lost its spiciness; the flavor of the pepper is no longer fresh.

This phenomenon is easily explained. Just as when you make a cup of tea, the volatile molecules are the first ones to be extracted, followed by the molecules that are more strongly bound, such as tannins, while some of the odorant molecules are lost. In the case of pepper, since piperine (the molecule responsible for its spiciness) is volatile, it is rapidly extracted, and then eliminated, whereas the tannins are extracted only gradually. The spiciness is lost and a sharpness (or astringency) asserts itself in its place.

Various techniques used in modern chemistry—though not yet, alas, in cooking—are improved versions of these traditional methods. A Soxhlet extractor permits continuous high-temperature extraction while rapidly recycling solvents. Enfleurage, an extreme form of maceration, involves placing delicate aromatic products (flowers, for example—hence the name) in contact with a neutral, solid fat. These elements are then hermetically sealed so that the evaporated volatile molecules are dissolved in the fat. Periodically the flowers are replaced with fresh ones. Once the fat is highly enriched in volatile molecules, it is melted in order to recover the essential oils dissolved in it.

Separating funnels and other similar devices are used in research laboratories to extract and divide both hot and cold liquids. Chemists generally put two nonmiscible liquids in a separation funnel (for cooking purposes, oil and water are good candidates, or alcohol and oil).

Adding a mixture of molecules, some of them soluble in water and others soluble in oil, one obtains an oily phase, on the one hand, and a watery phase, on the other, which capture different molecules. In the same way one can divide a flavor (of chanterelles, for example, using whole mushrooms) into two parts: one produced by the molecules that dissolve in oil, and the other from the molecules that dissolve in water.

Finally, the technique of distillation, at ambient or other pressures, could easily be employed to extract several different aromatic fractions of a given product. Although distillation is generally associated with the manufacture of alcohols, which is strictly regulated, no law prohibits the distillation of sauces or stocks, even of foods. Do you have any idea of the remarkable flavors that could be obtained in this way?

Now Jean has received another packet, again by round-about means, that answers the one Hélène received:

Let us come back to the anonymous Carthusian monk who referred to four winds, four temperaments, and so forth. At the time it was also thought that there were four primary colors. Since then science has conclusively demonstrated that this is false: three basic colors are enough to generate all the shades and tones of the palette, which can therefore be represented as forming a three-dimensional space.

Would four tastes similarly suffice to generate all known tastes? No—the false doctrine of the four tastes is what stands in our way today: just as the number of chemical elements is not four, as Aristotle believed, but exceeds a hundred; and just as the number of colors is not four, but infinitely large; so the number of tastes is not four, but probably infinite, like the number of smells. Licorice, for example, cannot be made out of only sweet, sour, bitter, and salt. By adhering to the unscientific theory of the four tastes, we remain stuck back in the Middle Ages. Cooking must be liberated.

As Inspector Belmont points out, the strange thing about these documents is the way they combine the ancient with the modern: there is a sort of continuous thread of culinary knowledge from antiquity up until the present day—as if a contemporary author had added to a palimpsest in which the learning of one generation was absorbed and assimilated by the next, and then incorporated in a new layer of writing. The text continues:

*Sapid molecules, perceived by the papillae that are distributed over the tongue and in the mouth, form an unexplored world: it was only a short time ago that the existence of a fifth taste, called umami, was internationally recognized (quite belatedly, and even then rather begrudgingly). The history of this development is bound up with that of glutamic acid, discovered in 1886 by the German chemist B. Ritthauser, who had tried to decompose gliadin, a protein found in bread.[69] Ritthauser went on to isolate monosodium glutamate (MSG). Then, in 1908, the Japanese chemist Kikunae Ikeda observed that glutamic acid was the sapid molecule present in a species of seaweed called kombu (*Laminaria japonica*). Ikeda used 40 kilograms of seaweed to recover 30 grams of glutamic acid. Then he patented a method for producing monosodium glutamate from wheat flour. In 1909, the Ajinomoto Company (from the Japanese phrase* aji no moto, *meaning "essence of taste") was formed to market MSG, which is easily manufactured from the gluten in wheat, an elastic substance obtained by kneading flour and water, then rinsing the lump of dough in a bowl of water in order to remove any white starchy powder.*

Umami, now accepted as a fifth taste, is associated with dashi, the Japanese broth made from kombu. This distinctive taste is due to two amino acids: glutamic acid and alanine. It is subtly different from MSG, and (contrary to what the producers of MSG claim) probably not a universal taste present in shellfish and members of the lily family (onions, garlic, shallots, and so on). For while it is true that these things contain glutamic acid, they also contain many other amino acids, each having its own particular taste. One ought to refer instead to the amino acid tastes since—well, you can see for yourself.

Finally, how do we perceive tastes? Just as we have only seven words to describe an infinite number of colors, we have an inadequate vocabulary for tastes. How many basic tastes are there? Neurophysiologists are actively studying this question, but their task is a difficult one, because we seldom perceive tastes in an isolated fashion: they are generally associated with smells, and their perception depends on a great many factors: training (in the case of trained tasters in laboratory studies), temperature, and so on. To be able to distinguish between them more clearly, try eating different foods while a gentle current of air is blown into your nose: since the odorant molecules are prevented from passing up through the retronasal fossae (which link the mouth and the nose, at the rear of the oral cavity), you perceive only the taste. In this way you will discover that there is not a single sweet taste, but several: sweetening agents all have different tastes and aftertastes. The descriptive terms currently in use for tastes are sweet, licorice, caramel, burnt sugar, bitter, sour, mentholated; and, for aftertastes, licorice, bitter, sweet, and metallic. The oral sensations are described in terms of body, dryness, astringency, roundness, irritation, and freshness.

Furthermore, we are all different: the compound called phenylthiocarbamide, for example, is perceived as bitter by certain individuals and as tasteless by others. These differences are genetic.[70] And salt in weak concentrations triggers a sensation similar to the one produced by sugar.[71] These tastes are not detected by particular areas of the tongue, as has often been claimed: most papillae display few affinities for one another, and they typically react to several substances. The Japanese physiologists Keiichi Tonosaki and Masaya Funakoshi have shown, for example, that, of 29 mouse taste cells reacting to sucrose (ordinary sugar), 26 also reacted to salt and 27 to chlorogenic acid.[72]

How tastes interact with one another is the great unknown. We are far from understanding why sugar and salt permeate mouth tissues, whereas bitterness leaves the palate entirely untouched.[73] And as for bitterness—which one? Some kinds of bitterness are combated by sugar, such as the one found in browned onions, but not the bitterness encountered in drinks containing quinine. Édouard Nignon, one of the great chefs of the early twentieth century, clearly grasped that there is not a single kind of bitterness, but several— which is what physiologists are demonstrating today.

Everything is confused. It is time to start over again from scratch, basing our inquiry on recent results in sensory neurophysiology. Most people correctly use the word "flavor" to describe the general sensation that they perceive while eating: a food can have a good flavor or a bad flavor. Flavor is the overall, synthetic sensation that we have prior to any subsequent attempt to break it down into its constituent elements.

Which sensations compose flavor? First, as we bring a food toward the mouth, we notice that it has a color, which partly determines our expectation of what it will taste like. The fact that we are mystified by unnaturally colored foods (try adding flavorless color agents to samples of apple jelly, for example, and conducting a blind taste test) is proof that color is a component of flavor. Tactile sensations are also a determining factor, but our cultural preference for eating with utensils has caused us to forget this fact (something worth thinking about—it may contain a seed of practical culinary progress).

As the food approaches the mouth, we perceive its smell. The smell of a food results from the evaporation of molecules initially present in it: the more volatile these molecules are, the greater the chance that they will stimulate large numbers of receptor cells in the nose. It should be noted that we sometimes call these molecules "aromas," which confuses them with the sensation that they produce. For the sake of clarity, we should insist on calling molecules that are perceived by the nose "odorant" molecules, while keeping in mind that some of them stimulate senses other than olfaction.

Now the food enters the mouth. Some of its molecules pass into the saliva, and subsequently bind with other molecules, known as receptors, on the surface of special cells in the buccal cavity. It is these so-called sapid molecules that give the sensation of taste. The cells bearing the receptors of these molecules are grouped together in the form of papillae (the small round nodes you see on the tongue, commonly known as taste buds).

In the mouth, chewing brings about the evaporation of other molecules, which rise up into the nose from the rear of the mouth through the retronasal fossae. This is also a part of olfaction.

Still other food molecules behave in different ways in the mouth. Some stimulate cells that signal pain and heat, producing the sensation of spiciness. Other sensor cells detect mechanical characteristics: thus we perceive hardness, softness, fattiness, moistness, and so on.

Nor should we forget the sense of hearing, which comes into play when we eat crispy or crunchy foods, for example, with the result that sounds propagated by the muscles and bones involved in mastication reach the ears.

All these sensations—of color, taste, and smell, of mechanical and thermal properties, proprioception, and so on—make up what we call flavor. Once perceived physiologically, they are interpreted by the brain, which associates flavors with qualities as a function of individual and social experience (memories, emotions, training, and so on).

Ought we therefore call the perception of the general sensation we call flavor "gustation"? There is no reason why we shouldn't— but in that case the perception of taste should be known by a different name: sapiction.

That's as far as we've gotten. Inspector Belmont seems to have taken an interest in the case. He's trying to be reassuring, but Jean and Hélène are both uneasy. Clearly they are being closely watched and followed, since the new packets of pages are now being delivered to them. And Hélène hasn't recovered from the shock of her car accident: she fears the arrival of each new packet.

A RECIPE WITH MANY TASTES

IN THEORY

To combat the false doctrine of the four tastes, nothing beats a recipe that involves more than four tastes, and, still better, that brings out these tastes in a way that is readily perceptible. To be sure, a recipe is not a demonstration, only a promising indication—and an invitation to learn more.

IN PRACTICE
BRAISED SQUAB WITH RED PEPPERS, CARDAMOM FRAGRANCE, AND SWEET-AND-SOUR RED CABBAGE

Squab is a young nestling pigeon that has not yet taken flight. It is very tender, and this tenderness is associated with a quite particular flavor.

The squab is roasted whole, and when still rather rare removed from the oven and left to rest on its breastbone, with the meat still attached. This allows the meat to relax while retaining its juices, which are diffused from the center of the bird, the least cooked part, toward the outside, which has become slightly dry and whose flavor has changed as a result of cooking. You then remove the breast fillets, reserving the thighs, wings, and carcass.

The sauce is made by a long, slow cooking of the carcass and reserved

pieces in wine, which allows sapid (or taste) molecules to be extracted from the meat, and gelatin from the bones and cartilage; some of these molecules react chemically with the molecules in the wine, while the ethanol and the most volatile odorant molecules evaporate. You then strain the liquid, adding to it some roasted cacao beans, and simmer it so that the sauce is enriched by the sapid molecules of the chocolate and the burnt taste disappears. Strain it a second time in order to obtain a clear sauce, then heat it again until it is hot (though not boiling) and infuse some green cardamom in it, covering the pan (you want to preserve all of the cardamom's odorant molecules).

Now place a sweet red pepper over the burner, turning it until the skin is charred on all sides; then remove the skin, cutting off the cap and extracting the tough internal parts and the seeds. Coat the pigeon fillets generously with butter and close them up inside the pepper with the peel from a lemon and a sprig of silver thyme. Cook rapidly in a very hot oven, then let rest for twenty minutes. Remove the pigeon and put it aside, discarding the aromatic ingredients, and finely dice the pepper, which is then sautéed in olive oil until crunchy. This will be served separately, a little like a salad.

The red cabbage is cut into very thin slices using a mandolin and immediately sautéed in butter (vegetables that are cut up and left exposed to the air take on a bad flavor). When the butter begins to foam, add some red wine, grenadine, and vinegar (the vinegar gives the cabbage a bit of crunchiness). Finally, add a few really nice black currants that have been macerated in white brandy.

At this point you finish the pigeon sauce, thickening it, if you like, with a dash of starch to accentuate its syrupy, adhesive quality. To complete the thickening, add a touch of bitter chocolate and a knob of butter, gently moving the pan back and forth (be sure not to stir the sauce with a whisk or spoon, which would ruin the sheen you want to achieve). This glistening effect is an essential aspect of the sauce: what you want

to end up with is the equivalent of a varnish on a painting, a layer that gives it a shiny transparence as well as depth. You have to pay very close attention, so that the sauce is just thick enough to coat each piece without sticking.

Finally you reheat the fillets, which until now have been left in their skin. Once they are hot, remove the skin and put it in the sauce, and then strain. Cut the fillets in thin slices, or into pieces that you thread onto skewers, and place them on top of the red cabbage.

The red cabbage brings both sweetness and sourness. The sauce has a residual bitterness that comes from the roasted chocolate and the infused cardamom. The wine contributes an acidity distinct from that of the cabbage. Two other flavors—from the onion in the aromatic garnish that accompanies the reheating of the fillets, together with a small head of garlic (unless the pan is rubbed with garlic beforehand)—are added to the preceding ones without, however, being confused with them. The garnish also includes carrot, which brings some sugar (or rather sugars, since it releases glucose and fructose as well as sucrose). In addition to these sapid molecules there are also astringent molecules (the tannins in the wine, for example).

Beyond my instructions for this recipe, which were to combine a great many different tastes, there is the artistic idea that the chocolate serves as a thickening agent, while also deepening both the color and flavor of the sauce. The squab has a wild flavor that is accentuated by the method of cooking. To achieve the desired result, you mustn't try for anything too nuanced: the effect must be powerful, emphasizing the bloody appearance of the bird (which has been choked rather than bled).

The dish depends for its effect, too, on a certain flavor that calls to mind old, tanned leather and forest undergrowth, with muted, sensuous notes. Obviously this is a winter dish. It would probably be a mistake, a proof of a lack of subtlety, to add wild mushrooms; only button mushrooms can be recommended for the braising stock. I like button mush-

rooms a lot, by the way, as a sauce base, because they have the same virtues as a veal stock that is used properly, which is to say discerningly, sparingly, and only in certain well-chosen cases.

YOUR TURN

Before setting out to make a recipe that involves more than four tastes, I invite you to discover the world of tastes experimentally. Take a small aquarium pump and connect the outlet tube to an improvised nose mask, which you can make with modeling clay; gently blow a slight current of air into your nose while you eat. The air current will prevent the odorant molecules from passing upward through the retronasal fossae and thus let you finally perceive the true taste of different foods.

Once you've tried this and convinced yourself that the world of tastes cannot be reduced to the canonical four terms, you will be able at last to walk along a culinary road that has been cleared of misleading preconceptions.

SEVENTEEN

THE DAWN OF THE RENAISSANCE

Toward the close of the Middle Ages, the idea took hold that artists must imagine, and that what they imagine must appear to be real. More than this, it came to be believed that artists must bring forth ideas from matter— a notion similar to that of the abstract painters of the twentieth century. We must nonetheless be careful to avoid anachronism: the urge to imitate nature was long to remain deeply rooted in the minds of artists.

IMAGINING

Near the entrance to the Luxembourg Gardens at the Rue de Vaugirard, Hélène and Jean are standing in line in front of the Musée du Sénat. In the fog, a couple dozen people are waiting ahead of them to be allowed in.

HÉLÈNE It's kind of you to come with me to see this exhibition of fifteenth-century painting. I thought you were interested only in modern art.

JEAN   Not at all. It's just that I don't know what to make of this repetition of the same motifs. Mary and the infant Jesus, for example—there must be thousands of them. No doubt you can enlighten me—and be my guide, because I get lost in the Louvre. In return I'll be your restaurant guide.

HÉLÈNE   Enlighten you—well, it will be all the easier since the latest packet of pages I've received has done half my work for me. This time it was placed in my hands.

JEAN   How?

HÉLÈNE   I was on my way to my lecture, calmly—actually no, not calmly—I don't know how it's been for you, but I haven't felt at all at ease lately, with everything that's been happening to us. I was walking along the Rue des Écoles, when someone came from behind and took me by the arm and said, "Take this, quick, and put it in your bag. Be careful." Then he rushed off ahead of me.

JEAN   What did he look like?

HÉLÈNE   Short, rather plump. He had short hair, and a very pronounced accent, Burgundian I'd say. Sideburns. A dark raincoat.

JEAN   Did you notify Jérôme?

HÉLÈNE   Yes, and he said we could meet this evening to talk about it.

JEAN   What, this evening? But I'd been counting on taking you out to dinner at—

HÉLÈNE   Ah, no, not tonight. Tomorrow?

JEAN (*a bit curtly*)   No, not tomorrow, I've got a meeting at work that's going to run late.

HÉLÈNE   Look, they're letting us in finally. And we're in luck—at this time of day there's no crowd. Ah, there's a very rare picture, by Cennino Cennini.

JEAN   Who's that?

HÉLÈNE   An Italian painter and writer about art, born in Siena around 1370 if I remember correctly—yes (*checking the plate next to the picture*). He died in Padua sometime in the early fifteenth century. Cennini was one of the first, at the end of the Middle Ages, to hold the view that the artist must imagine, and that his imaginings must seem real.[74]

JEAN   So that was the big change, was it—imagining? In the Middle Ages, as we know from the pages we've been receiving, it was all a matter of repetition. I was wondering when the artist was going to be able finally to imagine things—to make dreams real, to express whatever thoughts came to his mind. That's what art is to me, especially culinary art. Enough of these stews, pot-au-feus, daubes, cassoulets, choucroutes—

HÉLÈNE   Hold on, you're jumping ahead a few centuries. Cennini wasn't advocating an entirely unbridled imagination. For him, imagination had to remain within the limits of what was thought of as reality.

JEAN   Which was what?

HÉLÈNE   Well, let me give you a comparison—a culinary comparison, to make you happy. Let's begin by trying to imagine what could be done with a leek, for example. There are any number of possibilities: you could make a cheese with it, since the word *fromage* comes from the Latin for "form." The form in the case of cheese making is a strainer, which serves as a receptacle for the cheese after the whey has been drained off from the curd, which gives the cheese a shape. You could use the leek as a container instead. Or you could use it to make a layer cake, or even a piece of sculpture unsuited for human consumption, a little like what is done with spun sugar or carved ice. Cennini says that what is imagined must seem real—that the dish we imagine making with the leek must be leek-like.

JEAN   So it couldn't be a layer cake, then.

HÉLÈNE   No, you're right—the leek must remain as it is, a side dish.

JEAN   Why? Says who?

HÉLÈNE   Aristotle. Cennini's principle echoed the Aristotelian idea that a work of art, as an imitation of nature, must stick as closely as possible to the object that is represented: one must imitate, and the leek must remain a leek.

JEAN   In other words, any innovation that our age might devise is prohibited—but on what grounds?

HÉLÈNE   On the grounds that if our age has gone further, it is not because artists today are more intelligent or more learned than the philosophers of the past, but because "we are dwarfs sitting on the shoulders of giants."

JEAN   As Isaac Newton said!

HÉLÈNE   No—well, yes, he did say it; but he wasn't the first. Bernard of Chartres was. And Montesquieu, in the sixteenth century, expressed much the same idea in saying that we extend the reach of those who came before us.

But to come back to Cennini, I believe that the past is the past: culinary artists can never hope to put themselves back in his shoes. But this one idea of his—the need to imagine—will stay with them. Oh, look at this wonderful copy of Lodovico Castelvetro's edition of Aristotle's *Poetics!*[75]

JEAN   Who's Lodovico Castelvetro?

HÉLÈNE   He was a sixteenth-century Italian literary critic who formulated a new, stricter version of Aristotle's theory of the unity of time and space in art, especially drama. What a marvelous example of book production! The attention to detail is really—

JEAN   And the book next to it? That's not bad either.

HÉLÈNE   I don't know what that is. Let's look at the plate—ah, yes, Leon

Battista Alberti's treatise on painting. Alberti* held that a picture is "an open window on the world."[76]

JEAN   Like the plate for the cook, in a way.

HÉLÈNE   You think only of eating!

JEAN   No, not really. Well, yes and no. After all, you're fond of good food, too: the leek—who brought that up?

HÉLÈNE   That was only to please you!

JEAN   Well, it's true, even so. The plate, for a culinary craftsman, is a simple container in which the result of a piece of manual labor is deposited. A sort of constraint. For a culinary artist, on the other hand—I'm going to mention this idea to Cécile. She could do a lot with it in the new restaurant.

HÉLÈNE   So when are you going to open? Do you think Cécile will have enough time for two restaurants? Isn't Denis jealous of you being with Cécile all the time?

JEAN   All the time? Very little, actually. I've got my hands full handling the business side of things, dealing with the banks and the suppliers. Cécile's busy recruiting her new cooks and setting up the kitchen. I don't think we see each other *enough,* at least not if we're going to get everything organized properly—

HÉLÈNE   But Denis?

JEAN   Denis will be jealous no matter what happens. He's madly in love with Cécile and she's madly in love with him. Someone only has

---

*LEON BATTISTA ALBERTI (Genoa, 1404–Rome, 1475): Italian humanist and architect whose treatises on painting and architecture made him the first great theorist of art of the Renaissance. Among many other projects, Alberti produced drawings and wooden scale models for buildings in Rimini (the Malatesta temple), Florence (Rucellai Palace), and Mantua (Church of Sant'Andrea).

to come near either one of them for the other to show his claws. I wouldn't like that, living with someone who makes me her own, taking away my freedom.

HÉLÈNE I wouldn't mind. It's comforting to know that someone's looking after you. Think of the graduated scale in music: it doesn't have all the pitches, but that didn't prevent Bach from composing his extraordinary concertos. Within a certain framework, freedom remains.

JEAN Yes, but why impose this framework on yourself?

HÉLÈNE Oh, you can remain single, without any attachments, without a framework—without a plate, if you like. But if you want to have dinner for two, for example—

JEAN Hmmm . . . But you won't deny that, in art, the constraints of a period determine the style, and that the great artists manage more or less to escape the stylistic framework of their age.

The interesting thing, it seems to me, is that a picture doesn't have to have the same shape as Alberti's window, a rectangular wooden frame with the canvas that supports the painting stretched over it. It can be any number of things: a canvas in a round frame, or a canvas without any frame at all, or a picture in several framed pieces that you rearrange to suit your mood.

Just so, the classic round plate we're used to eating off of could be changed as well: today you see plates having various shapes—rectangular, square, triangular, what have you—and that are made out of equally varied materials—wood, metal, porcelain, and so on. The plate could even be divided into a series of containers in which the different parts of a dish are arranged.

HÉLÈNE Like the plates of raw vegetables that were popular a few years ago: one compartment for each kind? There's nothing new about that!

JEAN   How about a dish that is divided up and served on a series of plates, bowls, saucers, ramekins—

HÉLÈNE   Someone will have to explain to me how I'm supposed to eat it. This is getting awfully intellectual!

JEAN   And another thing, while I'm thinking of it: Alberti says that a painting lets us see the world. What world does the plate show us? Through a window one sees the real world. In a plate, Alberti would have us see nature: raw vegetables—crudités, to put the matter, uh, crudely. Nonetheless the world is also a world of human beings. Windows show factories, cities, and so on. Couldn't the plate also show human labor? Foods that have been transformed, manipulated—even synthesized? No aesthetic law prohibits us from imagining such a thing.

HÉLÈNE   I forgot to tell you that Alberti also adopted Plotinus's view that art must bring ideas out of matter. Can you imagine that in cooking?

JEAN   I don't know. You'd have to ask Cécile.

HÉLÈNE   Oh, look, we're coming to some works by Leonardo da Vinci. I told you that this exhibition was marvelous: the Louvre loaned the rarest pieces from its collections!

JEAN   I never quite understood what da Vinci was up to. There's the *Mona Lisa,* not my favorite picture, I must say; and then all those notebooks, where I can't work out whether he's drawing or doing science—

HÉLÈNE   What do you mean, he was a genius! And amazingly productive until a ripe old age: remember that after living most of his life in Florence and Milan he came to France at the invitation of François I, in 1516, I think it was, when he would have been in his sixties—three years before he died. Of course he's famous for the *Mona Lisa,* but he painted a great many other pictures as well—*The Virgin of the Rocks,* a Last Supper, *The Virgin and Child with Saint Anne,* which you see here.

He concerned himself with every branch of art—architecture and sculpture in addition to painting—and he also took an active interest in technology and the sciences. He designed a parachute made from a linen curtain and attached to a square frame; apparently engineers tested a device made from his designs a few years ago and it worked! Da Vinci observed, he drew, he sought to understand everything from whirlpools to the flight of birds. With regard to painting, his aesthetic point of view was clear: "That painting is worthiest of praise which displays the greatest resemblance to the things it wishes to render—thus are refuted those painters who wish to correct the things of nature."[77]

JEAN   Hmmm . . . Cooking won't get very far with that: we're still stuck with the problem of imitation.

WHEN THE LEEK
IS NO LONGER A SIDE DISH

IN THEORY

Why should a meal inevitably be composed of an appetizer, main course, a cheese, and a dessert? Why should the main course unvaryingly be composed of a meat or fish and a side dish? Why should sweet dishes always follow savory dishes? A serious reappraisal of traditional assumptions is required. Let's begin with the simplest question: the side dish. How can it be avoided?

IN PRACTICE
MARKET TERRINE

Vegetables are often served as side dishes: the very name expresses nothing but contempt for the role it assigns to them. Yet every product is entitled to enjoy the limelight. Indeed, ingredients usually thought of as masters can also be servants.

For example, foie gras that has been pushed through a sieve and heated in a stock can be whisked to obtain a foamy emulsion that Hervé calls "Chantilly foie gras." When combined with oysters, for example, this noble preparation can certainly play a leading role, but why not serve it as a side dish?

The white part of a leek, on the other hand, sliced open and stuffed with Chantilly foie gras, can be treated as the principal element of a main course, its centerpiece, rather than as a side dish. It assumes even greater importance in the terrine that I made several years ago by alternating layers of foie gras puree, made with Coleman's mustard, and large blanched leeks. This preparation was chilled in the refrigerator, and then served with red beet juice on top of a layer of jelly made by concentrating veal stock, with small gherkin cucumbers, capers, and a good *ravigote* sauce.

YOUR TURN

Take the most common side dish you know and give it the leading role, so that the vegetable is the central element of the dish, and the meat or fish secondary.

ESCAPING THE TYRANNY
OF THE ROUND PLATE

IN THEORY

Finding alternatives to round plates is not all that difficult, but coming up with meaningful alternatives, rather than doing something different simply for the sake of novelty, isn't so easy. There are many cultures that do not use Western-style plates, of course, and traveling will stimulate your imagination in this respect. The challenge is to adapt novel shapes to the idea of the dish.

IN PRACTICE
SORBETS AND SAUCE IN A "GUTTER"

Our plates happen to be round, but this is hardly inevitable. Today, square and triangular plates are common—and many other shapes remain to be explored.

A few years ago I came close to reviving the trencher of the Middle Ages, the slice of bread that served as a plate. In this case it was not quite the plate, since it rested on a square napkin of immaculate linen, with cheeses decoratively arranged on top of the bread.

I've also used "gutters"—long, rectangular, glazed earthenware receptacles with high sloping sides, so called for their resemblance to old street gutters—to serve small Spanish hot peppers known as *palamos,* macerated in olive oil and accompanied by an olive-oil sorbet (the oil is frozen and then scraped with a potato peeler) with white grapes macerated in Manzanilla and bay leaf.

This container amounted to something more than a lame attempt at originality, for by allowing me to order the various ingredients of the dish in a linear sequence, one after the other, while at the same time emphasizing their individual character, it was perfectly adapted to the effect that I was seeking to achieve. In the narrow bottom of the gutter I added a little oil and Manzanilla syrup. And to prevent the sorbet from running off in every direction as it melted, I lined the sides of the gutter with a mixture of dried cauliflower powder and almond and hazelnut powder.

I'm hardly the first person to do such a thing: Japanese cooks have long explored ways of retaining juices with the aid of ingeniously designed containers. Nonetheless this is an important aspect of culinary technique that requires further investigation. Yesterday, for example, I was unsatisfied with a black currant sorbet served with thin slices of carrot and some carrot juice. Similarly, I was unsatisfied with a reduction of Port and red wine in a dish that contained button mushrooms, kumquats, long narrow strips of rich *pâte sablée,* and a julienne of mango. Why was I unsatisfied? Because the shape of the plate didn't allow the spoon to pick up the juices that were mixed together—juices that, from the culinary point of view, had a real reason to be mixed together. Sometimes the problem can be solved by rearranging the ingredients, but in other cases it's necessary to change the container.

YOUR TURN

This time a simple game: look around you and try to imagine ways of using as plates or containers all the unusual objects you see. Don't be content simply with filling them with various dishes. Think carefully about the particular meaning of each dish and your reasons for putting it in a particular receptacle.

EIGHTEEN

FROM THE RENAISSANCE ONWARD

During the Renaissance, the artistic genre of the grotesque reunited contraries: the material and the spiritual, the inert and the animate, and so on. Although many philosophers and artists still hesitated to acknowledge taking the Greeks as their models, their advocacy of reason gradually began to free aesthetics from Christian principles.

OPENING DOORS

Inspector Belmont rings the bell of Hélène's apartment. Doors can be heard closing inside. Hélène then appears and lets him in.

JÉRÔME   Excuse me for being late.

HÉLÈNE   Please come in. Nothing today, nothing new.

JÉRÔME   Good. There's already a lot of material. Do you mind if I take a look at the last document you received?

HÉLÈNE   Here it is. With a sketch of a château in the Loire. The sketch is new. There's also some information about the Renaissance.

JÉRÔME   Let's see: *"With mannerism (and particularly Vasari), the 'drawing' is the visible expression of the concept formed in the mind; the concept derives from the contemplation of individual instances."* Who's Vasari?

HÉLÈNE   Vasari? Giorgio Vasari, born in Arezzo in 1511 and died in Florence in 1574. He was truly a man of his time: painter, architect, and writer on art. He is known above all for his *Lives of the Artists,* which talks a great deal about the Florentine school.

JÉRÔME   Say, you really know this stuff! Why don't we go have dinner? I haven't had anything to eat since eight o'clock this morning. It's on me.

HÉLÈNE   You mean—

JÉRÔME   Let's go, you'll be home soon enough if you've still got things to do. I know a quiet place not far from here. And you can explain things to me on the way. Bring all the documents you've got.

Hélène excuses herself and goes off to get ready. Jérôme looks around, takes a book from the bookcase, sits down, sets the book on the table, gets up, walks around the table, comes back and sits down. He seems satisfied.

After rather a long while changing clothes and putting on makeup, Hélène rejoins him and they leave the apartment, descending one of those old Parisian staircases whose carpet is held in place by gold rods. They get in Jérôme's car and drive to a brasserie in the fifteenth arrondissement. A waiter shows them to a table. Hélène takes out her papers and hands them to Jérôme.

JÉRÔME   All right, let's pick up where we left off: *"A little after Vasari, painting was assigned the mission of externalizing the 'drawing' directly* *formed in the mind.[78] Already in 1548, Francesco Robortello* had published a commentary on Aristotle's* Poetics *in which he twisted the Greek philosopher's words to make him say that poetry must edify and persuade the public.[79] Aristotle was talking more about demand than supply."*

That last phrase is surprising—very modern, makes Aristotle sound like an economist. It's clear that the text has been written recently. That gives me an idea—The earlier pages were addressed to you, right? Tell me about yourself.

At the same moment Jean is having dinner with Denis at Cécile's restaurant.

JEAN   This is really going too far. We confide our worries to him and he takes advantage by trying to come on to her.

DENIS   Good for him, no? After all, Hélène's not your type, right?

JEAN   Not exactly. What I said was that I wasn't happy about her bringing her friend along to Les Eyzies—

DENIS   And also that she's a know-it-all.

JEAN   No, I do very much admire her knowledge of art history. This can really be of help to Cécile. Oh, there she is—Cécile!

CÉCILE *(coming over to their table)* Yes?

JEAN   I copied out for you a passage from the last packet that talks about the grotesque.

---

*FRANCESCO ROBORTELLO (Franciscus Robortellus; Udine, 1516–Padua, 1567): Renaissance humanist who taught philosophy and rhetoric at universities throughout Italy. His editions of newly rediscovered works by ancient authors, notably Aristotle's *Poetics*, which had a great influence on seventeenth-century theories of comedy and dramatic writing, laid the basis for the modern hermeneutical approach to textual analysis.

CÉCILE (*taking a seat*) · The grotesque?

JEAN   An artistic genre that combines the bizarre, the ridiculous, and the shocking, as your friend Hélène puts it. The text quotes a Russian critic, L. E. Pinsky: *"In the grotesque, life passes through all its stages, from the material to the spiritual, from the inert to the animate, and so on. The scope of its concerns and its homogeneity are what give it its unity. In bringing together those things that are distant from one another, in combining those things that exclude each other, in going against customary ways of thinking, the grotesque in art is a cousin to the paradox in logic."*[80]

CÉCILE   And why did you copy all that out for me?

JEAN   At first glance, the grotesque seems an entertaining idea, nothing more; but it implies a whole range of culinary possibilities: bringing together things that are far apart, violating received notions—

CÉCILE   Let me think about it—

She starts to get up.

JEAN   Wait, there were a lot of other things going on in the Renaissance. Here, for example: *"Francisco Pacheco, in his treatise on painting, held that the beautiful is a result both of imitation and of the concept: 'For perfection consists in a going back and forth that leads from Ideas to the natural model, and from the natural model to Ideas.'"*[81]

DENIS   A reconciliation of Plato and Aristotle, in a sense.

CÉCILE   Yes, but what am I to do with it in the kitchen? As a practical matter, all of this business about ideas and contraries resolves nothing. The thing I have to be concerned with above all is flavor—and making sure that the dish pleases my customers. When will that happen again? Are they going to say it's good?

JEAN   You remember Augustine said that things give pleasure because they are beautiful? Well, the last page we received says the opposite. Look here. It begins with a discussion of Spinoza,* and a quotation—

DENIS   That's surprising: the note is much longer than usual. There seem to be several authors. What I find puzzling is that the book that was originally given to Hélène seemed so old. How can a book be old when the authors are from different periods, and one of them seems to be modern? Anyway, what's the quote from Spinoza?

JEAN   *"So it is established from all this that we do not endeavor, will, seek after, or desire something because we judge it to be good, but on the contrary we judge something to be good because we endeavor, will, seek after, or desire it."*[82]

DENIS   No wonder the religious authorities made things uncomfortable for Spinoza—he contradicted the great St. Augustine!

JEAN   Hold on, there's an explication: *"The ideas of Spinoza put an end*

---

*BARUCH SPINOZA (Benedict de Spinoza; Amsterdam, 1632–The Hague, 1677): Dutch philosopher who as a young man studied to be a rabbi. On being banished from the Jewish community of his native city for heterodox opinions in 1656, Spinoza earned his living as an optical lens grinder. The publication of the *Principles of the Philosophy of Descartes* (1663), and especially of the *Tractatus Theologico-Philosophicus* (1670), attracted the hostile attention of religious authorities. His other works—*Ethics, On the Improvement of the Understanding,* and *Tractatus Theologico-Politicus*—were published posthumously.

Spinoza sought to loosen the constraints of religious orthodoxy, placing emphasis upon the joy that knowledge brings. Knowledge of nature, which is to say of God, requires understanding the causes that give all creatures, including human beings, their characteristic attributes. Of nature itself (which Spinoza called substance), human beings perceive only two attributes: physical extension and thought. There exist three modes of knowledge: belief, reasoning, and rational intuition. In his political philosophy, Spinoza defended freedom of expression and tolerance of dissenting opinions.

to the medieval idea that the world is full of resonances with the world
of God. To talk of resonance is to talk of harmony."

CÉCILE   That's more up my alley. For example, some of my chef friends think there's a "succulence limit" that one must aim for in cooking meats. They believe in the culinary equivalent of harmonious tones, or chords: there is only one way of cooking a particular meat, and the cook's task is to discover such preexisting harmonies, or resonances, as though they've fallen from the sky.

I fear that this is only a prejudice, a personal preference that one dresses up in fine phrases to prevent it from being examined critically—a sort of laziness, in other words, that avoids searching for other methods of cooking, for other ways of obtaining harmonies. With regard to matching wines and foods, for example, this way of thinking has long condemned us to serving Muscadet with shellfish, when so many other wines would be suitable choices. The range of what is acceptable is greater today than it was, but gourmets continue to believe that some pairings are absolute! As for harmonious combinations in cooking, it's easier to believe that what has been done until now is what must be done than to look for other possibilities—and so one goes on doing what has always been done.

DENIS   Yes, but it's no use denouncing mistaken beliefs. One must try above all to open up doors, darling.

JEAN   Let's rejoice in the fact that so many types of cooking are possible, that there are so many culinary chords to be played. It's up to us to imagine the possibilities, to search for marvelous new sensations by exploring new methods and proportions of ingredients.

A SURPRISING CHORD USING ONLY TWO INGREDIENTS

IN THEORY

The question of whether there exist culinary chords, or ideal combinations, haunts cooking still today. Gourmets are forever trying to match dishes and wines, but why should anyone suppose that a certain dish and a certain wine go together in the first place? Is the imagined harmony physical or cultural in nature? With a bit of work, couldn't a talented cook arrive at unexpected harmonies?

IN PRACTICE
MORELS WITH LICORICE

Soak dry morels of good quality (which is to say large morels) in warm water overnight. Wash them carefully. Brown them in olive oil after having very slightly salted and sweetened them. Add spring water and licorice powder. Cover and cook very gently for several hours until they are crystallized. In this way you will obtain two distinct flavors, morel and licorice. At the last moment, off heat, add some chestnut cream that has been softened with fresh cream. If you like, accentuate the savory sensation by adding some salt crystals coated with olive oil.

I happened to stumble across this surprising combination in the course of my culinary investigations, but the reason for it is clear enough: the smoky quality of the morels is reinforced by the licorice. Surprisingly, the sweetness does not dispel the saltiness. Slow cooking develops the flavor of the morels in a quite remarkable way, and the licorice envelops this flavor. The chestnut cream lengthens all these tastes and flavors in the mouth. The result is that famous "nose" that oenophiles call Russian leather.

YOUR TURN

Go ahead, just for the fun of it: take the two most opposite ingredients you can think of and try to unite them in a single dish. This isn't easy to do. You need to approach the problem in the same way matchmakers once brought young couples together: don't consider only their flavor, but also their texture and taste.

NINETEEN

THE ENLIGHTENMENT
IN THE WEST AND THE EAST

Whereas in the eighteenth century, in the West, the idea took hold that a beautiful painting should arouse in the viewer thoughts of things already seen or of things that could possibly be seen, Chinese painters of the period made no distinction between the beauty of a work and the moral character of the artist. In the extreme case, a technically superb work was thought to be worth nothing if the artist did not have the requisite personal qualities. Through work and meditation the artist was expected to make himself a peerless technician who had so thoroughly learned the rules of painting that he was able finally to dispense with them.

THE WELLSPRING OF MY HEART

Three men follow Jean after he leaves Cécile's restaurant. Turning the corner they come to a side street where Jean had parked his car. As he is

*searching for his key, one of the men comes up from behind and takes
him by the arms.*

JEAN   Hey, let me go—what are you doing, you bastards? Help! Help!

*Without a word, another of the three men goes through Jean's pockets,
removing the contents and taking his briefcase.*

JEAN   My papers! My papers!

MAN WHO WENT THROUGH JEAN'S POCKETS *(to the others)*   Okay,
let go of him.

A car comes: the three men get in and the car roars off. Jean runs after it.

JEAN   Bastards! My papers!

A woman appears.

WOMAN   Follow me at once.

JEAN   Excuse me?

WOMAN   Follow me. Hurry.

JEAN   Where to?

WOMAN   Follow me. The last word in cooking. Don't make it look like
we're together. See the white van at the end of the street? Get in the front,
in the passenger seat.

JEAN *(to himself)*   Well, what have I got to lose?

*He gets into the van. The woman follows and climbs in back through the
unlocked rear doors. The van pulls away from the curb at once.*

JEAN *(to the driver)*   Who are you?

DRIVER   You'll find out later. First we have to go get Hélène. When
they realize you don't have what they're looking for, she's the one—

JEAN   Why?

DRIVER   They'll think she's the next link in the chain. For the moment I can't say anything more.

The van rolls through Paris, then arrives in front of Hélène's building. The driver looks up at the windows. The lights in Hélène's apartment are on.

DRIVER   Go up and get her, but be quick about it.

JEAN   All right, but you'll tell me—

DRIVER   Hurry, they'll be here any moment.

Jean takes the elevator and rings the bell at Hélène's door.

HÉLÈNE   Jean? What's happened to you? Your jacket is torn.

JEAN   Grab your coat, please, and come quickly. The guys who want that book will be here any moment.

HÉLÈNE   But I don't have anything! Jérôme's got all the pages.

JEAN   These guys don't know that, and they're thugs. Hurry up!

Hélène takes her coat, closes the door to her apartment, and follows Jean down the staircase; they go out through the lobby and get in the van, which drives off just as the car carrying Jean's attackers pulls up.

DRIVER   You're safe. They won't dare try anything with us, because they know that we'll destroy the documents rather than hand them over.

JEAN   What's this whole thing about?

DRIVER   You'll know soon enough. At the Musée Camondo.

HÉLÈNE   But that's where I went with Denis and Cécile!

DRIVER   Which we had been planning for you two to visit. Then our plans changed.

HÉLÈNE   What?

The driver doesn't reply and drives on in silence. The van pulls up in front of the old Camondo mansion. The driver gets out and looks around.

DRIVER   Nobody. Come inside.

Jean and Hélène get out and follow the driver and the woman who had approached Jean. The driver indicates a door to the right of the court-yard. Jean and Hélène go inside. A short, plump man is waiting for them.

SHORT MAN   Be seated. The man in charge will be coming.

HÉLÈNE   But what's going on? You—I recognize you! You're the one who gave me the last page.

SHORT MAN   Yes. Read these. Quickly.

The man departs, leaving Jean and Hélène alone in the room. Too stunned to react, they sit down on a bench in front of a large wooden table and begin reading:

> *In the eighteenth century, the German painter Anton Raphael Mengs* wrote: "Painting is one of the three Fine Arts whose object is the imitation of truth, which is to say the appearance of all visi-ble things."[83]*
>
> *Here we have something new: this time it is a question of truth, of the appearance of all visible things. It is not said that the painter ought to imitate nature, but truth! Mengs goes on to say: "Paint-ing . . . insofar as it is an Art, is only the way of placing colors, which,*

---

*ANTON RAPHAEL MENGS (Aussig, 1728–Rome, 1779): German painter born in Bohe-mia whose father was also an artist, specializing in miniatures. A representative of the neoclassicist movement, in reaction to the prevailing Rococo style, Mengs was elected a member of the Academy of Dresden and, along with the German archeolo-gist J. J. Winckelmann, enthusiastically promoted the study of Greco-Roman artifacts and monuments. He was also the author of an influential treatise, *Considerations on Beauty and Taste in Painting* (1762).

*depending on their arrangement and their modification, can arouse
in the viewer ideas of things already seen or that it is possible for
him to see."*

*Arouse ideas of things already seen or that can be seen? Here
again we have a fine novelty, which many artists could turn to their
advantage: could not cooking in its turn arouse ideas—thoughts,
as we would say—of things already eaten or of things that it is possible to eat? How would you actually go about arousing these
thoughts?*

*During this period a distinction was made between artisans and
artists: Denis Diderot* says in his* Encyclopedia *that the artist works
with his hands, whereas artisans are practitioners of the minor arts.*[84]

*Moreover, every artist now had the right to have his own style.
It therefore becomes clearer why Comte de Buffon,† in saying that
"Style is the man himself," was saying something very new.*[85]

*In this Buffon displays certain affinities with Far Eastern thinkers
of the period. In the same year Buffon was born, the Chinese painter
Shitao (also known as Friar Bitter-Melon) wrote in his* Treatise on
the Philosophy of Painting: *"The high artistic quality of the author
is necessarily accompanied by his high moral quality."*[86] *Shitao and*

---

*DENIS DIDEROT (Langres, 1713–Paris, 1784): One of the greatest minds of the eigh-
teenth century, Diderot aimed at the creation neither of a complete philosophical system nor of a unified body of work. His learning was immense, and his interests ranged
from philosophy and aesthetics to literature, the theater, politics, and publishing. He
relied frequently on the device of soliloquy, which gave his writings a lively and accessible style. Indefatigably curious and alert to paradox, Diderot remains best known
as the editor (with Jean Le Rond d'Alembert) of the *Encyclopedia,* published in twenty-
eight volumes between 1751 and 1772.

†GEORGES-LOUIS LECLERC, COMTE DE BUFFON (Montbard, 1707–Paris, 1788): French
naturalist, mathematician, biologist, and writer. The author of the vast *Natural History,* published in fifteen volumes between 1749 and 1767, Buffon's theories had a
profound influence on two generations of naturalists, notably among them Jean-
Baptiste de Lamarck and Charles Darwin.

*other painters of his time in China and Japan regarded association
with the world as mere "dust," for it distanced them from the Truth
of the work. Truth of the work! Not a concept easily grasped by self-
proclaimed culinary artists today, who cook for money, for power,
and for any other reason than culinary Art!*

HÉLÈNE   Look—the page that follows isn't written in the same hand.

JEAN   Yes, that struck me right away. There are two different styles of
writing—and only two. What does this page say?

*Art and gesture. The Chinese tradition opposes the artisan, who is
content with reproducing outward appearances, to the artist, who
transcribes the contents of his intellect. The painter does not seek
to imitate nature, but to reproduce the act by which nature creates.
Leonardo da Vinci, despite upholding a contrary theory, can also
be seen as an exemplar of this tradition.*

*In the art of the Far East, the gesture of the artist is very impor-
tant. For example, a drawing done with the hand raised is more prized
than one done with the arm resting on a surface, because it requires
greater concentration, greater preparation and control. Shitao remarks in the* Treatise: *"Spiritual motivation precedes the brush."*[87]
*Isn't that the motto one finds engraved above the entrance to the
Musée de Compagnonnage in Tours: "The head guides the hand"?*

*Shitao goes on to say, in the same vein: "Painting emanates from
the intellect; whether it concerns the beauty of mountains, flowers. . . ."*[88] *Here he recalls the idea of an earlier Chinese painter, Deng
Chun:* *"What is the only rule? To convey the mind."*

---

*DENG CHUN (dates unknown: active twelfth century): A government official under the
Southern Song dynasty who became acquainted with painting as a young man through
his family's extensive collection. A historian rather than a theorist of aesthetics, unlike earlier authors, his treatise *Huaji* (1167) was nonetheless the most important record
of painters and paintings in China between 1070 and 1160.

The artist must therefore be a wholly upright man. His head must be free, cleansed of the dust of the world: "If one does not paint with a free wrist, errors in painting will ensue."[89] *The wrist is not free if the head that guides it is not filled with the motion that the head commands.*

How is the motion of the hand to be controlled? This gesture must be carefully considered, for it is everything: "However far you go, however high you climb, you must begin with a single step. Thus the One Brush Stroke embraces everything, as far as the most inaccessible distance, and of ten thousand millions of strokes of the brush there is not one whose beginning and end do not ultimately reside in the One Brush Stroke whose control belongs only to man."[90]

And this is why art is difficult: "The One Brush Stroke suffices to reveal the master: the other strokes cannot correct the first; a thousand instruments of an orchestra will not correct the wrong note of one of them."[91]

How is the requisite skill acquired? Through the widest possible learning. As Confucius* said: "A gentleman is not a pot." This means that his capacities, or abilities, are not limited to a particular function or purpose, as in the case of a utensil or tool.[92]

How are the arts to be taught? Rules are necessary for beginners: "The possession of the rule, in its fullness, leads back to the absence of rules . . . but whoever desires to be without rule must first possess the rules."[93] *In other words, the artist is emancipated from the rules of his art only after long and arduous practice. Moreover, this training can be undergone only by an apprentice, who must perfect both his technique and his thought under the tutelage of a*

---

*CONFUCIUS (K'ung-Fu-tsu; Zu, Shandong Province, 551–Zu, Shandong Province, 479 B.C.E.): Scholar and statesman whose social and political doctrines, summarized in the *Analects,* were erected into a state religion upheld by Chinese emperors for more than two thousand years, from the Han dynasty until the early twentieth century. His influence on Chinese civilization remains unrivaled.

master of the art, not a craftsman: Chinese tradition cites the example of a wheelwright who, though he makes perfect wheels, is incapable of teaching this skill, because it falls within the province not of technique but of the mind.

Once mastery has been achieved, Shitao says, the artist detaches himself from rules: "From the moment that one knows the rule, one must devote oneself to transforming it."[94] In this way it becomes possible to avoid academicism, freeing art from traditional assumptions and prejudices. To those who asked him who were his masters, the eighth-century Chinese painter Zhang Zao replied that he recognized none other than nature and his heart (that is, his mind): "I have for a master only nature, outside myself, and, within myself, the wellspring of my heart."[95]

The ancient Greek physician Hippocrates* said: "Life is short, the art long, opportunity fleeting, experiment treacherous, judgment difficult."[96] More than two thousand years later, the Chinese painter Dai Xi† echoed this view: "To have ink [i.e., technique] is easy, but to have the brush [thought] is difficult; to have the brush and ink is easy, too, but what is difficult is no longer to have any trace of the brush or of the ink."[97]

HÉLÈNE   Jean, I'm a little afraid. This whole story—Jérôme said that—

---

*HIPPOCRATES (Cos, *ca* 460–Larissa, *ca* 370 B.C.E.): Greek physician born into a family of priest-physicians, the Asclepiads. Considered the father of Western medicine for having decisively separated the healing arts from their ancient religious context, Hippocrates was the author of a number of works, which, together with those of his followers, form the Hippocratic corpus. The Hippocratic oath, with its injunction "Above all, do no harm," is still administered to doctors on their graduation from medical school.

†DAI XI (1801–1860): Prominent government official, from a scholarly family in Hangzhou province, who is remembered in particular for his struggle against the cultivation of opium in Canton. Dai Xi was also one of the most famous painters of his time, noted especially for his landscapes.

JEAN   Let's talk about Jérôme, why don't we? We go to him for help and he takes advantage of it to—

HÉLÈNE   Please, don't say anything.

JEAN   I insist. It's perfectly clear that he's taking advantage. He pounces on every pretty girl who passes his way.

HÉLÈNE   No, I assure you. And besides, I'm not even pretty. With my glasses, always lost in my love of the past—

JEAN   That's not true, and you know it. You're always smartly dressed, always attractive—I love your hair, your face, your eyes, your love of the past! Hélène—

HÉLÈNE   No, not now, Jean, please.

The door through which the short man had left now suddenly opens. The lights are turned out, leaving Jean and Hélène in the dark. Hélène takes Jean's hand as he haltingly makes his way toward the barely illuminated opening of the doorway. They walk a few steps—and suddenly find themselves in the street, where it is raining. The door closes behind them.

JEAN   Now what? I don't understand anything anymore—do you really think they brought us here just to read a few pages about Chinese painting?

HÉLÈNE   You're forgetting the three guys who attacked you and who were about to come after me. What are we going to do?

JEAN   Let's go to the restaurant and talk to Denis and Cécile. Then we can decide.

HÉLÈNE   First we've got to call Jérôme—

JEAN   No! I'll file a complaint at the police station tomorrow—and tell Jérôme that I don't want him to come near you.

HÉLÈNE   What gives you the right—

JEAN   The right? This is what gives me the right!

He takes Hélène in his arms.

HÉLÈNE   Jean, Jean!

They passionately kiss. When Hélène regains her breath, she snuggles up against him. They kiss again, but Hélène is shivering.

JEAN   Let's hurry, you're going to catch cold.

Holding Hélène by the waist, he urges her forward. Before long, they arrive at the restaurant.

DENIS (*peering through the window of the front door*)   Jean, what are you doing there—and Hélène?

JEAN   Let us in, we're soaked.

CÉCILE   Hélène, my dear—come in, you look upset.

A few moments later they are all seated around the bar. Jean and Hélène are drinking hot toddies.

CÉCILE   Hélène, do feel free to spend the night with us. We're driving home in a moment.

HÉLÈNE   Do you mind? I'm exhausted.

JEAN   Wouldn't you rather—

HÉLÈNE   Jean, no. I've got an early lecture tomorrow. Denis and Cécile are right next to the Sorbonne.

JEAN   All right. Very well. Will I see you tomorrow?

HÉLÈNE   Sure—do you want to have lunch? I'll be finished at 1 P.M.

JEAN   Let's have lunch, then. Okay, I'm going home. This time I'm in no danger: they took my briefcase and I've got only my wallet and keys.

DENIS   Be careful just the same.

THE REMEMBRANCE OF THINGS ALREADY EATEN

IN THEORY

Stimulating a familiar sensation in the absence of the ingredient with which it is associated—what a fine task for the cook! Here we are far from the glucids (carbohydrates), lipids (fats), and protids (proteins) that obsess the food industry, which forgets that when we eat we are partaking of a culture as well. Nonetheless, though the task is noble, it is also formidable, given that a particular food is apt to produce different sensations depending on where we are from and what we grew up eating. Why should roasted flour, for example, make us think of chocolate?

IN PRACTICE
ROASTED FLOUR COOKIE

This is Hervé's idea: a cookie made with roasted flour that reminds one of the flavor of chocolate, even though it is made only of flour, egg, and butter.

To make these cookies involves nothing more than putting the flour under the broiler or salamander until it turns a blond color. In this way you avoid the tasteless and over-rich flavor of raw flour and, more importantly, cause a flavor somewhere between that of a boletus mushroom and chocolate to appear.

Next mix the roasted flour with yolks from eggs cooked at 66°C (about 151°F), butter, and a bit of salt. Press this mixture into round shapes and cook them in the oven until the butter melts, thickening the flour granules so that they bind together.

Cover each cookie with a thin layer of melted chocolate (the "moustache") and serve it on a tube of sugar-coated chocolate along with roasted nuts (hazelnuts, almonds, pistachios) and crystallized citron.

The moustache is a sort of hat that tops off the story with its crunchiness. The cookie beneath crumbles very easily, and its flavor suggests the presence of chocolate that isn't there. The sugar-coating prolongs the phantom flavor. The dessert itself is designed so that you can pick it up by the sides with your fingers and experience a succession of flavors.

YOUR TURN

The simplicity of Pierre's execution of this idea adds to its beauty. He shows us that, depending on the case, cooks can choose to lay emphasis on the texture, taste, smell, or appearance of a dish. Any aspect can be turned to good account.

Can you come up with an example of your own that will arouse memories of a familiar flavor without using the ingredient that ordinarily gives rise to it? Can you make the final note of a chord heard without actually playing it?

TWENTY

NATURE OVERCOME

In the early nineteenth century, the German poet and scientist Johann Wolfgang von Goethe held that, in the symbolist conception of art, objects do not exist in and of themselves, but rather by virtue of a higher realm of being to which they give access. Symbolism is therefore different from allegory, for which the object exists only by virtue of its symbolic value. In Goethe's view, beauty is an embodiment of the universal in the specific.

Together with the poet Friedrich von Schiller, Goethe identified "retarding" or "impeding" themes in epic poetry, an idea that was later to be adopted by the Russian linguist V. I. Propp in analyzing folktales. Adapted to cooking, it suggests a way of constructing a dish by concentrating upon the consistency, or texture, of its ingredients.

STORYTELLING

Hélène meets Jean at a small bistro near the Sorbonne. He is waiting for her, reading the paper, and startles when she gently touches his arm.

243

HÉLÈNE   Jean! I didn't get a wink of sleep all night. I'm whipped. All these stories, and then (*Jean tries to give her a kiss*)—please, not in front of everybody, come on. A lot of these people are colleagues of mine. Let's go sit in the corner over there where it's quieter. So you got home last night without any problem?

JEAN   Yes—

HÉLÈNE   You know, I've been thinking about *The Quintessential Art*. It seems to be a sort of treatise of culinary aesthetics that two camps are fighting over: on the one side, the people who are writing it, and on the other, people who want to have it. And we're in the middle. I don't really understand why we're caught up in all of this. There must be some connection with Denis and Cécile, since they were robbed too, but lately everything's been happening to us.

JEAN   That's what I was thinking. And yet we're very different.

HÉLÈNE   Yes, me and my love of the past, my glasses (*she suppresses a smile*)—

JEAN   And me?

HÉLÈNE   You? You live in the present, in the world of food, which you know very well, and also in the future, with your restaurant projects and the like.

JEAN   That doesn't explain why we're the ones receiving the packets of new pages now. By the way, I reported the theft of my briefcase and the attack to the police this morning. And I called Jérôme to tell him that I want him to leave you alone. He pretended not to know what I was talking about, but I know I'm not mistaken.

HÉLÈNE   Jean—come on now, sit next to me. What are you going to have? (*Looking up at the waiter*) A mixed salad and a bottle of sparkling water, please.

JEAN   I'll have the andouillette. With the house mashed potatoes. Tell me, Hélène, I was wondering: are you learning something from these pages or do you already know everything that's in them?

HÉLÈNE   Oh, I don't know everything—but it's my specialty, after all, aesthetics and art history. The latest pages have brought us up to the eighteenth century in China, with Shitao. I think I could write you a page on the eighteenth century in the West. (*She starts to look for a pad, then thinks of the butcher paper that covers the table.*) Why don't I just write on the tablecloth? All right, let's see:

Johann Wolfgang von Goethe (1749-1832): A leader of the Sturm und Drang movement who first came to prominence with his play Götz von Berlichingen (1773) and his novel The Sorrows of Young Werther (1774). He knew Italy well and was actively involved in politics, having served as chief minister of state under the Grand Duke of Weimar for ten years, and took part in the failed invasion of Revolutionary France in 1792. A close friend of the poet and dramatist Friedrich von Schiller, Goethe was also interested in science and published Metamorphosis of Plants (1790) and Theory of Colors (1810). This mixture of science and art led Goethe to practice a more classical style of art, which assumed an autobiographical and symbolic form.

JEAN   Dates and all, bravo! You could write the notes for our old book! But we still need the aesthetic commentary.

HÉLÈNE   One moment.

In his writings on art, Goethe defines what later critics have called syntheticism as a romantic aesthetic tendency to see every work as the result of an interpenetration of two opposites, whose contradiction is resolved into a happy synthesis.[98]

JEAN   You mean like Aristotle and catharsis? One might imagine that the cook composes the dish in such a way that only by eating all of it does the diner take pleasure from it.

HÉLÈNE   How would one do this? It appears difficult—

JEAN   Yes, but not impossible. Ideas are needed to guide art—culinary art no less than any other.

HÉLÈNE   Ideas, or feelings?

JEAN   Why not both?

HÉLÈNE   You're right. Shall I go on?

> Goethe also held that, in the symbolist conception of art, objects do not exist in and of themselves, but rather by virtue of a higher realm of being to which they give access.

This is different from allegory, you see. In the case of allegory, the object exists for its symbolic value alone.

JEAN   I see that, yes, but still it seems very close to the aesthetics of the Middle Ages.

HÉLÈNE   Except that now God isn't necessarily there. Besides (*she resumes writing*):

> Goethe was also a pioneer of naturalism, a school of thought that drew upon the theory of resemblance in defining a work of art by reference to the object that it imitates. He remained attached to the Greek idea of equilibrium, insisting that excess must be avoided—

JEAN   But, in the end, he lost out and the Romantics won.

HÉLÈNE   Yes, but Goethe was a very interesting figure. I often recall a remark that summarizes his attitude toward art. No poet is deserving of the name, he said, who only gives voice to his subjective feelings; a poet is someone who takes possession of the world and expresses it.[99]

JEAN   It's true—there are too many people who take themselves to be writers simply because they recount their feelings and what's happened to them, possibly changing the names of people and places. Who gives a damn? Talking about oneself doesn't qualify as literature—at least not without some artistic elaboration!

Similarly, in cooking, one isn't an artist if one knows only how to produce dishes that a few people find pleasing. There's no chance of universality in that. This is what I call the paradox of culinary art: how is it that when Japanese, Americans, Indians, and Europeans, say, eat the food of a great cook, they all agree that it's good, even though they're from different food cultures? This is certainly a case, as Goethe put it, of the artist appropriating and expressing the world.

HÉLÈNE   I should also note this passage from Goethe: *"As soon as the artist selects a natural object, it no longer belongs to nature. We may even say that he creates it at this very moment, when he perceives in the object what is significant, characteristic and interesting, or better, when he imbues it with a higher value."*[100]

JEAN   Marvelous—this is the fatal blow that fells all those who put ingredients first. I'll propose to you a translation into culinary theory: an ingredient no longer belongs to nature once a cook has gotten hold of it. It's true, because the job of the cook is exactly that, to transform. Nothing the cook does is natural. Cooking is a paradise of artificiality.

On the other hand, I don't agree with Goethe when he says—again, I'm trying to establish a rough equivalence—that the cook can even be said to create the work because he brings out what is significant, characteristic, and interesting about it. This is too limiting: if the cook doesn't want to bring out these things, he is perfectly within his rights. Down with rules! We need to go beyond these aesthetics, which after all are two centuries old.

HÉLÈNE   Goethe had something to say about that as well. I don't remember exactly, but it's got something to do with the true artist being someone who strives for artistic truth by working in accordance with principles, whereas the artist who follows only blind instinct seeks only the appearance of reality. The former leads art to its highest peaks, the latter to its lowest depths.[101]

JEAN   Yes, but I'm not so happy with this moralizing way of decreeing what is art and what is not—

HÉLÈNE   Say, the reference to law makes me think of Goethe's correspondence with Schiller. (*She makes another note*)

> *Friedrich von Schiller, born in Marbach in 1759 and died—*

Where was it now? Ah, yes, Weimar:

> *and died in Weimar in 1805. His historical dramas resembled both classical tragedy and the plays of Shakespeare. His dramatic theories greatly influenced French Romantic writers. He also wrote lyric poetry.*

Now, what was the line from Goethe's letter to Schiller? Oh, yes: *"One main quality of the epic poem is that it constantly goes forward and backward—hence all retarding motifs are epical."*[102] For Goethe, the epic poem par excellence was the *Odyssey*.

You see, one knows from the beginning of the *Odyssey* that Ulysses is going to go back home, to Ithaca, but he is delayed—for years.

JEAN   This is an intriguing idea. A little like Propp's notion that some episodes in a story are like opening parentheses, which signal a digression, a straying away from the narrative path, and others, which lead back toward the story's destination, are like closing parentheses.[103]

HÉLÈNE   Sorry, what's this bit about parentheses?

JEAN   Ah, my turn to play the teacher! Vladimir Iakovlevich Propp, Russian linguist, who studied Russian folktales. He observed that all such tales are constructed in the same way: they consist of successions of events

that are like opening parentheses, together with closing parentheses that correspond to them later in the story.

For example, a prince goes out from a castle to slay a dragon: this is an opening parenthesis. Later he will come back to the castle: closing parenthesis. But before coming back, the hero avoids stepping on a toad (another parenthesis opens); later on he has to slay the dragon with a magic sword, and this sword is given to him by an enchanter, who turns out to be the toad that was saved from being crushed (parenthesis closed).

At bottom, this business of parentheses is a natural device for the purposes of communication. A tale is like a road that you make your listeners travel along. You must lead them from one place to another. If you turn off from the road, to the left, for example, this is like an opening parenthesis; but at some point you must come back, that is, you must close the parenthesis by turning back to the right. You can come back right away, or much later, but you have to come back at some point or risk losing your way.

HÉLÈNE (*laughing*)   And in cooking?

JEAN   In cooking? Uh, well, I imagine that a plate of food is like a story. At the beginning the plate is full, and at the end it is empty. Between these two places the diner will have traveled along a road. And this road will have to be laid out.

HÉLÈNE   But going forward and back?

JEAN   I'll need to think about this some more. Has Goethe given us any other hints that might be helpful?

HÉLÈNE   I don't know, let me look at my notes. Yes, there's this, again from a letter to Schiller: *"I was trying to subordinate the law of retardation to a higher one; it seems to be subordinate to the one which demands of a good poem that, even before reading it, one should know, even has*

to know, the ending. And really, the how must be the center of interest. In this way, curiosity has no part in such a work; its purpose lies, as you say, in every point of the movement."[104]

JEAN   One would have thought Shitao wrote this. To transpose the idea to cooking, one knows the plate will be empty at the end, but it is the road of flavor that matters—which, as it happens, is quite true: the succession of flavors is fundamental. And it is exactly this road that has to be prepared. Cécile was saying the same thing the other day: the chewing, the perception of flavors, has to be structured.

HÉLÈNE   Wait, here's another one. A letter from Schiller to Goethe this time: *"I believe that there are two kinds of retardation, one concerning the path, the other the walking"*[105]—in other words, the road traveled and the traveling itself.

JEAN   The traveling—that's another thing. Wait, I've got it. In the *Odyssey,* we know that Ulysses will arrive home in the end, but before this expected conclusion is reached he will have to contend with Circe and the Cyclops, navigate his way between Scylla and Charybdis, resist the temptations of the Lotus-Eaters, be rescued by Nausicaa, and so on.

In cooking, we find an analogy to these episodes of epic poetry: we know that the plate will be empty in the end, but we have to make our way forward in order to arrive at this destination. And the more slowly we make our way, the better it will be. This is why the consistency, the texture, of a dish is so important!

HÉLÈNE   How many kinds of consistency are there?

JEAN   There are all sorts—from liquids, which are drunk rather than eaten, to solids, which are too hard to chew except in very small mouthfuls, so long as they can be easily broken up. And everything in between.

It's interesting to note that the emulsions, foams, and gels that are so

popular today represent the next state of consistency after liquids, the next rung on the ladder leading to solids: they are all soft. To go beyond these, we need to look at the natural world and the foods we actually eat. Think of turbot, for example, which has an altogether extraordinary texture when it's perfectly cooked. Or pigeon. What accounts for the wonderful consistency of its meat? Or salmon roe or red currants, and the delicious juice that is released once their hard envelopes are pierced.

In all these cases one finds a liquid, or a gel, or an emulsion, or a foam inside some hard envelope. The envelope of a fish, for example, is made of muscle fibers. The same goes for meat, fruits, and vegetables, whose tissues are made out of cells that have different shapes and sizes.

HÉLÈNE   My, you sound like Denis.

JEAN   Yes, well, it's not very hard: you have only to look at an overcooked pot-au-feu to see the fibers of the meat, or chop up the flesh of a fish.

The characteristics of these natural systems could be artificially reproduced. For example, suppose we cook some macaroni and then arrange them vertically in a glass: this would give us the fiber envelope. Then pour in a very flavorful gelatinous stock and let it cool: the liquid that is trapped between the macaroni seals them together, whereas the liquid that passes inside them becomes a quivering jelly. When you turn the macaroni out of the glass you obtain a sort of artificial "flesh," whose flavor is released in the course of chewing, once you've gotten through the firm layer of the macaroni. We've now climbed up another rung on the ladder of textures, and we can keep on going!

HÉLÈNE   Oh look, it's getting late. I've got to go back.

JEAN   Me, too, but we don't have a conclusion for our episode.

HÉLÈNE   That won't take but a moment—so much has been written about

Romanticism and the urge to imitate the ancients. I recall the words of the German painter Runge* (*she begins to write again*):

> "We are no longer Greeks. . . . The works of art of all periods show us in a perfectly clear manner that the human race has transformed itself, that no era has ever repeated itself. Why then should we have the unfortunate idea of issuing a call to arms in the name of ancient art?"[106]

Hélène and Jean get up and leave. A tall man who had been hunched over the bar comes over to the table, pushes away the glasses and plates, removes the butcher paper on which Hélène has been writing, and departs without saying a word to anyone.

GOING TOO FAR

IN THEORY

Let's try to unite the medieval rule of moderation (not too much salt, not too much pepper) with the Chinese idea that only an artist who has managed to free himself from rules can be considered accomplished. Applied to cooking, this combination of contraries presents the chef with one

---

*PHILIPP OTTO RUNGE (Wolgast, 1777–Hamburg, 1810): German painter, designer, writer, and theoretician of art. One of the leading figures of the early nineteenth-century German Romantic movement (along with Caspar David Friedrich), Runge's writings include *The Color Sphere* (1810) in addition to an extensive correspondence edited by his older brother, Daniel Runge, and published posthumously.

of the greatest challenges: creating a work of art that goes too far while at the same time preserving its essential ability to please, enchant, and stir the emotions.

IN PRACTICE
HARE CONFIT WITH RED CURRANT JELLY,
STEWED BUTTERNUT SQUASH ALONE AND WITH CHESTNUTS,
QUINCE PASTE, AND FLAVORED CREAM SAUCES

Sometimes the cook ends up with a dish that is unfinished, imperfect. For example, if a dish includes various kinds of vegetable- and fruit-flavored cream sauces (artichoke, quince, butternut squash, parsnip, carrot, and so on), you wind up with too much of a muchness, which wears out the flavor and undermines the point of the dish.

Even so, you go ahead and serve the dish, because no obvious solution to the problem occurs to you: the dish exists, and it isn't uninteresting; but it still needs more work, and the solution may not occur to you until years later. That's no reason to abandon the dish, which contributes its share of new ideas just the same. The cook should have the right to make mistakes, so long as he tries to correct them.

This dish with hare and squash was my attempt to correct the problem created by the cream sauces. The hare confit itself is good, but the stewed butternut squash (a kind of winter squash whose flavor is reminiscent of nutmeg) introduces a contradiction that is aggravated by its juxtaposition with still more stewed butternut squash, this time made with chestnuts. The quince paste gives the whole thing a very thick consistency, while nonetheless contributing a fragrance that is an indispensable part of the overall effect.

How far can one deliberately push the limits of excess? In comedy, repetition works only if it is openly acknowledged and emphasized. Serving two versions of stewed squash together would usually be unbearably heavy, but by also including the fruit- and vegetable-flavored cream sauces

I had made it clear that the repetition was deliberate, not an unintended piece of clumsiness. In other words, repetition to the point of excess *was* the point of the dish!

The hare confit and butternut squash rose up from a disk of red currant jelly, an idea that pleased me—I needed a juice of some sort to set the stage. The center of the dish was sour, with the flavored cream sauces placed around it. Some of these sauces were plain, but others were seasoned, particularly with red pepper, which created a lastingly warm sensation in the mouth.

YOUR TURN

This time your guests are liable to suffer if you're not careful: I don't dare imagine what they'll feel like if you offer them dishes that are *completely* excessive! To make the inedible edible, you will have to practice long and hard—and be prepared to test the results yourself. But think how proud you'll feel when you're finally able to serve your friends a dish in which moderation is thrown to the winds—to everyone's delight!

STRUCTURING FLAVOR SPACE

IN THEORY

Inspired by Goethe and Schiller, I set to work a few years ago to devise mathematical formulas that would provide new principles for spatially organizing the elements of a dish—principles to which Pierre has attempted to give culinary expression. This is only one example of how such formulas can be applied. Ordinary checkerboards can't be eaten, of course. But what if they are constructed out of textures and flavors?

IN PRACTICE
A SCALLOP AND TRUFFLE CHECKERBOARD

One can create an epic style of cooking by introducing "impeding" themes, just as Homer did in delaying Ulysses' return to Ithaca in the *Odyssey*. In culinary terms, it is a question of adding layers of chewiness in order to make a story—which must be constructed out of textures and flavors—go on and on. One way of doing this is to build a checkerboard in three dimensions. A checkerboard in two dimensions is the familiar board on which one plays checkers. A checkerboard in three dimensions is a slab made by alternating cubes of two kinds of food that differ from one another in texture or flavor, or both.

Consider this checkerboard of scallops and truffles that I served at my restaurant during the winter of 2002. Long parallelepipeds of each ingredient were stuck together with melted butter, then pressed together in plastic wrap and put in the refrigerator. Once sufficiently firm to be sliced, the packet was cut perpendicularly to the axis of the parallelepipeds, yielding a checkerboard that was then transferred to a hot plate and put under the salamander. The result was elegant—and good.

Scallops and truffles are a classic combination in French haute cuisine. But why should we be content with the same old recipes? Here, once again, setting the stage properly is the main thing. But there are also technical considerations: the dish is good only if the products are of the highest quality (after all, there are scallops, and then there are scallops; there are truffles, and then there are truffles), and only if the execution is perfect.

Oh, yes—this checkerboard is served with a very flavorful chicken stock (not easy to make, by the way: it is absolutely essential that "false flavors" be avoided by blanching the chicken first and after that skimming off the scum from the surface at frequent intervals along with any oily liquid that has risen to the top), along with parmesan and truffle juice.

Ultimately, a dish such as this hangs together mainly because of the painstaking attention to detail in giving effect to the initial idea.

YOUR TURN

We leave it to you to devise your own checkerboards, taking care to assure that there is nothing slapdash about the execution, no matter what prior decisions you've made about flavor and texture. To obtain a beautiful result, visually, you have to think carefully about the technical aspects of the dish, and keep in mind also that smaller portions will be more readily welcomed by your guests than larger ones. In any case, if you want them to appreciate the structure of the dish, you need to construct it mouthful by mouthful. Have fun!

PART FIVE

THE PRESENT AND FUTURE OF COOKING

TWENTY-ONE

THE MANY STRANDS OF MODERNITY

In the early nineteenth century, Friedrich Hegel held that beauty is not to be confused with the work of art itself, for a work of art is artificial whereas beauty may be natural as well. At about the same time, Honoré de Balzac suggested that the purpose of art is not to copy nature, but to express it. Eugène Delacroix liberated painting in urging the painter to seek the means for rendering nature and its effects in his own imagination: "Painting has no need for a subject." In reaction against naturalism, the poets of the symbolist movement sought to suggest the most subtle nuances of impressions and feelings through the musical quality of words and the elevation of subjectively experienced reality to the level of idea and symbol. Elsewhere neoclassicism gave way to impressionism. In all the arts it was a time of ferment and brilliant experimentation. In cooking, however, little changed.

───────────

IMAGINING FLAVORS THAT HAVE NEVER EXISTED

Jean is in a hotel room with the air conditioning turned on. Double bed, sofa, wicker chair, a big television (turned off), a blue pastel painting. Outside the sky is blue, with a view of the water.

Hélène,

I've only been away for two days and already I miss you. The blue sky of the West Indies is much grayer than the sky of Paris because you are not with me. For the first time, I enjoy neither my trip nor the pleasure of being with colleagues who are also friends. I can't wait to return to Paris. And during the day I can't wait to come back to my hotel room and prepare the next chapter of our joint project on culinary aesthetics. I devoured the materials that you gave me. Take a look, would you, at what I've managed to draw from them, in the fashion of our old book on the quintessential art of cooking. I've drafted only short paragraphs, because the nineteenth century is so rich, filled with movements of all sorts.

> *Friedrich Wilhelm Joseph von Schelling (Leonberg, Wurtembourg, 1775–Bad Ragaz, Switzerland, 1854): German philosopher and pan-theist. In the lectures that formed the basis of* Philosophy of Art *(1802–1805), Schelling said that beauty is "the infinite expressed in a finite way."[107] This goes back to an old medieval idea, only God has now become the infinite.*
>
> *Schelling also held that the artist does not imitate nature, but enters into competition with it. In cooking, this is a matter of going beyond the ingredients themselves and creating flavors that have never existed, which will take their place alongside natural flavors. How? With the aid of molecules that will be like the tubes of colors that painters use today: no one any longer cares whether these mixtures of pigments are natural or not. What matters is that they*

succeed in rendering the tones that artists dream of using. Can't we imagine that the day will come that cooks will use flavoring agents, natural and artificial alike, to give dishes the flavors they dream of?

Georg Wilhelm Friedrich Hegel (Stuttgart, 1770–Berlin, 1831): German philosopher, professor at the universities of Jena, Heidelberg, and Berlin, who sought to promote human fulfillment by seeking to resolve the opposition between reality and thought. Hegel maintained that beauty is not to be confused with works of art, for works of art are artificial whereas beauty may also be natural.

In cooking, having freed ourselves from the cult of the ingredient, we hold that a cassoulet may be beautiful, without this beauty being that of the beans or of the confit or of any of its other ingredients.

Arthur Schopenhauer (Danzig, 1788–Frankfurt, 1860): German philosopher who detected in the will to live—the law to which all living beings are subject—the origin of the suffering that he sought to alleviate through aesthetic experience. Schopenhauer's pessimistic philosophy had great influence, notably upon Nietzsche. In The World as Will and Representation *(1818), he wrote: "The work of art is only a means of facilitating that knowledge in which [aesthetic] pleasure consists."*[108] *This idea greatly influenced Wagner and the symbolists.*

Marie-Henri Beyle (Grenoble, 1783–Paris, 1842): French writer, officer of the Sixth Dragoons and later a quartermaster in Napoleon's armies during the wars of the Revolution and the Empire whose experience in Italy made a lasting impression on him. After the fall of Napoleon in 1814, Beyle settled in Milan, where he wrote essays on music and painting, as well as an account of his travels, which he published under the name Stendhal. He went on to publish On Love *(1822), and an essay on Romanticism in which he defended prose tragedy and advocated the abandonment of classical rules. Though still unrecognized, he was able to bring out* Armance *in 1827 and then* The Red and the Black *in 1830. He went back to Italy as a con-*

sul and, while on leave in Paris, wrote The Charterhouse of Parma
(1839). In his History of Painting in Italy, *published in 1817, he wrote:
"Painting is only constructed morality."*[109]

This is an interesting idea. What "constructed morality" would amount
to in cooking I haven't a clue. Who could help us? I move on to Delacroix:

> *Eugène Delacroix (Saint-Maurice, Val-de-Marne, 1789–Paris, 1863):
> French painter, famous for his talent as a colorist and as a leader
> of the Romantic school. Known for his large canvases, Delacroix also
> illustrated Goethe's* Faust *with lithographs. His* Journal *contains a
> wealth of aesthetic ideas in the form of aphorisms such as "The artist
> must seek the means of rendering nature and its effects in his own
> imagination" and "Painting has no need of a subject."*[110] *The cook
> is free! At last. And cooking does not have to be legible.*

I know that you have argued just the opposite, that cooking must be legible. This is something we have all discussed at length before. Let me sum-
marize what's been said so that we'll have a permanent record.

> *First of all, regional cuisines, classical or modern, are legible: when
> I eat them, I understand that I'm eating a regional dish. In the case
> of culinary craftsmen, who make the same traditional dishes (good,
> bad, or indifferent) over and over again, the legibility is greater still:
> when I eat a dish of choucroute, for example, I know that I'm eat-
> ing something from Alsace. The story being told is clear, and there-
> fore easily understood.*
>
> *You will recall that we compared cooking to stories told by cooks.
> As in painting and the other arts, the cook doesn't assemble in-
> gredients at random; he chooses them with care, because he has a
> feeling for how they should go together. For the diner, no less than
> someone who listens to a story or reads a book, there's a need to
> understand. A story that strays too far from the usual conventions of
> storytelling, whose elements are rambling and disjointed, is incom-
> prehensible, and therefore disliked.*

Which suggests that cooking must also be legible. Anyone who doubts that culinary artists must take care to organize their stories properly, in order to achieve a particular purpose, will see after a moment's reflection that the general construction of a dish matters as much as the details of its presentation: when we don't know how to "read" dishes consisting of a number of separate elements, we don't know where to begin. For cooking is not the same as music, where a story is told by a succession of notes, or a figurative picture, where the eye almost automatically perceives juxtapositions among painted objects.

For all these reasons, then, we decided that legibility is obligatory. But having now had the opportunity to consider what Delacroix says, I am forced to conclude that it is optional. Cooking has no need of a subject. I hear you say: yes, but if we don't recognize the form of what we're eating, we won't eat—we're not prepared to go that far. A point worth thinking about.

Delacroix also said: *"Every complete aesthetic pleasure is the synthesis of a sensory pleasure, a formal pleasure, and a purely emotional pleasure."*[111] This is probably something that's also worth thinking about. But let me move on to Balzac for the moment:

Honoré de Balzac (Tours, 1799–Paris, 1850): Prolific writer, author of the Human Comedy *(17 vols., 1842–1847), a series of novels that describe French society between the Revolution and the July Monarchy. More than two thousand characters chasing after power, money, love . . .*

Balzac wrote: *"The mission of art is not to copy nature, but to express it,"*[112] and *"Art's greatest efforts are invariably a timid counterfeit of the effects of nature."*[113] It seems to me that Delacroix was way ahead of Balzac. Nonetheless let me transpose: *For Balzac, one must not try to recreate the flavor of an apricot by mixing together the flavor of an orange and a carrot, but to freely interpret the flavor of an apricot. Yet another person who seeks to limit possibilities!*

Now then, you'll be proud of me for this next one. Someone in your field:

> *Walter Horatio Pater (London, 1839–Oxford, 1894), British writer and critic, champion of aestheticism, and author of influential studies on the Italian Renaissance.*

And here are two notes in keeping with the spirit of our old book:

> *Aestheticism: an artistic idea emphasizing formal refinement and virtuosity; also an English literary and artistic tendency of the last third of the nineteenth century, part of a broader movement advocating art for art's sake, in opposition to naturalism.*
>
> *Naturalism: a literary and artistic school of the nineteenth century that, through the application of the methods of positive science to art, sought to reproduce reality in all its aspects, even the most ordinary, with perfect objectivity. In the fine arts it called for the faithful imitation of nature, in opposition to both stylization and idealism (according to which everything is reduced to thought and subordinate to it), as well as to symbolism.*

With regard to symbolism, I found that this movement came into existence in 1886 with the manifesto published that year by the Franco-Greek poet Jean Moréas in *Le Figaro:*

> *Moréas brought together poets who sought to suggest the most subtle nuances of impressions and feelings through the musical quality of words and the elevation of subjectively experienced reality to the level of idea and symbol. In painting, the symbolist movement was represented by artists such as Gustave Moreau.*

In cooking today, so many years after the battles of the nineteenth century, a symbolist movement has yet to be invented. Should we say that symbolist cooking would seek to suggest the nuances of impressions and feelings through the gustatory qualities of a dish? Cécile would love to tackle a problem like this!

All right, now I come to another point of disagreement. You remember our discussion about art, history, and philosophy? You maintained that aesthetics is a branch of history, while I maintained that it belongs instead to philosophy. Plato, Aristotle, Hegel—and now Nietzsche:

> *Friedrich Nietzsche (Röchel, near Lützen, 1844–Weimar, 1900): German philosopher, son of a Protestant minister, who studied classical philosophy before going on to teach at the University of Basel. After resigning his post he led a wandering and solitary existence, before finally going mad in 1889. A close friend of Richard Wagner for a time, and strongly influenced by his reading of Arthur Schopenhauer, Nietzsche frequently resorted to aphorism and poetic forms of expression. "Art," he held, "makes the sight of life bearable by laying over it the veil of unclear thinking."[114] Or again: "Art is not merely imitation of the reality of nature but rather a metaphysical supplement of the reality of nature, placed alongside it for its overcoming."[115]*

This time culinary artifice is legitimized, with regard to the artistic component of cooking. A veil is not nature. And artistic cooking is legitimized as well: it is no longer a question of giving a roasted chicken the flavor of a roasted chicken, as Curnonsky insisted, but of using a roasted chicken to overcome the roasted chicken of artisanal tradition. At last!

And yet artists still hesitated between nature and artifice. Paul Cézanne*

---

*PAUL CÉZANNE (Aix-en-Provence, 1839–Aix-en-Provence, 1906): French painter who, like the impressionists, relied on small brush strokes in combination with large patches of color to represent compact forms, structured by light. Toward the end of his life he moved away from impressionist technique in an attempt to express the eternal, intrinsic character of naturally occurring forms through a series of basic shapes. He ex-

said that the landscape *"thinks itself in me . . . and I am its consciousness."*[116] And Claude Debussy:* *"Is it not more profitable to see the sun rise than to hear the* Pastoral Symphony *of Beethoven?"*[117]

Finally, I took advantage of a quiet moment one evening to read the writings you gave me by Baudelaire.† There is this observation, with which I am in perfect agreement as far as it concerns cooking: *"There is a great difference between a piece that is done and a piece that is finished: in general, a piece that is done is not finished, and a very finished piece may not be done at all."*[118] Observe how true this is in cooking: really, I do not understand why some people refuse the status of art to what certain cooks create. In my opinion, these people have never come anywhere near such a thing in their lives, and judge without even knowing it exists. They should be sent to Cécile's restaurant at once.

I don't know why it is, but Baudelaire has made me see—finally!—that composition must be distinguished from execution. Yes, there are culi-

---

celled at portraiture, figure drawings, still lifes, and landscapes (notably among them Mount Sainte-Victoire); seaside bathers were a favorite subject. His influence on some of the major currents in late nineteenth-century and early twentieth-century art (fauvism, cubism, abstraction) was crucial.

*CLAUDE DEBUSSY (Saint-Germain-en-Laye, 1862–Paris, 1918): French composer whose independent spirit allowed him to escape Wagner's influence in opera, for which he created a new style of recitative. In his works for piano and orchestra Debussy achieved a fresh and exquisite refinement of sound.

†CHARLES BAUDELAIRE (Paris, 1821–Paris, 1867): Poet who carried on the Romantic movement in France while remaining faithful to the rules of traditional prosody. His poetry expressed the tragedy of human fate and a vision of the universe in which he discovered secret correspondences. Along with *The Flowers of Evil* (1857), for which he was charged with immorality, Baudelaire's critical work (notably *Aesthetic Curiosities* and *Romantic Art,* both published in 1868) and his *Little Poems in Prose* (1869) were fundamental documents of late nineteenth-century thinking about modernity.

nary artists who compose, and there are others who execute. Why didn't I understand this earlier?

I've also come to understand that originality, which Baudelaire talks about, poses a problem for cooking: since cooking is visceral, it's not clear that one can cook the way one paints. Our species is protected by food neophobia, the reflex that prevents us from eating what we do not know. This protects us against toxic plants, as Denis has already pointed out, but it is also a brake on the development of culinary art.

Baudelaire posed in connection with painting the question that we've been discussing in connection with cooking: how does one judge? One can evaluate the appearance of a dish, the sensations it arouses in us when we look at it, and how they fit with what we then experience in the mouth. But is this correspondence really necessary? Baudelaire replies poetically: *"To the wind that blows tomorrow, no one lends an ear."*[119] And again: *"The melody leaves behind a profound memory in the mind."*[120]

One of the most easily transposable of Baudelaire's ideas is this: *"A good way of telling whether a picture is melodious is to look at it from quite a distance, so that neither the subject nor the lines can be made out. If it is melodious, it already has a meaning, and it has already taken its place in the repertoire of memories."*[121] I can see myself at the table, not literally stepping back to look at the plate, but consciously detaching my critical faculties from the sensations that envelop me in the presence of a fine culinary work of art. If the dish claims its place in the repertoire of my memories, it's a good sign. This is a piece of advice, by the way, that I'm going to give to my food critic friends: let time do its work, and judge according to what you remember.

And now to close—romantically, Hélène, may I? *"An eclectic,"* Baudelaire says, *"is a weak man, for he is a man without love."*[122] I assure you that I'm not weak!

—JEAN

EXPRESSING NATURE

IN THEORY

The question of nature—reproduced, imitated, imagined, evoked—has not ceased to occupy philosophers of art. In cooking it has made its presence felt as well, in large part because until recently ingredients were seasonal. Nicolas Appert, a maker of fruit conserves who discovered the technique of preserving food by canning or bottling in 1795, made a decisive advance (recognized shortly afterward by Grimod de la Reynière) because he succeeded in abolishing the seasons. Whereas until then foods were difficult to keep, Appert's discovery made it possible to improve upon the traditional practice of salting them, or covering them with sugar, or putting them in fat. Today, of course, we are accustomed to seeing exquisite strawberries that have come from the other side of the world, but equally remarkable products can be found in our own markets at the right time of year, and often even the most avant-garde chefs feel a sort of duty to make their cooking suit the season. Ah, the taste of the first green beans when they've just been picked! The freshness of those first heads of lettuce, and the milky juice you can see in their leaves and stems!

IN PRACTICE
FLOWER RAVIOLI

First let's make a stock by heating some fennel, at the height of its flavor, in a covered pot of spring water with a slightly aromatic base of oregano, onion, and the green part of a leek. Then let's thicken the stock with some agar so we get a texture that's firmer than that of gelatin and, more importantly, that produces more varied sensations when it is consumed: once you bite through the somewhat rubbery resistance of the outside layer, the stock becomes liquid again.

Slice this jellied stock into rectangular sheets and on top of each one put some ricotta cheese, mascarpone, chervil, baby spinach leaves, and cilantro. Cover this layer with edible flowers such as violets, pansies, pineapple sage, or borage, and then fold it by pulling one side over to meet the other to make transparent ravioli.

The ravioli are served with some chanterelle mushrooms that have been just barely moistened with melted butter, together with a soft butter-almond paste. Take some chilled butter and knead it with the liquid from the mushrooms, heavily seasoned with black pepper, and some fresh almonds; later in the season you might think of adding some apricot pulp (the combination of apricot, almond, and chanterelle is very interesting, by the way). You can also add an egg yolk that has been cooked at 63°C (about 145°F)—still almost raw yet slightly thickened, while preserving its moist and cool freshness.

All the ingredients of this dish evoke the spirit of springtime and renewal. The fennel lends it a verdant freshness, and the flowers announce the season by their very presence, all the more as they are visible through the transparent jelly. The pungency—from the flowers, the pepper, and the chanterelles—has a seasonal liveliness as well. Still, it's not to everyone's taste, and needs to be toned down a bit. The sensation of spiciness should be prominent, but not aggressively so. The almonds serve to soften the edge somewhat.

Everything considered, the dish may actually be a little too spicy to call to mind springtime, but the presentation, the idea of the dish, certainly does. We need to learn to look behind what we perceive, to taste behind what we taste.

YOUR TURN

For many of us, making a seasonal dish is only a matter of using seasonal products. For an aesthetic tradition that proclaims the primacy of mind over matter, however, it is also necessary that the idea of the dish evoke the season. The preceding example shows us the way. Can you think of something in the same vein as this surprising recipe?

TWENTY-TWO

YESTERDAY

During the troubled years that saw the rise of Nazism in Germany, the Bauhaus sought to reconceive the teaching of architecture, design, and art. Carrying on a great tradition that went back to Leonardo da Vinci, this school looked to science for inspiration. Its faculty included Wassily Kandinsky, one of the great pioneers of abstract art, who sought to illuminate the human heart.

THE BAUHAUS AND BEYOND

Denis and Jean are walking down a street. Denis is carrying a big briefcase and Jean is dressed in light colors.

DENIS   So, we haven't seen much of you lately.

JEAN   I was away on business. And Hélène and I have been working together.

DENIS   Working? Billing and cooing, you mean. I knew you were a con-
noisseur, but this—

JEAN   No, I'm serious. Well, we do bill and coo, if you like. But since
we've been together we haven't received any more packets of new pages.
Troubles over. And besides, we're continuing the history ourselves.

DENIS   What history?

JEAN   You know—the old book on culinary aesthetics. Hélène knows a
great deal, of course, and she's got an extraordinary library. As for me,
I've got a lot of experience in restaurants—

DENIS   You mean you're so fond of food that you've been to every one
and you've eaten a lot!

JEAN   Yes, but right now my experience is coming in handy. Take a
look at what we came up with last night.

Denis reads:

> *Heinrich Wölfflin (Winterthur, 1864–Zurich, 1945): Art historian, pro-
> fessor at the universities of Basel, Berlin, Munich, and Zurich, whose
> landmark* Principles of Art History *(1915) inquired into the inner
> motivations of the great artists of the past in seeking to explain
> the evolution of styles and, in particular, the opposition between
> the classical and the baroque. Wölfflin's concern with techniques,
> forms, and visual possibilities,*[123] *led him to insist that technical analy-
> sis of artistic practice needed to be supplemented by a broader ap-
> proach drawing upon psychology and social history.*
>
> *Wölfflin's insights need to be taken into account in considering
> gustatory forms and possibilities. We must make an inventory first,
> before trying to draw up classifications.*

DENIS   This really does sound like *The Quintessential Art.*

JEAN   The credit is mostly Hélène's. We're having a lot of fun.

DENIS   And to think you're doing all this in the bedroom—

JEAN   Stop. If you must know, well, yes, I'm sleeping with Hélène, and she's sleeping with me. And we're happy. Which doesn't prevent me from doing my job, nor Hélène from doing hers—nor the two of us from working together on this project.

DENIS   And why *are* you working together on it?

JEAN   Why? Why do you spend your days doing calculations? More than once you've quoted the words of your friend Jean-Claude Pecker to me: "In this leaden age, when money takes the place of moral value . . ." Let me complete the sentence for you: In this leaden age, when money takes the place of moral value, knowledge is the most beautiful thing of all—after love. Do you want me to ask Cécile if she holds another opinion?

DENIS   No, no, don't bother. Come on, don't be upset. Let me read the rest. Ah, the handwriting here is different—

JEAN   Just like in that old book: two hands, a single text.

DENIS   I see you've even added some recipes.

JEAN   Yes, I asked Pierre Gagnaire to suggest some.

DENIS   Okay, let me read further:

> We go on now to Das Staatliche Bauhaus—better known simply as the Bauhaus—a school established in Germany by the painter and architect Walter Gropius (Berlin, 1883–Boston, 1969). This school, and the aesthetic philosophy it embodied, came into existence in Weimar in the spring of 1919, subsequently moving to Dessau and Berlin; the German police closed the school down in Berlin on 10 April 1933.[124] In the interval it created a great many novel works of architecture and design, whose aim was to prevent human beings from becoming the slaves of machines.
>
> In the words of the Swiss painter Paul Klee (Münchenbuchsee, near Berne, 1879–Muralto, near Locarno, 1940), who taught at the Bauhaus: "Art must reveal and make visible the invisible."[125] Ac-

cording to another faculty member, the German painter Oskar Schlemmer (Stuttgart, 1888–Baden-Baden, 1943): "The Bauhaus is an opening to all that is new, to all that moves in the world. It is a will to assimilate." [126]

Gropius, in his 1919 manifesto, declared that art cannot be taught. At the same time, "There is no basic difference between the artist and the artisan. The artist is just an elevated version of the artisan. Thank heavens, during rare moments of light that are beyond his control, art flourishes unconsciously from the work of his hands, but the knowledge of the basics of his work is indispensable to any artist. It is the source of all creative production." [127]

Instruction at the Bauhaus was based on the assumption that forms and colors enjoyed an objective existence and were governed by laws: "Alongside a technical and artisanal training," Gropius wrote, "the creator must also learn the language of forms in order to be able to visually express his ideas. He must acquire a scientific knowledge of objective facts: a theoretical basis, capable of guiding his creative hand, and an objective basis on which a great number of individuals will be able to rely in order to work together in harmony." [128]

An interesting school, from which we can draw culinary lessons, especially at a time when the status of the cook has been shaken by the growth of the food industry and the proliferation of chain restaurants and institutional cafeterias (in schools, hospitals, prisons, and so on). Can we not imagine the day when, alongside a technical and artisanal training, the culinary artist must also learn the language of flavors in order to express his ideas? Following Gropius, we would require in particular that, as part of their basic training, cooks receive instruction in the scientific basis of flavor. But this is not enough, for in that case aspiring artists would remain at the technical level, without having yet acquired the language of flavors.

The Bauhaus thought in terms of elementary shapes: triangle, square, circle. In cooking, these correspond to the flavor of pure ingredients (raw or cooked? alone or in combination?). Let's roll up

*our sleeves and try to elaborate the language of flavors that holds
the key to a resolutely modern culinary art. Time to get to work!*

Well, you've certainly got a lot on your plate! Years of work.

JEAN   That's right—and we've got to get started at once: every minute
we delay is a minute lost for the cause of culinary art. I'm thinking about
founding a society of cooks and neurophysiologists of flavor in order to
further this research.

DENIS   Ah, you speak next of Kandinsky. Cécile and I both love his work.
What do you say about him? Let's see:

*Wassily Kandinsky (Moscow, 1866–Neuilly-sur-Seine, 1944): Russian
painter who became a naturalized German citizen, then a French
citizen; one of the founders of the* Blaue Reiter *in Munich and, after
1910, one of the great pioneers of abstract art. He began teaching
at the Bauhaus in 1922, then settled in Paris as a refugee from the
Nazis in 1933. His writings include* Concerning the Spiritual in Art
*(1911), which appealed to "inner necessity" to justify freedom of in-
vention and lyricism, and* Point and Line to Plane *(1926).*

That much I know. What else?

*In promoting abstract art, Kandinsky turned his back on figurative
representation. What is abstract art? In the case of painting, it refuses to recognize the authority of an external subject: colors and
lines, being relieved of any representational function, are responsible instead for assuring the harmony of the work.*

*And what of abstract cuisine? It involves using edible ingredients
to create flavors that are not those of the ingredients themselves—
the opposite of what Curnonsky wanted, finally. For the abstract
cook, a chicken may be only a texture, with an oyster flavor perhaps,
so long as the urge to create something beautiful is at work. Why
should we limit ourselves to making chicken taste like chicken? Nothing obliges us to do so.*

In Concerning the Spiritual in Art, *Kandinsky argued that the viewer "seeks in a work of art a mere imitation of nature which can serve some definite purpose (for example a portrait in the ordinary sense) or a presentment of nature according to a certain convention ('impressionist' painting), or some inner feeling expressed in terms of natural form (as we say—a picture with* Stimmung*)."*[129] *Or again: "A man, a tree, an apple, all were used by Cézanne in the creation of something that is called a 'picture,' and which is a piece of true inward and artistic harmony. . . . To attain this end he requires as a starting point nothing but the object to be painted (human being or whatever it may be), and then the methods that belong to painting alone, colour and form."*[130]

The abstract is what Kandinsky sometimes calls an "inner tendency," other times an inner nature, feeling, or need. In art, he says, there is "another kind of external similarity [between different periods] which is founded on a fundamental truth. When there is a similarity of inner tendency in the whole moral and spiritual atmosphere, a similarity of ideals, at first closely pursued but later lost to sight, a similarity in the inner feeling of any one period to that of another, the logical result will be a revival of the external forms which served to express those inner feelings in an earlier age. An example of this today is our sympathy, our spiritual relationship, with the Primitives."[131]

"When religion, science and morality are shaken," Kandinsky goes on to say, "the last two by the strong hand of Nietzsche, and when the outer supports threaten to fall, man turns his gaze from externals in onto himself. Literature, music and art are the first and most sensitive spheres in which this spiritual revolution makes itself felt."[132]

And he concludes: "There is no 'must' in art, because art is free."[133] *Is this true?*

Or again: "The artist must have something to say, for mastery over form is not his goal but rather the adapting of form to its inner meaning."[134] *And finally: "That is beautiful which is produced by the inner need, which springs from the soul."*[135]

Obviously, the detractors of abstract art will say that it is anar-chic. But what a marvelous thing it would be for a culinary artist to embrace the purpose that Kandinsky envisioned, quoting the Ger-man composer Robert Schumann (Zwickay, 1810–Bonn, 1856): "To send light into the darkness of men's hearts—such is the duty of the artist."[136] *How can this goal be reached in practice? Kandinsky gives some hints, citing the example of poetry: "The apt use of a word (in its poetical meaning), repetition of this word, twice, three times or even more frequently, according to the need of the poem, will not only tend to intensify the inner harmony but also bring to light unsuspected spiritual properties of the word itself. Further than that, frequent repetition of a word (again a favourite game of chil-dren, which is forgotten in [later] life) deprives the word of its orig-inal external meaning. Similarly, in drawing, the abstract message of the object drawn tends to be forgotten and its meaning lost."*[137]

Translated into cooking terms: the skillful use of a flavor, the in-wardly necessary repetition of this flavor in various parts of a sin-gle dish, makes it possible to bring out the spiritual properties of this flavor.

Why insist on repetition in particular? Kandinsky explains: "To let the eye stray over a palette, splashed with many colors, produces a dual result. In the first place one receives a purely physical sen-sation, one of pleasure and contentment at the varied and beauti ful colors"—as when, for example, we eat a dessert. "The eye is either warmed"—like the palate by a spicy dish—"or else soothed and cooled"—like the finger that touches ice cream. "But these physi-cal sensations can only be of short duration. They are merely super-ficial and leave no lasting impression, for the soul is unaffected." Just as one feels only the physical sensation of cold, on touching the ice cream, and forgets this sensation once the finger is warm again, so "the effect of the colors is forgotten when the eye is turned away." And just as the physical sensation of the cold of the ice cream, when it penetrates more deeply, arouses other more profound sen-sations and may set in motion a train of mental events, so "the su-

perficial impression of varied colour may be the starting point of a whole chain of related sensations."[138]

All this, you see, is readily transposed to the field of cooking. There's no time to lose if we are to create an abstract cuisine. At last, after millennia of stagnation, we've earned the right!

Kandinsky's conviction that abstraction allows the artist to free himself from the forms of the external world and to devote himself to inner languages is one that culinary artists can share if they also accept that beauty proceeds from an inner necessity of the soul.

DENIS   Well—I love Kandinsky's work, but I didn't know he was such a mystic! Incredible.

JEAN   It's a bit crazy, I agree—but think of the possibilities for an abstract cuisine! I spoke about this to Cécile—

DENIS   I know, it really got her to thinking—she seems to like the idea. She wants the new restaurant to be a place for experimentation. It's a risky proposition in some ways, but it seems to me that the time is ripe for developing an abstract approach to cooking. In any case, she has my support.

Shall we continue?

The American art historian Meyer Schapiro (Šiauliai [Shavel], Lithuania, 1904–New York, 1996) observed that students of prehistoric art are well aware that the flat surface we associate with a painting was the result of thousands of years of evolution.[139] *Thus, too, in cooking, the plate—the equivalent of the picture frame—emerged only relatively recently. Questions to be explored: Is there any reason to preserve this convention? Should we exchange our plates and bowls for something different? Change our way of arranging them? Our way of serving meals? After all, the Romans ate in a reclining position.*

Paul Klee again: "Art does not reflect the visible; it makes [the unseen] visible."[140] *Once again the old idea of revelation. To be developed.*

The French painter Fernand Léger (Argentan, 1881–Gif-sur-Yvette, 1955), who practiced a form of cubism, elaborated an essentially plastic language based on the dynamism of modern life and contrasts of form and meaning in order finally to reintegrate moral and social values. He considered one of the aims of figurative painting to be the creation of images that are equally "valid" in every part of the canvas.[141]

It will be necessary to try to develop a sort of culinary cubism by experimenting with new ways of combining elements in the plate, the order in which they are eaten, and so on.

In the "Manifesto of Futurist Cuisine" (1931), the Italian poet Filippo Tommaso Marinetti (Alexandria, Egypt, 1876–Bellagio, 1944) wrote: "It is necessary that everyone have the sensation of eating works of art."[142] *The manifesto published recipes by "airpoets": paradoxical associations and heretical combinations of ingredients involving miniaturization, accumulation, and transgression. The dishes are metaphors. Marinetti had an aesthetic bias, but he was mistaken about beauty: what he proposed has nothing to do with flavor. It is a formal game—the worst outcome imaginable for cooking.*

I see you declare your own bias in these notes.

JEAN   Yes, but then so does the old book, which is very personal. So—

DENIS   You're right. I notice, too, that now you're linking together brief remarks in a rather disjointed way.

JEAN   That's because we're talking about figures who are almost our contemporaries—they're too close for us to see them clearly. It will take another century for those who continue our work adding to *The Quintessential Art* to smooth out these rough edges.

DENIS   Okay, let's go on:

Jean-Paul Sartre (Paris, 1905–Paris, 1980): "One is accustomed, since

cubism, to declare that a picture must not represent or imitate re-
ality, but that it must itself constitute an object."[143]

Well, that's not new: we've come across this idea before.

JEAN   You're right, but we put it in because it's expressed in a way that cooks will find helpful. It's a sort of authorization for them to create as they see fit, without reference to any particular point of departure. It's no longer a question of making a purée of turnips, or oranges, or pota-toes that tastes like turnip or orange or potato, nor of a roasted chicken that tastes like a roasted chicken. It's now a question of choosing ingre-dients and culinary techniques—I say "culinary," but one could do away with the adjective: ingredients and techniques, then, in order to make something. Something unknown, new. An object—

DENIS   A UEO—

JEAN   Huh?

DENIS   Unidentified Edible Object.

JEAN   Call it what you will, but I don't like the pejorative connotation. Can't we finally imagine marvelous and unknown things, and rid our-selves of the old food neophobia of our primate cousins?

DENIS   You're right. Besides, this has been Cécile's dream for a long time. Let's go on with your chronological ramble though the twentieth century, shall we?

> *Maurice Merleau-Ponty (Rochefort, 1908–Paris, 1961): French philoso-*
> *pher who used phenomenology (a philosophical method developed*
> *by Edmund Husserl with the aim of giving philosophy a rigorous*
> *scientific basis), to elucidate the psychological processes on which*
> *scientific practice is founded. In* Signs *(1960), Merleau-Ponty spoke*
> *of "already stylized perception."*[144] *That is, style extends and sys-*
> *tematizes the work of perception in symbolically dividing up real-*
> *ity. An idea that needs to be examined further.*

Martin Heidegger (Messkirch, Baden, 1889–Messkirch, 1976): A student of Husserl who taught at the University of Marburg and later at Fribourg-en-Brisgau, where as an enthusiastic Nazi party member he served briefly as rector: "The work of art," Heidegger said, "does not imitate an already given reality; it brings forth a truth of the objects represented, reliability, which is established presence."[145] An old idea!

In The Voices of Silence (1951), André Malraux (Paris, 1901–Créteil, 1976) wrote: "Just as a musician likes music and not nightingales, a poet verse and not sunsets, a painter is not a man who likes figures and landscapes: he is first of all a man who loves pictures."[146] This is one of those quotes that perfectly illustrates the notion that a remark is interesting if the opposite of it is interesting as well. One can imagine musicians who like nightingales, and also music that renders the beauty of their song.

In cooking? The culinary artist can have a thousand objectives. He may like the flavor of a roasted chicken, or he may seek to create his personal version of the flavor of a roasted chicken, or . . .

Malraux again: "The artist creates not so much in order to express himself as he expresses himself in order to create."[147] This is a very modern idea—aiming at creation rather than expression. Culinary art might be mistrustful of it, but one can imagine various sorts of cooks: those who are primarily interested in experimentation, those who cook because they wish to give their interpretation of a dish, those whose interest is mainly in creating new dishes, and so on.

The French art historian and critic Pierre Francastel (Paris, 1900–Paris, 1970) rejected attempts to distinguish between art and technique. All technique, Francastel claimed, involves an element of skill and leaves room for choice.[148] He wasn't wrong, but the Bauhaus had already answered him: artisanal cooking involves an element of skill while leaving room for choice—and happily so, but artistic cooking aims at something else.

Paul Claudel (Villeneuve-sur-Fère, 1868–Paris, 1955): Poet, drama-

*tist, and diplomat who sought to show in his plays that the contra-
dictory aspirations of mankind, the conflict between the flesh and
the spirit, can be resolved only through an overcoming of the self
and recognition of God's love. In his* Journal *(1968) he wrote: "Art
imitates nature, not in its effects, however these may be, but in its
causes, in its 'manner,' in its techniques."*[149] *Is this still imitation?
Claudel seems rather closer to ancient Chinese ideas!*

*Jacques Lacan (Paris, 1901–Paris, 1981): French psychoanalyst who
insisted on distinguishing between the real, the imaginary, and the
symbolic—a genuinely novel insight that deserves to be investigated
further in connection with cooking, for these three aspects are the
basis of a complete cuisine.*

What do you mean by "a complete cuisine"?

JEAN   Think of our roasted chicken. There is the roasted chicken itself.
There are also the thoughts and feelings that the roasted chicken evokes
through the flavor that the cook has given it: thoughts of rotisseries turning in the delicatessen window, all sorts of things, I don't know. And then
there is the symbolism of the roasted chicken. In the case of a chicken
it's hard to say, but for a leg of lamb there's the symbolism of the lamb,
the Easter lamb, for example.

In any case, there's something there to structure the cook's creativity,
and—

DENIS   Oh, you really have left no stone unturned! I find the following:

*According to the American philosopher George Dickie (Palmetto,
Florida, 1926–), the work of modern art may be any production that
the art world has decided to call a work of art.*[150]

JEAN   It's not the best reference we've managed to find, I grant you,
but it does give some idea of what needs to be avoided. Imagine, a dish
in which an "artist" has put anything he likes. I want no part of that.

DENIS   Nor do I. Culinary art is limited because we eat it. We can't stand apart from it. Ah, Umberto Eco. I know him for his wonderful novel *The Name of the Rose,* of course, but I wonder what you've taken from his writings on aesthetics:

> *"Nowadays, the tendency is to believe that, while art has some qualities of uniqueness, this is not attributable to its independence from nature and experience. We look upon art as a focus of lived experiences, given order and form by our normal imaginative processes. Artistic particularity arises from the manner in which the order and form are made concrete and offered to perception."* [151]

This reminds me of the philosopher Jean-Luc Chalumeau's remark that "interpretations are functions that transform material objects into works of art." [152]

And your conclusion is what?

> *Anne Cauquelin, the French painter and philosopher, remarks that contemporary art "forces belief [that there is such a thing as art] to come out from its lair, forces expectations to take shape (in a tone of lamentation [I know quite well that what I see is contemporary art, but, even so, art is something different], but no matter)."* [153]

You've really done a good job. But does your history end there?

JEAN   No, Hélène and I have decided to carry on with it. You remember Lu Wenfu's words: "To forget the past is a grave error, but to neglect the future is a still greater error." So we have decided to explore two paths: looking at what science fiction writers have imagined and searching on our own. And we'd like you two to join us in this work, around a table. What do you say?

DENIS   Why, of course! After all, it was around a table that all this began. And Cécile couldn't bear the thought of not doing her part.

ON ABSTRACT CUISINE

IN THEORY

For a long time culinary art was "figurative": when a flavor is announced by means of a visible element, when the flavors of the ingredients in a dish are allowed to assert themselves, this amounts to the same thing as visually representing objects that exist—trees, houses, people, and so on. Painting went beyond this stage, with the advent of abstraction; cooking did not. Ratatouille is nonetheless an invitation to work in this direction, to use foods to create flavors that are not those of the foods themselves. At last, a nonfigurative cuisine!

IN PRACTICE

A RATATOUILLE OF CHANTERELLES, EGGPLANT, AND APRICOTS

I like the classic ratatouille, because it reveals the personality of the cook. The exercise is obligatory because of the ingredients: tomatoes, eggplant, squash, peppers, garlic. The quality of the vegetables, the way in which they are cut up, the pot in which they are cooked, the heat at which they are cooked, how they are stirred (not too much, lest you end up with a slimy mush)—all these things tell us something about the cook. A ratatouille may be bad when it is too oily (think of a botched mayonnaise), or when the eggplant is undercooked, or when all the ingredients merge to form a purée of indistinct consistency. Conversely, a ratatouille can be delicious when all the ingredients are cooked just the right length of time, when the seasoning is well balanced, when the individual flavors sing.

The classic version is nonetheless a figurative dish. To go beyond it, I propose to cook some chanterelle mushrooms with eggplant and apricots (very ripe Bergeron apricots), letting the three ingredients stew together so that they lose their individuality. They are all seasonal products, but their combination is unusual. The eggplant should have a beautiful violet color. It should be very firm, with the seeds removed, and cut in a small dice, leaving the skin on. Frying the eggplant cubes in olive oil makes them very crunchy and gives them a quite bitter taste.

The mushrooms are more difficult to cook than the eggplant, because they have to be given many qualities at once. I suggest simplifying matters by using small chanterelles from Brive, with their tiny button caps, and quickly sautéing them so that their spiciness is not lost.

You then combine the eggplant, the chanterelles, and the apricots in a pot, cover, and add a few drops of water or stock to produce a bit of steam. As they soften and break down, the three ingredients lose their individuality and become more civilized, so to speak. The result, in terms of flavor, is no longer figurative.

YOUR TURN

By this point you have tackled such difficult exercises that you are now ready to face the hardest one of all—one that is also perfectly modern, and no longer fifty years behind the other modern arts. Here we set out along a new and vitally important road, far from nature, deep into the land of art. When will food critics be prepared to recognize the praiseworthy efforts of those who embark upon this course?

GIVING THE FLAVOR OF ONE THING TO SOMETHING ELSE

IN THEORY

On several occasions we have given hints, while leaving the rest to your imagination. Here the challenge is to take an ingredient and sublimate one of its characteristics in order to produce something new—to tell an unexpected culinary story.

IN PRACTICE
TARRAGON-FLAVORED MARSHMALLOWS

The technical idea behind this recipe comes from the marshmallow, which children love more than almost anything else for its softness. As adults, we chew a marshmallow without giving it a second thought, but it can be given any number of flavors. Why not use tandoori spices, for example, or tarragon?

I especially enjoy singing this song with tarragon, because its anise flavor is sufficiently precise that it can be deliberately distorted, unlike complex flavors, which tend to be rather muffled. If you use parsley, the distortion will not be as pronounced, but you can be more daring and use rose water, vanilla, or coffee.

Serve the flavored marshmallow with a green-bean salad, for example: the green of the beans and the tarragon makes the combination even stronger. You may also consider serving it with a piece of poultry, in order to evoke memories of chicken with tarragon. Or, of course, with a piece of red tuna coated with a caramelized soy-sauce glaze.

YOUR TURN

Constructing a story involves associating one thing with another: don't try to begin by "singing a song," as Pierre does here. Start out more simply by playing with one ingredient. What textures does it make you think of? What flavors? What events in your life? What smells? What seasons? What colors? What sounds? Then think about combining this ingredient with others that are linked to it through the associations you have found. Start constructing a story and follow where it leads you.

INSISTENCE AND REPETITION

IN THEORY

Music makes considerable use of repetition and insistence. One thinks, for example, of variations on a theme. Painting often uses emphasis—contrasts between foreground and background, with repeated motifs—to reinforce an underlying idea. In literature one cannot help but think of the "lung" that Molière harps upon in the consultation scene of *The Love Doctor* (1665), a comedy of repetition. All of this goes to show, contrary to the opinion of certain academic authors, that repetition is a mistake only when it is unintended.

IN PRACTICE
RISOTTO VARIATIONS

Not too long ago I served a dish of white truffles and cèpes at the restaurant, prepared three ways: with rice (cooked as you would in a classic risotto), with bulgur wheat (cooked in chicken stock), and with quinoa (cooked in chicken stock with a bit of cream).

This amounted to three interpretations of risotto since, in addition to using wheat and quinoa, incorporating cèpes and truffles in a classic risotto made it decidedly unclassic! Strictly speaking, this was a case of insistence rather than repetition: instead of using a traditional element as a centerpiece, the risotto was itself distorted as an invitation to do something new. And, with each of the three grains, unity is imposed by the white truffle, which supplies the flavor, rather than the consistency, that the grains play off of.

Why does the dish need to be so insistent, so emphatic? I love white truffles, but I don't have the same standing as a cook from Alba: I'm not from there, I don't have Italian ancestors, I've never worked in Italy. Nonetheless, why should I deprive myself of a note on the culinary piano? I therefore claim the right to practice another style, to make the truffle live in a different way. I'm doing something in my own way: the truffle serves me, I don't serve it!

YOUR TURN

Be careful not to confuse insistence with variation, which we experimented with earlier in chapter 9. To repeat is to reproduce something without changing it.

TWENTY-THREE

AND TOMORROW?

Why should modern culinary art lag behind the other arts? There is no reason in principle why current research should not produce novel ideas— but philosophers and scientists and cooks will have to work hand in hand if we are to succeed in liberating cooking from the tyranny of what we have been eating for so long.

THE QUINTE ESSENCE

At Cécile's restaurant. It is closed, and all the lights are off except for a small lamp on a table near the kitchen at which Denis, Hélène, Jean, and Cécile are seated.

CÉCILE   How different everything seems since our dinner a few months ago when that old book came into our hands! But the mystery remains: why the sudden appearance of the book, which is then stolen, followed by packets of loose pages, attacks—

DENIS   And then, all of a sudden, total silence.

JEAN   As I was saying to you the other day, everything quieted down the moment Hélène and I began continuing the work of *The Quintessential Art.*

HÉLÈNE   We've even managed to reconstitute the beginning, which was stolen. I've—

A man enters, tall, thin, with shining eyes—as though they contained stars. Cécile gets up to tell him that the restaurant is closed.

CÉCILE   Excuse me—

MAN (*addressing Hélène*)   You're wrong—

JEAN (*standing up*)   What do you mean she's wrong? And first of all, who are—

HÉLÈNE   I recognize him: he's the one who gave me the book, in Geneviève's shop.

MAN   Yes, that was me. I'm going to explain everything—and tell you why you are wrong to try to reconstitute *The Quintessential Art.* The book was finished when it was stolen, and if you write it all over again, as you are doing now, new troubles will arise. May I sit down with you?

CÉCILE   Please do.

MAN   My name is Tendret. I am a descendant of Lucien Tendret, who wrote a book entitled *La Table au pays de Brillat-Savarin* in 1892. My ancestor knew Brillat-Savarin well, and upon his death inherited some of his books. Among them was a work on culinary theory, entitled *The Quintessential Art,* annotated by several hands.

DENIS   A book that's unknown to booksellers specializing in culinary literature! Even the bibliographer Oberlé fails to mention it in his catalogue.

TENDRET   Yes, unknown because unique. The book was the fruit of a long tradition. You know that cooks, like other artisans, are organized in fraternities, associations, guilds, and so forth. One of these, the oldest, was created in Paris under the Romans, who called their settlement Lutetia. Contrary to the usual belief, the Gauls were not barbarians, nor was Gaul a vast wild forest. The land was cultivated, and rich by virtue of its temperate climate, which favored a diversity of vegetation and animal life. Cooking, of course, already flourished among the Gauls. And when the Romans came, native cooks feared for the independence of their craft; in concert with the druids, they created a secret society, in which membership was reserved to those who sought a kind of "truth" in local products.

DENIS   Truth? This is a mere fable—

TENDRET   It was naive, yes, but these people had ancestral tastes—traditional tastes, if you like—that they wished to preserve, because they knew that invaders always seek to impose their own tastes and ways of eating. And besides, the Gauls already had developed their own techniques of cooking! The secret society they founded still exists today. Naturally we no longer look for inspiration to memories of our Gallic ancestors: for my part, I have a Polish great-grandfather on my mother's side, as well as a great-great-grandfather from the south of Spain whose family probably came from North Africa; and, on my father's side, a great-great-grandmother who gave us our slightly slanting eyes. In short, it's not a question of nationalism. The Quinte Essence—

JEAN   The what?

TENDRET   The Quinte Essence. This is the name that was given to our society around 1000 C.E., when distillation was discovered and the cooks of our society understood its importance. Our aim is to further the progress of culinary art, by critically examining traditional techniques and modernizing them, with due care and deliberation—because if not everything old is good, not everything old is bad either. The same is true for the new: not everything new is bad, nor is everything new good. As far as our culinary heritage is concerned, this poses a very difficult question: what can we change without losing the best of what we have received from the past?

DENIS   But as far as technology is concerned, cooks in earlier times had only fire—no stainless steel or any of the other things we take for granted today. Surely their cooking techniques cannot be taken as models?

TENDRET   This isn't quite true. Ignore for the moment the question of how dishes were made and think of the dishes themselves. Why do you suppose recipes thought to be new are so often found in old cookbooks? Because genuine innovation, through the invention of new combinations, is difficult. Take your wife, for example. She has been cooking every day for about twenty years. That comes to about 7,000 days, or almost 15,000 meals. You must consider that many of her "novel" combinations have already been tried by some other cook, who has spent perhaps forty years in the kitchen. Many things have been tried—and the result of these experiments has been recorded for posterity only by the Quinte Essence. It is a treasure—that small minds would like to get hold of. The ones who stole the book.

JEAN   And these recipes are what the book contained?

TENDRET   No, certainly not. The book was only the key. Aesthetic ideas are much more powerful, more fertile, than particular combinations of flavors. Besides, the theft itself is unimportant: either the thieves understood the spirit that animated the book, in which case they would have immediately adopted an intelligent approach to cooking; or they understood nothing, and so the book was useless to them. Nor would they have been able to make any money from it, because the book isn't really very old, even if the knowledge that it contains is.

HÉLÈNE   But why did you give me this book at Geneviève's shop?

TENDRET   Because I was charged with transmitting the precious document that recorded the history of our researches to a young chef who could make them bear fruit. I am happy to say, madame (*addressing himself now to Cécile*), that you were the one who was chosen.

HÉLÈNE   Why then did you give it to me—

TENDRET   The book? Because we knew that you would be having dinner together. And we thought that you would leave the book with the person who could make the best use of it.

HÉLÈNE   But then why did you keep sending pages to me after that? And to Jean as well?

TENDRET   Because we quickly understood that we could accomplish still more than we had originally imagined possible. We discovered that you understood the past perfectly and that your, ah, friend Jean is a man who lives in the present but also anticipates new developments, that he is a visionary. Together you ally the past with the future. Our expectations were borne out by events: you passed the tests we set for the two of you, and we have even seen you continue our work!

JEAN   That was taking a chance. What if things hadn't worked out between Hélène and me? Besides, a few months ago—

HÉLÈNE   Jean, please!

TENDRET   Yes, anything could have happened. But the four of you are friends, and you embody the qualities necessary to go forward. First, there is cooking, the basis of our enterprise. Then there is the past, without which the present has no meaning, and the future, which is in the process of coming to be. You, sir (*turning toward Denis*), have a rational, disciplined mind that stimulates your wife's talent. And you, madame, have an artistic bent that you ceaselessly cultivate. The Quinte Essence marvels at your work. We have seen it again over the last few days—

CÉCILE   But then you must watch us all the time!

TENDRET   First we judged you, then we protected you. The people who stole the book are not soft-hearted. Now that the book has been recovered, we will not make the same mistake again, of letting it leave its hiding place. I have come to tell you that, whatever you do, you must not write it again: the existence of another edition will inevitably rekindle the spirit of covetousness. That would be an error. The time has come to transmit the book's aesthetic ideas to a broad audience. But not before having imagined the future. Our society will be dissolved on that day, and on that day only.

DENIS   Why?

TENDRET   Because we finally decided that knowledge—ideas—must be shared. There is no danger of losing a body of technical, practical learning, because it is continually being reinvented. True wealth is found in human nature, in each and every human being. Moreover, we have already destroyed the documents that transmitted this secret learning. The simple fact of their existence aroused the desire to possess them. In any case the practical knowledge that they contained is already available to anyone who wants to look for it. It is diffused by means of cookbooks, of course, but one finds it sculpted in symbolic form as well, in cathedrals, or else embodied in ancient monuments, as at Cluny, Lascaux—

JEAN   The guide at Les Eyzies! That was you!

TENDRET   Yes. Prehistoric sites, which go much farther back in time than the founding of the Quinte Essence, are full of signs that the artist can decode. Ideas matter more than technique, and more than what we took to be "truth."

DENIS   What a responsibility, putting an end to a society that has existed for more than two thousand years!

TENDRET   It was a difficult decision, yes—but it is necessary to end what must be ended, in order to bring forth still better things. Who can regret that an end was put to slavery, for example? The time has come. Yes, it is time—to prepare the future. You haven't worked very hard at this yet. And the Quinte Essence, which places the future of cooking in your hands, in a sense, has decided that you will have your reward only when you have completed this work.

JEAN   Reward?

TENDRET   Do you remember "the last word in cooking"?

DENIS   But you yourself have said that everything is known, publicly available.

TENDRET   Of course, but you forget that your wife would give anything to have it, this last word.

CÉCILE   Right now, especially! I cast about, I try things, I try out new ideas. They bubble away, and yet I'm still unsatisfied.

TENDRET   That's rather a good thing, isn't it?

CÉCILE   Perhaps so. How can you rest when you're never pleased with what you have done?

TENDRET   Yes, I see—This is a sign.

CÉCILE   A sign—of what?

TENDRET   That you need the knowledge that we promise. I must be going. I hope we will meet again soon.

He leaves as abruptly as he came in.

JEAN   What a story! Imagine, a Gallic secret society—the sort of thing one finds only in novels and plays.

HÉLÈNE   I know—but I'm happy it's all over. Even without the pages coming to us out of the blue and all the other incidents, you see, I wasn't really at ease. What worries me now (*she smiles, looking at Jean*) is that they seem to think that our love will last forever.

JEAN   Forever!

He gets up, takes Hélène in his arms and kisses her. Wordlessly, she snuggles up against him.

CÉCILE   Ah, look at the lovers. This is something to celebrate! All right, I'll open it.

She gets up and comes back with a bottle whose label is curled and crumbling at the edges.

DENIS   What's that?

CÉCILE   A hundred-year-old Gewürztraminer. It was given to me by my grandfather, and I decided I'd save it for a very special occasion. And this *is* a very special occasion, isn't it?

JEAN   Yes—but what will you bring out for us if we discover the last word in cooking for you?

DENIS   Don't worry, she's holding—something in reserve.

HÉLÈNE   In the meantime there's still a lot to be done. Jean, shouldn't we take the first steps?

DENIS   Oh, no—Cécile and I have to be part of it.

HÉLÈNE   It's only a question of getting started. I've got an idea. Next Sunday, let's all of us get together here and make a meal, using what we've learned. The main thing is that we find a way to help Cécile get out of her rut.

CÉCILE   Okay. Next Sunday.

A QUINTESSENTIAL EXERCISE

IN THEORY

Quintessence: the word may be taken literally or not. Literally, quintessence is a concentrated extract. But it may also be an idea. What if one sets oneself the task of combining the two senses of the term in a single dish?

IN PRACTICE
GREEN CRAB REDUCTION

For me, quintessence is something that has an excess of flavor, more than it normally does, since the flavor is intensified by being carried to its own extreme.

For several years now I've made a reduction of green crab by taking crabs in their shell and sprinkling them with oil, then crushing them and cooking them in a mixture of very dry white wine (10 percent alcohol), fish fumet, and water with an aromatic garnish (carrot, onion, thyme, bay leaf, garlic, and citrus peels). The cooking must be done slowly, in a covered pot so that all the odorant molecules remain in the resulting bisque.

The stock is skimmed at regular intervals, but it would be better still to perform a perfect filtering when the cooking is done. I don't have the special apparatus that Hervé uses in the laboratory (and in any case cooks would need something sturdy, made out of stainless steel rather than glass), so we do it the old-fashioned way, straining the bisque after two or three hours through a chinois, and then let it slowly reduce, on top of the stove, for another two or three hours. At that point we strain it again, and then reduce it still further in order to obtain a very flavorful syrup.

At my old restaurant in Saint-Étienne I used to serve this quintessence with a fish terrine that was prepared with four different textures. Its highly concentrated power made it easier to appreciate the particular qualities of the various textures.

In the version I serve now in Paris, the crab quintessence is also used as a condiment, only this time to accentuate the flavor of beef marrow, along with some lettuce, which gives a bit of crunchiness, in contrast to the soft, smooth consistency of the marrow.

YOUR TURN

Here the invitation to the cook is to produce simultaneously a concentrated extract and the idea of a pure flavor. Before trying to do this yourself, you will need first to have mastered concentration, reduction, distillation, and the problem of extraction in general. There are a great many technical details to consider. For example, to concentrate a broth, a stock, or a fumet, is it better to bring the liquid to a roiling boil, or to slowly reduce it over a very low flame?

TWENTY-FOUR

SIMPLICITY AND COMPLETENESS

Will we eat nutritive tablets or food pills in the future? No, this is a fantasy. Evolution has taken millions of years to forge a palate in human beings that cooking must satisfy. This implies that our food must have smell, taste, freshness, spiciness, texture, and so on. All the senses must be stimulated, because culinary art is a complete art, but one that must aim at simplicity as well.

―――――――――

WIELDING OCKHAM'S RAZOR IN THE KITCHEN

The following Sunday, in the closed restaurant. Outside it is dark. Inside only the lights in the kitchen are on. A table in the dining room is set with silverware and crystal glasses. Hélène, Cécile, Denis, and Jean are seated around it. In the middle of the table, a bottle of Vosne-Romanée.

DENIS   I've done a lot of work over the last week myself. My greatest discovery is an address by the chemist Marcellin Berthelot, a professor at the Collège de France who was also Minister of Public Instruction (in Goblet's cabinet of 1886–1887) and Minister of Foreign Affairs (under Bourgeois in 1895–1896), and the recipient of honors of all kinds. On 5 April 1894, the occasion of a banquet hosted by the Chemical Manufacturers' Association, he delivered an utterly remarkable speech entitled "In the Year 2000." Just wait, you'll see. And don't forget that it is now more than a century later:

> Gentlemen, I thank you for being so kind as to invite us to your banquet and for having brought together at this fraternal feast, presided over by the public-spirited gentleman who sits in front of me, the servants of our scientific laboratories, among whose number I have been honored to count myself for almost a half-century now, and the managing directors of our industrial factories, in which the nation's wealth is created. . . . Need I remind you of the advances that have been made during the course of the century that is now drawing to a close: the manufacture of sulfuric acid and artificial soda, the bleaching and coloring of fabrics, beet sugar, therapeutic alkaloids, gas lighting, gilding and silver-leafing, and so many other inventions due to our predecessors? Without praising our own work too highly, we may declare that the inventions of the present age are certainly not less important: electrochemistry is now transforming the old metallurgy and revolutionizing its centuries-old practices; explosive materials are being developed through advances in thermochemistry, bringing about in the arts of mining and war the convergence of all-powerful energies; and organic synthesis, in particular, the achievement of our generation, now lavishes its wonders on the invention of coloring materials, perfumes, and therapeutic and antiseptic agents.
>
> But even if these advances are considerable, each of us foresees many others: no one should doubt that the future of chemistry will be still greater than its past. . . . Let me, then, tell you of my dreams: the present moment is propitious, for it is after drinking that one confides in others.

Much has been said about the future state of human societies. I would like, in my turn, to imagine what they will be like in the year 2000—from the purely chemical point of view, of course, for we are talking about chemistry at this table.

At that time, there will no longer be agriculture, or herdsmen, or farmers in the world: the problem of sustaining life through the cultivation of the soil will have been eliminated by chemistry! There will no longer be coal mines in the earth, nor any other subterranean industries, and therefore no miners' strikes! The problem of fuel will have been eliminated, through the convergence of chemistry and physics. There will no longer be any customs inspectors, nor protectionism, wars, or borders bathed in human blood. Aerial navigation, its engines derived from chemical energies, will have relegated these outdated institutions to the past. We shall then be quite prepared to realize the dreams of socialism—provided that a spiritual chemistry can be discovered that changes the moral nature of mankind as profoundly as our chemistry is transforming physical nature!

Here, then, we have a great many promises. How are they to be realized? That is what I am going to tell you.

The fundamental problem of industry consists in discovering inexhaustible sources of energy and in renewing them with little or no effort.

Already we have seen the strength of human arms replaced by that of steam, which is to say by chemical energy derived from the burning of coal. But this agent must be arduously extracted from within the earth, and the proportion of it is constantly diminished. A better way must be found. Now the principle of this invention is easily conceived: we must use solar heat, we must use the heat found at the center of our own planet. The unceasing advances of science give rise to the legitimate hope of capturing these sources of unlimited energy. . . . But let us come back to the subject at hand, which is to say chemistry. In either case, whether one is talking about a source of calorific or electrical energy, it is a question of finding a source of chemical energy. With such a source, the manufacture of all chemical products becomes simple and economical, at any time, at any place, at any point on the surface of the globe.

It is here that we shall find an economical solution to perhaps the greatest problem that comes within the competence of chemistry, namely, the manufacture of food products. In principle, it is already resolved: the synthesis of fats and oils was achieved forty years ago, that of sugars and carbohydrates has been accomplished in our own time, and the synthesis of substances derived from nitrogen is not far off. The problem of nutrition, let it not be forgotten, is therefore a chemical problem. Once energy can be cheaply obtained, there will be scarcely any delay in manufacturing foods from nothing, carbon being derived from carbonic acid, hydrogen taken from water, and nitrogen and oxygen drawn from the atmosphere.

What vegetables have done until now, with the aid of energy taken from the world around us, we are already managing to do, and will in the future do in a much better, more extensive, and more perfect way than nature: for such is the power of chemical synthesis.

The day will come when each of us shall feed himself by taking a small nitrogen tablet, a small clump of fat, a small piece of starch, and a small vial of aromatic spices adjusted to one's own personal taste— all this manufactured cheaply in inexhaustible quantities by our factories; all this independently of irregular seasons, of rain and drought, of the heat that desiccates plants, of the frost that destroys the hope of fruition; all this free, at last, from these pathogenic microbes that are the source of epidemics and the enemies of human life.

On that day, chemistry will have brought about in the world a radical revolution, whose scope no one can calculate; no longer will there be fields covered with crops, or vineyards, or plains filled with cattle. Mankind will gain in gentleness and morality, because it will cease to live by means of carnage and the destruction of living creatures. There will no longer be any distinction between fertile and barren regions. It may even be that deserts will become the preferred abode of human civilizations, because they will be more salubrious than the pest-ridden alluvial plains and marshlands, fertilized with putrefaction, that today are the seats of our agriculture.

Do not suppose that, in this universal empire of chemical force, art, beauty, and the charm of human life are fated to disappear. If the surface of the earth should cease to be used—and, let it be said, in a very low voice—by the geometrical works of the farmer, as today, it will then be covered again with greenery, trees, and flowers; the earth will become a vast garden, watered by the effusion of underground springs, in which the human race will live in abundance and in the joy of the golden age of legend.

Yet you must not suppose that it will therefore live in sloth and moral corruption. Work is part of happiness: who knows this better than the chemists present here? Now it is said in the Wisdom of Solomon that whoever increases knowledge increases work. In the golden age that awaits us, everyone shall work more than ever before. Now, the man who works is good, for work is the source of every virtue. In this renewed world, everyone will work with zeal, because he will enjoy the fruit of his work; everyone will find in this rightful and complete remuneration the means to raise his intellectual, moral, and aesthetic development to the highest point.

Gentlemen, as these dreams and others are fulfilled, it will still be true to say that happiness is acquired through action, and in action raised up to its highest intensity through the reign of science.

Such is my hope, which triumphs throughout the world, as the old Christian saying has it; such is our ideal for everyone! It is the hope of the Chemical Manufacturers' Association. I raise my glass to work, to justice, and to the happiness of humanity![154]

JEAN   That's crazy! Promises, promises—I can't believe Berthelot was naive enough to believe what he was saying. In any case, we don't have these nutritive tablets of his, thank goodness!

HÉLÈNE   What do you mean we don't have them? Of course we do: think of the energy bars that mountain climbers eat and the fragrances used in processed foods. And then there's the vogue for gels, foams, soft—

JEAN   I mean that none of us eats this way every day. My friends who farm in the Gers, in the Southwest, continue to raise their geese outdoors, and grow their vegetables—

DENIS   You're right. Berthelot was quite mistaken: for the most part we continue to eat the same things we did a century, two centuries, three centuries ago. Should it come as a surprise that, whereas science text-books become outdated, cookbooks do not? Cécile still uses recipes from Nicolas de Bonnefons, whose *Le Jardinier François* appeared in 1651.

CÉCILE   Yes, but I adapt them.

DENIS   You adapt them, but you continue to cook the way people did in the past. The same textures, the same combinations—or, at least, the same type of textures and combinations. The style has changed, but not the basics.

Oh, yes, I found another interesting text. From Gustave Le Rouge—

HÉLÈNE   Gustave Le Rouge? The writer whom Blaise Cendrars* admired?

*BLAISE CENDRARS (La Chaux-de-Fonds, 1887–Paris, 1961): Swiss-born French writer whose travels, real and imaginary, were the principal source of inspiration for his po-etry and prose works, notably *Gold* (1925). Wounded in the First World War, his right arm was amputated above the elbow, depriving him of the hand he was used to writing with.

DENIS   The very same. In his novel *The War of the Vampires,* published in 1909, Le Rouge imagined something he called "Vitalose."

JEAN   A sort of vitamin supplement, you mean?

DENIS   Not exactly—it's more sensual than Berthelot's nutritive tablets, as you'll see:

> Before him was a sort of tray holding an immense number of tiny bottles; next to this, a plate containing a pink jelly and a carafe filled with a violet liquid.
>
> The captain took a bit of jelly, moistened it with a drop of liquid from one of the vials, and consumed it with relish. . . .
>
> "This pink jelly is a complete food, chemically prepared, containing only the nitrogens and carbons necessary to the organism, without any of the useless or harmful matter that encloses animal and vegetable substances. . . . Thanks to these vials, I can give my Vitalose—that is the name of the complete food—any flavor I want."
>
> And Georges read the labels with amazement: trout essence, salt-meadow lamb essence, partridge essence, salmon essence, almond essence, etc., etc. All possible dishes were summed up there, quintessentialized in a few drops of fragrance.[155]

Le Rouge had gotten the idea for Vitalose from a work of proto-science fiction by Tiphaigne de la Roche, *Giphantie,* published in 1760.

HÉLÈNE   It's funny that you should mention literature, because I've been thinking along some of the same lines. We all agree that a dish presents a series of questions: What does it say? What does it say to me in particular? What does it mean? What does it make me think it means? For it to be memorable, and legible, certain conditions must be satisfied, as in painting. For example, there must be a foreground, something clear, which speaks to us immediately, and a background, which fills out the scene and sets off the foreground. A foreground is easier to imagine in literature, something simple that can be taken in at a glance; in cooking it is what guarantees the legibility of a dish, and ensures that the dish will be memorable, because one remembers the essential idea. This raises the question of simplicity.

DENIS   And so we meet up again: I had prepared something on this subject as well. The question of simplicity arises in science as in art. Albert Einstein,* for example, said "Our experience hitherto justifies us in believing that nature is the realization of the simplest conceivable mathematical ideas."[156] When Einstein was working out the general theory of relativity, he chose the least complicated set of suitable equations, for, as he said, "God would not have passed up the opportunity to make the world this simple."[157] And yet, nature is simple only to a first approximation—

JEAN   And a work of art, particularly a culinary work of art, is also a simplification. The cook makes a choice, and retains those things that best express his idea.

DENIS   In cooking, as in mathematics, one might employ the motto of Alfred North Whitehead, the English philosopher and mathematician who published the three-volume *Principia Mathematica* (1910–1913) with Bertrand Russell: "Seek simplicity and distrust it."[158]

*ALBERT EINSTEIN (Ulm, 1879–Princeton, 1955): German-born physicist, naturalized as a Swiss citizen in 1900 and then, having fled the Nazis, as an American citizen in 1940. His theory of relativity, formulated in restricted form in 1905 and extended in 1915, explained an extraordinary range of phenomena on both the atomic and cosmological scales and supplied the basis for a general account of the universe. Einstein's later career was devoted to an unsuccessful attempt to develop a unified field theory in which gravitation and electromagnetism are seen as different manifestations of a single fundamental force. His religious faith was intensely personal and unorthodox, recalling that of Spinoza.

Thus Galileo,* the father of the experimental method in science, selected the simplest equation to describe the fall of bodies, but this formula did not take altitude into account, and Newton† corrected the error by slightly complicating it. Yet Newton himself had confidence in the parsimony of nature: "Nature is pleased with simplicity, and affects not the pomp of superfluous causes."[159] Kepler‡ spent years defending the idea that the planets describe circular orbits, on the ground that the circle is the simplest closed curve, and finally admitted the ellipse as a necessary evil in order to protect astronomy against worse evils. (*Denis pauses for a moment and looks at his friends*). And I am surprised that Hélène has not remarked that these scientists were preceded by the English theologian William of Ockham.

---

*GALILEO GALILEI (Pisa, 1564–Arcetri, 1642): Italian physicist, mathematician, and astronomer, one of the founders of modern experimental science and a foremost defender of the individual's right to freedom of thought, whose open support for Copernicus's heliocentric theory brought him into conflict with the Church. His *Dialogue Concerning the Two Chief World Systems* (1632) was condemned and Galileo was sentenced to life imprisonment. Living under house arrest at his villa near Florence, he wrote a treatise on physics that was smuggled out of Italy and published in Holland as *Two New Sciences* (1638).

†ISAAC NEWTON (Woolsthorpe, near Grantham, 1642–Kensington, 1727): English physicist and mathematician. His early work on mechanics, later published as *Philosophiae naturalis principia mathematica* (1687), which explained Galileo's results on falling bodies and Johannes Kepler's three laws of planetary motions by the means of the calculus (independently invented by Newton and Gottfried Wilhelm Leibniz), remains perhaps the most influential book of science ever written. In addition to his pioneering work in optics and fluid mechanics, Newton devoted much of his energies in later years, unsuccessfully, to research on alchemy.

‡JOHANNES KEPLER (Wurtemburg, 1571–Regensburg, 1630): German astronomer and physicist whose attempts to work out the orbit of Mars on Copernican principles led him to the discovery of the laws of planetary motion. Working in Prague, where he had sought refuge from anti-Protestant persecution, and then Linz, after the outbreak of civil war, Kepler was also the founder of the geometrical study of optics as well as a mystic and an active enthusiast of astrology.

HÉLÈNE   That's because Jean told me that he found me pretentious and pedantic.

JEAN   What? No, I told you that at the beginning—

HÉLÈNE   I'm teasing, darling. Yes, I immediately thought of Ockham and his "razor." Ockham was born in a village of the same name in Surrey, in England, in 1285 and died in Munich in 1347 or 1349, no one knows for sure. He was an excommunicated Franciscan monk and one of the chief defenders of nominalism. Using a logic based on the analysis of language, Ockham combated the belief in the reality of universal substances. If I remember correctly, his principle of parsimony is *Essentia non sunt multiplicanda praeter necessitatem.*

JEAN   Which means?

HÉLÈNE   Entities are not to be multiplied unnecessarily. Roughly, the idea is that one ought to make as few assumptions as possible. But in art this is a rather doubtful principle. Think of Baroque painting. Think of Dürer,* who multiplied entities right and left. Think of Hieronymous Bosch,† whose pictures are nothing but multiplications.

---

*ALBRECHT DÜRER (Nuremburg, 1471–Nuremburg, 1528): German painter and engraver who united the dominant Italian and Dutch styles of his time. One of the greatest painters of the Northern Renaissance, he achieved still greater renown for his engravings, particularly the fifteen woodcut panels of the *Apocalypse* (ca 1498) and the copper engraving *Melancholia* (1514), whose rich symbolism expresses man's anxiety in the face of the new learning of the age.

†HIERONYMOUS BOSCH ('s Hertogenbosch, ca 1450–'s Hertogenbosch, ca 1516): Dutch painter whose mystical compositions, filled to overflowing with fanciful creatures and bizarre, apparently irrational imagery, have been seen by some as a precursor of twentieth-century surrealism. *The Garden of Earthly Delights* (ca 1500), the most famous and perplexing of Bosch's pictures, is usually understood to be a damning portrait of man's chronic sinfulness, but its true significance remains a matter of dispute.

CÉCILE   The artist, unlike the scientist, has a choice.

JEAN   Look at Rabelais,* in literature: everything is multiplied and exaggerated in his work!

HÉLÈNE   We really must talk about style one day. Cécile, what is your style? Or rather, what are your styles? Picasso† had his blue and rose periods—

DENIS   The greatest mystery of all, I believe, is emotion. The question of style leads one to say to Cécile, "Tell me who you are, and I will know your style."

CÉCILE   This is precisely the question I've been asking myself lately. I can force myself to do classical cooking, regional cooking, modern cooking, but I'm more or less satisfied only when I always do the same thing. It's said that writers write only one book, and that all the others are repetitions of the first. I fear that it may be the same in cooking. I can mix things up, but I feel at ease only in a single style, a style that moves me. And yet with a single style, I feel hemmed in—

JEAN   One mustn't overintellectualize. There is technique, which helps

---

*FRANÇOIS RABELAIS (La Devinière, near Chinon, ca 1483–Paris, 1553): French writer and physician who originally trained for the priesthood, studying ancient languages, before turning violently against the Church. His best known fiction, a series of five volumes (1534–1564) recounting the scandalous exploits and insatiable appetites of two legendary giants, Gargantua and Pantagruel, scathingly attacked scholasticism, the ignorance of monks, the absurdity of war, and the temporal power of organized religion. The ribald virtuosity of Rabelais's language anticipated the experiments of twentieth-century writers such as James Joyce.

†PABLO PICASSO (Málaga, 1881–Mougins, 1973): Spanish artist, the most famous painter of the twentieth century, renowned also for his work as an engraver, sculptor, and ceramicist. Endlessly inventive, Picasso revolutionized traditional forms of representation by his development of novel techniques, notably cubism and collage, in combination with elements drawn from older styles.

the cook tell stories with a foreground and a background, and so on; but Denis is right, the real question is emotion. A dish may make me want to cry or laugh or become angry—but for that to happen, the culinary artist must have cried himself, must have laughed, or become angry—

HÉLÈNE   I don't agree! Have you forgotten Diderot's *Paradox of the Actor,* in which he took issue with a common opinion of the day, namely, that a good tragic actor is able to move the audience only when he himself is consumed by the very passions that he expresses?

Nothing could be more wrong, Diderot argued: "In life, the spectacle of real pain leaves us indifferent if the person in whom it manifests itself does not have the actor's capacity for expression. It is when the actor in us is aroused that we obtain effects that sincerity does not permit us to obtain. Moreover, to portray one's own character leads one to play in a petty way, and the peculiar skill of the actor consists in stepping out of his own character in order to imitate any other."[160]

The actor must, by the exercise of his craft, attain the consummate mastery of means; he must acquire a technique that may be applied only by actors who are capable of detachment: "The sensitive man is too much at the mercy of his diaphragm to be a great king, a great politician, a great magistrate, a profound observer, and consequently a sublime imitator of nature."[161]

DENIS   That's all very fine, but it's of no help to Cécile. This type of advice, just like that of Shitao, promises only that you will toil away in obscurity, with no assurance that your labor will ever be recognized. Why shouldn't we instead look to reason for guidance?

JEAN   Your old obsession.

DENIS   Yes, but you will observe how far history has proved me right. The best example is the mathematization of chance, which seemed quite impossible and yet led to the theory of probability. Can flavors be quantified? Tastes? Smells? I propose that we scrutinize the culinary record and draw up an inventory of fundamental tastes, flavors, and smells; that we search for constants, basic ideas, variations—

HÉLÈNE   In other words, identify the norm and the deviation from the norm—

DENIS   In a way, yes, but mainly what I'm suggesting is that we try to exercise reason wherever possible, search for the meaning of—

HÉLÈNE   Even an art historian like Erwin Panofsky* searched for conventions among different works. In cooking, the way in which the various elements of a dish are presented is a similar sort of convention.

DENIS   No, that's not at all what I meant. I'm proposing that we begin by undertaking a grand project of culinary analysis. We might, for example, analyze the flavors of a particular dish by measuring the proportions of acid, fat, tomato, and so on. These proportions could be represented by means of a geometric figure—a star-shaped diagram, for instance (*He draws on a pad of paper*).

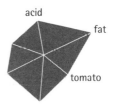

In this way, you see, a gustatory form can be expressed as a geometrical form. Mind you, I don't say that this is the only way of going about it. One could also work in vector space, with

---

*ERWIN PANOFSKY (Hanover, 1892–Princeton, 1968): German-born historian of art and essayist who accepted a permanent appointment in the United States in 1935, following the Nazi seizure of power. His pioneering studies of the "hidden" symbolism and iconography in early Dutch painting, particularly in connection with Jan van Eyck and Albrecht Dürer, remain landmarks in the modern understanding of the art of the Northern Renaissance. Panofsky also wrote about music and film, and counted among his close friends Wolfgang Pauli, a leading figure in the early history of quantum physics.

vectors varying as a function of time, in order to describe variations in flavor.

HÉLÈNE   Oh my, this is getting complicated.

DENIS   Let's not be afraid of words. Instead of making a star-shaped diagram, where the length of the rays is proportional to the intensity of each component, one could represent the same dish by a series of numbers that signify the intensity of sourness, of fatty flavor, of tomato flavor, and so on.

CÉCILE   Denis, this isn't going to help me tomorrow. How am I to go about this, as a practical matter?

DENIS   You're right, this is a project for the distant or, shall we say, not-so-near future. But in the meantime you can always draw upon what has been useful in other arts.

HÉLÈNE   I've been thinking about this myself: the constant in both music and painting is foreground and background, the chorus and the song. If we really are machines for recognizing patterns, as you say, we have to be able to recognize fundamental forms, and the song is the most legible of these. The rest serves to enrich perception.

CÉCILE   But this, my friends, is something that I'm already doing! You're going to have to find something else for me to do!

JEAN   I don't know. If the conventional is understood, why not be unconventional? That would be shocking.

CÉCILE   So it would be—and what do we do after that? The problem with this little game of surprise-your-guest is it doesn't last very long. The first bite is the surprise, the second lets you figure it out, and by the third bite you're already tired of the game. No, I'm searching for something that is both simple and beautiful—

JEAN   The quinte essence! And what about the promise of our secret friends?

CÉCILE   Exactly. Rather than going on as we have been, more or less blindly groping our way forward, let's begin by going back to the beginning: bouillon. What do you say we make one after our meal?

THE ART OF PARING DOWN

IN THEORY

Recall Shitao's "one brush stroke," which he holds to be the acme of art: one stroke, a single pared-down stroke, and the work is born—perfect from the moment of its existence, without any need for retouching. There is also the tale of an emperor of China who, after commissioning a work, waited for many years and then, his patience worn thin, sent emissaries to the artist to inquire after his progress. They found the artist seated, the work not yet begun. Infuriated at the news, the emperor set out to see the artist in person, though the artist had warned that the emperor's impatience threatened to spoil everything. The artist then took a charcoal crayon made from the wood of a spindle tree and, with a single stroke, drew a chariot drawn by wild ducks. Mounting the chariot, he was at once swept away into the skies, far from the emperor's wrath. One stroke, perfectly refined. Can the like of it be imagined in cooking?

IN PRACTICE
AN EGG COOKED JUST SO

In this recipe, everything depends on the bright orange yolk of an egg that sits at the summit. The rest functions as an accessory—supporting, highlighting, setting the stage.

The recipe is simple. First make a fine purée of chervil root and coat the bottom of a soup plate with it.

Then make a simple extract of parsley by gently simmering some parsley that has been ground in a mortar until a sort of froth rises on a crest of brown water. Take this intensely green, almost fluorescent liquid and dribble it in a circle on the surface of the chervil root purée.

Next separate the white from the yolk of an egg that has been cooked in the oven to a temperature of 66°C (150.8°F). At this precise temperature the white of the egg is cooked, but it is still very tender, with a consistency somewhere between milky and fluffy. Whisk it together with the pulp of a passion fruit, whose juice seems to "cook" the egg white. This preparation is then placed inside the disk described by the parsley extract.

Finally, at the center of the dish, like a cherry on top of a cake, place the egg yolk, a superb orange ball that sits enthroned against a spare background. Next to the egg one might also put an outer ribbed leaf of Romaine lettuce, very quickly sautéed in butter, or, better yet, a small leaf of Belgian endive. The endive brings a stringy chewiness, but you mustn't cook it more than a moment or two or it will lose its slightly crunchy texture.

Why chervil root? Because it has the same kind of supple texture as the egg, and a delicate flavor that goes well with that of the yolk, neither struggling against it or being conquered by it.

The seasoning? In the delicate registers I am playing upon here, something gentle is needed: cream and milk, salt, nutmeg . . .

YOUR TURN

Achieving simplicity in cooking, as in the other arts, requires a great deal of work! One must learn to eliminate everything that is superfluous. Start with a classic dish, if you like, and try to identify what is indispensable, what is necessary. Then pare down, strip away the inessential, and you will learn the reason for the ingredients that remain.

ICONOCLASM

IN THEORY

Absolute license, in art, is the end of art—and utterly without interest. By contrast, iconoclasm is not an insane sort of "deconstruction," only a struggle against idols—a struggle that aims at building up rather than dismantling. The Argentinean writer Jorge Luis Borges said that there are two kinds of envy: black envy, which seeks to destroy what it does not have, and white envy, which seeks to make what it has better. It is something like this benign form of envy that Pierre is trying to suggest here in connection with iconoclasm. How do we overcome, go beyond our idols— Marie-Antoine Carême, Escoffier, Urbain Dubois, Dartois Laguipière, Nignon, and all the other great chefs of the past—in order to make cooking better?

IN PRACTICE
SPONGE CAKE WITH BUTTON MUSHROOMS

Obviously, the iconoclasm that I have in mind is not a gratuitous piece of deconstruction. The combination of a *baba,* or sponge cake, with button mushrooms is not meant to shock; on the contrary, it's almost an obligatory exercise from the point of view of flavor. This is not a dish created in support of an idea, but a piece of iconoclasm that results from a genuinely harmonious association of ingredients.

For this recipe you need a perfectly ordinary sponge cake, placed in a shallow dish. Then—because its ability to absorb a great deal of liquid is one of the cake's most important characteristics— soak it with a reduction of red wine with tea and fruit peels, a little like a concentrated sangria.

Next add the traditional rum syrup, here in the form of a jelly seasoned with black pepper, and a very good pastry cream that has been vigorously whisked with lots of butter.

Finally, on top of the foamy pastry cream, arrange some very small, raw button mushrooms.

The principle of the dish is the same as a tart with a flaky crust, raw mushrooms, and vanilla pastry cream. The effect is very harmonious, for the mushroom asserts itself without being at all aggressive, its mild crunchiness agreeably counterbalancing the cushion-like softness of the cake.

YOUR TURN

Iconoclasm? For the artist, this ought to be the rule rather than the exception. Having learned much from past masters, he must free himself from their influence if he is to keep from stuttering.

As a practical exercise, why not see if you can devise an iconoclastic version of Escoffier's peach Melba?

TWENTY-FIVE

THE ILLUSION
OF THE PERFECT BOUILLON

Bouillon is the soul of the household, as the nineteenth-century chef Jules Gouffé remarked. Gouffé was one of the first to introduce a degree of precision in recipes. And it is true that bouillons (or stocks) are essential in cooking, both at home and in restaurants, for they are used to make consommés, soups, and sauces, and also used as a moistening liquid. But despite thousands of years of practice making them, we still do not know if they should be cooked for an hour, ten hours, or a hundred hours; nor do we know if their flavor is better in an earthenware pot, as some authors have claimed, or whether the pot must be covered during cooking, or indeed many other things.

EMOTION FIRST AND FOREMOST

The same characters, a little later in the evening. A few mignardises are left on the table. Before each person, a glass of dark golden cognac. Jean and Denis are comfortably settled into their chairs. Hélène is curled up on hers, and Cécile is standing, her elbows on the table.

CÉCILE   And so, what do you think of my bouillon?

HÉLÈNE   The wonderful thing about a bouillon is that it doesn't admit of any affectation. You can't play the game of changing plates with it. Solid foods can be arranged on bread trenchers, or on fabrics or chinaware, or in glasses, or what have you; but a bouillon comes in a bowl—whether square or round, or large like a soup plate, it's still a bowl, and the only thing that matters is the bouillon in it. Even if with a little effort we could imagine new kinds of container, it's the bouillon that will remain the focus of our attention—

DENIS   Right, no embellishments are possible. And no ordering of ingredients in one sequence or another, nothing like boustrophedon or tricks of perspective—none of these devices can be used. There's no raised rim on a plate to put spices on, barely any depth. Everything must be in the bouillon.

CÉCILE   Exactly. One could even insist on serving it in simple dark bowls, so that effects of light and depth can't be manipulated. And none of those games with letters that we used to play with alphabet pasta when we were little. As for the question of the story—

JEAN   The story?

CÉCILE   Yes, you remember—every dish must tell a story. But which story does the bouillon tell? How can we invent new flavors and help culinary art rescue bouillon from the ordinariness of everyday bouillon?

HÉLÈNE   Through metaphor?

CÉCILE   Metaphor? What do you mean?

JEAN   Perhaps that metaphor is both the recreation of the sensible world and a form of recreation, or amusement? I don't intend this simply as a play on words. Let me explain. A painter who paints Mount Sainte-Victoire not only reproduces, but re-creates as well, because he or she is a figurative painter. The analogue of the mountain in this case is the bouillon you make at home for your family, without any fuss, simply by cooking some meat in water.

Taking this homemade bouillon a step further, you get a consommé, which has still more of a bouillon flavor than bouillon itself, because the meat is cooked in bouillon rather than water! Perfect clarity, powerful taste—it's got everything.

HÉLÈNE   That's an interesting idea. I was thinking of something else altogether—a metaphor like "the little girl's roses," which refers to cheeks that are pink like roses: the flower stands for the girl's face. In the same way, why shouldn't we go beyond a bouillon, re-creating it to make something new that has the flavor of a bouillon, only in another context?

JEAN   I'd love to, darling, but it's already been done: there's an entire school of deconstructionist cooks who make a pot-au-feu with the meat in the form of a quenelle, the bouillon in the form of a gel, accompanied by thin slices of gherkin pickles, and so on. It's all rather facile—but, then again, it's fashionable.

CÉCILE   Fashion's not something to be avoided, you know. It gives pleasure to people by making them feel they're with it.

DENIS   Yes, it satisfies a certain urge to be sociable. Being in step with this or that fashion means belonging to a group, being recognized as a member of the group rather than an outsider. As a social animal, I'm happy to be in the group, which is where evolution says I ought to be.

CÉCILE   Maybe you're right. But here's a suggestion: let me throw out a bunch of ideas that I've been thinking about and perhaps you can help me see them more clearly.

DENIS   We'll still be here tomorrow!

CÉCILE   No, you know perfectly well that I always end up reaching for my usual bag of tricks.

JEAN   Let's give it a try.

CÉCILE   First, the question of quantity. To achieve a delicate result, you mustn't give your guests too much to eat.

DENIS   This leads to what is known as alliesthesia: when you eat too much of a certain food, a sort of sensory fatigue accompanies the feeling of being full—in the same way as when you enter a room that has a musty smell, you smell the mustiness at first, but then before long you don't smell it any more.

JEAN   Yet Brillat-Savarin said the opposite: "The most delicious rarity loses its influence when its quantity is stingy."[162]

CÉCILE   There's some truth in both opinions, I think. There musn't be too much or too little. I make it my business to see to that. In the case of a bouillon, you can play with the proportion in relation to the bowl. It's like when you fill up a glass: there's an ideal level for the liquid that's difficult to explain, but easy to determine when you put your mind to it. For this, intuition suffices.

Okay, another idea: the presentation, or visual display, of a dish can either enhance the flavor or skew the perception of it.

HÉLÈNE   Which means what?

CÉCILE   For example, if I use diced carrot in a dish in which the flavor of carrot is present, the sight of the carrot intensifies the flavor. In this case I'm relying on the faculty that is unconsciously activated when we drink wine: if I drink white wine that has been colored red, I perceive it as being red and describe it with words for red objects—Morello cherries, for instance—even if the coloring agents I use have absolutely no flavor. Conversely, if I use carrots in a dish that is based on a winter squash, my stage setting is thrown off.

HÉLÈNE   "Setting the stage"—you often use this phrase.

CÉCILE   Yes, it's like "telling a story" or "making a dish legible." All these things are at the heart of what I do. And telling fairy tales is hard work, let me tell you! But the idea of setting the stage is extremely suggestive. For example, a dish of choucroute reminds people in France of Alsace; whether I add to it or cut something out, it's still Alsace. And yet the addition or subtraction yields something novel, a variation on a familiar theme. The interesting thing is that even ingredients that have been omitted can be tasted, simply because of the context in which normally they're always found.

JEAN   You're right, legibility is critical—we've talked about it a hundred times. Still today so many restaurants simply throw dishes together. You don't know how you're supposed to eat what's on your plate. Each item separately? Everything together?

HÉLÈNE   It's the same in music or painting or literature, isn't it? Musicians know that if their listeners aren't able to recognize the song, the melody, then the music won't be memorable. Painters talk about preparing in advance the path that the viewer's eye is meant to follow in taking in a scene. And writers reinforce a basic story line with set phrases that are meant to stick in the reader's mind, a little like formulas or epithets, in order to emphasize aspects of a character's personality or to structure the story. But I see more similarities between painting and cooking than between cooking and music or literature. In music, melody is "synchronic," it flows; in literature, the narrative unfolds. In cooking and painting, by contrast, the fork and the eye pass from one element of a dish to another at the pleasure of—at whose pleasure, I wonder?

CÉCILE   At the pleasure of the composer, if he or she has done her work well. There must be a visible logic.

DENIS   Your theorizing is all very well and good, but it collapses in the case of a broth, a simple bouillon, where each spoonful is identical to the preceding one! Here, the flavor counts for everything—

JEAN   Yes, until alliesthesia sets in and you don't taste it any more!

CÉCILE   I wonder—

JEAN   You wonder what?

CÉCILE   If we're not barking up the completely wrong tree!

JEAN   Why?

CÉCILE   Because the perfect bouillon doesn't exist—any more than things have to taste like what they are. Idealism is always seductive, but it's an illusion just the same. Why should I search for just one bouillon, when there are a thousand bouillons waiting to be discovered? Depending on how I feel, depending on how I read my guests' mood, depending on the weather, the time of year, the products that I find in the market, I can imagine any number of bouillons. Clear bouillons, cloudy ones, strong ones, light ones—

HÉLÈNE   I was beginning to wonder the same thing just a moment ago. One shouldn't try to intellectualize too much. There is the question of technique, which the cook must perfectly master, but the song of one's cooking can't be reduced to schools, to preconceived ideas or theories. The heart of the matter is emotion. Tell me who you are, and I will tell you how you ought to cook.

DENIS   The first part of what you say is right, but not the second part. Yes, emotion is necessary, but no, the cook can't be limited to a single style of cooking. Like Picasso, cooks should be allowed to go through periods, to practice different styles, as they like and depending on the possibilities that they can squeeze out of each one of them. Yes, cooks must abandon themselves to their art, must embrace it, but they must also be free to change their aesthetic ideas at any moment. Above all, cooks must please—*that* is the Mystery!

JEAN   No morality matters any more, no theory, no technique. Cécile, make me laugh or cry, with a bouillon, a simple bouillon.

DENIS   You're right, method is of no use whatsoever. Recall that the Greek word *méthodos* signifies an efficient mode of reasoning that avoids the wastefulness of nature.[163] It's good for technical, artisanal work, but not for art. I can remember two occasions when I've cried from emotion while eating. I don't even know if it was from pleasure, or pain, or sadness—No, it was simply from emotion.

The first time (*Denis looks at Cécile*) was shortly after we met. You'd decided to close the restaurant and to cook for me, for me alone. You thought about it, for weeks, and then one day you set a date. I watched you cook, you almost didn't speak, concentrated on the idea of cooking for me. And at the table I cried with happiness. What I ate was the love that you gave me. Not ingredients, not lipids or protids or glucids—no, it was love.

The second time we were with very good friends, in Alsace. We had all ordered different main courses, and it was one of those evenings when we were remaking the world. Over appetizers we began by talking politics, and happily all our noble ideas were in harmony with one another. When the main courses came, we were so filled with the spirit of sharing that each of us wanted the others to taste his dish, rather than keep it all to himself. This act of sharing was deeply moving. I no longer remember what we had on our plates, but I do remember having tears in my eyes.

JEAN   A brute like you?

HÉLÈNE   Don't make fun, Jean.

CÉCILE   So, Denis, you say that the last word in cooking is love? Love in the bouillon?

HÉLÈNE   And all the rest is style, which must express the personality of the artist.

JEAN   Yes, style matters, because it is a manifestation. But the main thing, which so often escapes our notice, is the love of the person who cooks for you, and the love of those who share the meal with you.

THE SAME INGREDIENT IN DIFFERENT FORMS

IN THEORY

The humble bouillon epitomizes both the noble past and the glorious future of cooking; indeed, it is the main character of our drama in a way. Yet the fundamental distinction in matters of food and gastronomy, even more basic than a bouillon, is between the raw and the cooked. The artful simplicity of Pierre's preparations that follow suggests the wisdom of combining the two—a simplicity well known to generations of painters in both the East and the West.

IN PRACTICE
RAW AND COOKED ASPARAGUS

Cook some asparagus spears in boiling water that has been slightly salted. Then let them cool, separate the tips from the stalks, and sauté the stalks in butter, adding from time to time a teaspoon of water in order to prevent the butter from turning brown.

Then mix the tips and the sautéed stalks with some cream, chopped truffle, and a little parmesan. The asparagus is present in two ways that complement each other.

You can exaggerate the effect by leaving the stalks raw instead, cutting them into segments and mixing them with the truffle cream, and placing the cooked tips on top. This way the tender, smooth-flavored tips stand in contrast to the raw, crunchy stalks, which have a fresher, greener flavor.

You can continue in the same fashion with the classic preparations of asparagus served with hollandaise or mayonnaise, again leaving the stalks raw and poaching or boiling the tips.

In all these cases, the idea of serving uncooked asparagus stalks is a simple one, but its appeal grew in reaction to the banquet cuisine of the 1960s and the obsession with prime beef fillets and racks of lamb. Cooks today are learning to transform things that this older style of cooking, ignoring their wonderful virtues, threw away: the leaves of Romaine lettuce that used to be fed to rabbits, for example, now have a proud place in "fine cooking." My friend Michel Bras even serves raw broccoli stalks.

No matter how simple or inexpensive food products may be, in matters of culinary art the only thing that matters is the artistry with which these products are used. After all, the great painters have not disdained using the humble charcoal crayon!

YOUR TURN

When a vegetable is taken out of the ground, enzymes are activated and form new compounds that change its flavor while altering the texture and possibly the taste and smell as well. What we are accustomed to call "raw" is only something that hasn't been subjected to the ordeal of fire—a relatively minor distinction in one sense.

The fact remains, however, that the flavors of foods that have not been heated are very different from those of the same foods that have been cooked by heating. Why, then, shouldn't we use both? What can you imagine doing with a vegetable such as the radish, which is usually eaten raw rather than cooked?

NOTES

1   See Leonardo da Vinci, *The Notebooks of Leonardo da Vinci,* ed. and trans. Edward MacCurdy, 2 vols. (New York: Reynal and Hitchcock, 1938), 1:88. [The reference is to Leonardo's famous remark that "love of anything is the offspring of knowledge, love being more fervent in proportion as knowledge is certain; and this certainty springs from a thorough knowledge of all those parts which united compose the whole of the thing which ought to be loved."—Trans.]

2   Madame de Staël, *Corinne, ou l'Italie* (Paris, 1807).

3   Jean Anthelme Brillat-Savarin, *La physiologie du goût* (Paris, 1825); see *The Physiology of Taste, Or, Meditations on Transcendental Gastronomy,* trans. M. F. K. Fisher (Washington, D.C.: Counterpoint, 1999), 3.

4   René Descartes, *Discours de la méthode* (Leiden, 1637), part 2; see *Oeuvres de Descartes,* ed. Charles Adam and Paul Tannery, 2nd ed., 11 volumes (Paris: Vrin, 1974–1976), 6:11–21.

5   André Gide, *Journal 1889–1939* (Paris: Gallimard, 1948), November 1892.

6   Brillat-Savarin, *Physiology of Taste,* 7.

7   François Marin, *La suite des dons de Comus* (Paris, 1742).

8   Ernest Renan, *Souvenirs d'enfance et de jeunesse* (Paris: Calmann-Lévy, 1883).

9   See Kakuzō Okakura, *Book of Tea* (New York: Putnam's Sons, 1906).

10   See preface to Shitao, *Les propos sur la peinture du moine Citrouille-amère,* ed. and trans. Pierre Ryckmans (Paris: Hermann, 2000).

11 Quoted in Curnonsky and Gaston Derys, *Gaietés et curiosités gastronomiques* (Paris: Delagrave, 1933), 19. [Maincave's heretical ideas about traditional cooking attracted the attention of the gastronomic bard Raoul Ponchon ("our last Bacchic poet," in Guillaume Apollinaire's phrase), who devoted a number of playful verses to them; and the 1922 edition of the Almanach de Cocagne, edited by Bertrand Guégan and dedicated to "true Gourmets and Francs-Buveurs," contained a warm tribute to the ingenious dishes Maincave created as a company cook during the war, using herbs collected near the trenches. Maincave's futuristic theories also influenced Filippo Tommaso Marinetti (see note 142 below).—Trans.]

12 John Meurig Thomas, "Kirill I. Zamaraev (1939–96)—Experiment, the child of error and effort—Obituary," *Chemistry—A European Journal* (February 1997): 184–185.

13 Lu Wenfu, *Vie et passion d'un gastronome chinois* (Paris: Philippe Picquier, 1996), 164.

14 See *Lycurgus* 10.1–3, in *Plutarch's Lives,* 11 vols., trans. Bernardotte Perrin (Cambridge, Mass.: Harvard University Press, 1914–1926), 1:233–235.

15 Quoted in Françoise Dolto, *Autoportrait d'une psychoanalyste* (Paris: Seuil, 1989).

16 John Stuart Mill, "Nature," in *Three Essays on Religion* (London: Longman, Green, Reader and Dyer, 1874), 28–29.

17 Ibid., 62.

18 Ibid., 5–6.

19 See Daniel Vézina, *Ma route des saveurs au Québec* (Quebec City: Laurie Raphael Restaurant, 2001).

20 Meyer Schapiro, *Theory and Philosophy of Art: Style, Artist, and Society* (New York: George Braziller, 1994), 51.

21 Ibid., 54.

22 Ibid., 59.

23 Schapiro, *Theory and Philosophy of Art,* 1.

24 See Erwin Panofsky, *Idea: A Concept in Art Theory,* trans. Joseph J. S. Peake (Columbia: University of South Carolina Press, 1968).

25 See Cicero, *De inventione* 2.1.1, and Pliny, *Historia Naturalis* 31.64.

26 The Canon of Polyclitus, quoted by Galen, *De Placita Hippocratis et Platonis;* see Erwin Panofsky, *Meaning in the Visual Arts* (Harmondsworth: Penguin Books, 1970), 96.

27 Vitruvius, *De architectura* 1.2.4; see *On Architecture,* ed. and trans. Frank Granger, 2 vols. (Cambridge, Mass.: Harvard University Press, 1995), 1:27.

28 See Plato, *Republic* 10.603b, and the discussion in Jean-Luc Chalumeau, *Les théories de l'art* (Paris: Vuibert, 2002), 21; also Renée Bouveresse, *L'expérience esthétique* (Paris: Armand Colin, 1998), 13.

29   See Aristotle, *Rhetoric* 1366a 33, and the discussion in Umberto Eco, *Art and Beauty in the Middle Ages,* trans. Hugh Bredin (New Haven: Yale University Press, 1986), 22–23.

30   Aristotle, *Poetics* 1447a 14–16; the English versions here and below are from Richard McKeon, ed. and trans., *The Basic Works of Aristotle* (New York: Random House, 1941).

31   Aristotle, *Poetics* 1448b 4–9.

32   See ibid., passim, esp. chap. 9–14 (1451a 36–1454a 15).

33   Aristotle, *Poetics* 1454b 7–8.

34   Aristotle, *Poetics* 1451a 36–39.

35   Aristotle, *Politics* 1281b 7–14.

36   Aristotle, *Metaphysics* 1032a 32–33.

37   Apollonius of Tyana 6.19, in C. L. Kayser, ed., *Flavii Philostrati Opera,* 2 vols. (Hildesheim: Olms, 1964), 1:118.

38   See *Enneads* 5.8.1 in Plotinus, *Enneads,* ed. and trans. A. H. Armstrong, 7 vols. (Cambridge, Mass: Harvard University Press, 1968–1988).

39   Plotinus, *Enneads* 1.62.

40   Saint Augustine, *De Vera Religione* 32, 59; see *Of True Religion,* trans. J. H. S. Burleigh (Chicago: Regnery, 1959), 56–57, and Eco, *Art and Beauty in the Middle Ages,* 71–72.

41   Saint Thomas Aquinas, *Summa Theologiae* I, 39, 8; quoted in Eco, *Art and Beauty in the Middle Ages,* 71.

42   Aquinas, *Summa Theologiae* I, 5, 4 ad. 1; quoted in Eco, *Art and Beauty in the Middle Ages,* 70.

43   Macrobius, *Commentarii in Somnium Scipionis* 2.12.11; see *Commentary on the Dream of Scipio,* ed. and trans. William Harris Stahl (New York: Columbia University Press, 1952), and Eco, *Art and Beauty in the Middle Ages,* 35.

44   See Martin Gardner, "Fibonacci and Lucas Numbers," in *Mathematical Circus* (Washington, D.C.: Mathematical Association of America, 1992).

45   See H. E. Huntley, *The Divine Proportion* (New York: Dover Books, 1970) and Marguerite Neveux, *Le nombre d'or: Radiographie d'un mythe* (Paris: Seuil, 1995).

46   Boethius, *De institutione musica* 1.10; quoted in Eco, *Art and Beauty in the Middle Ages,* 31.

47   Alcuin, *Dialogus de Rhetorica et Virtutibus,* in J.-P. Migne, ed., *Patrilogiae Cursus Completus: Series Latina,* 221 vols. (Paris, 1844–1890), 101: cols. 919–950; see Eco, *Art and Beauty in the Middle Ages,* 38–39.

48   Eco, *Art and Beauty in the Middle Ages,* 41–42.

49   Ibid., 5n.

50   See ibid., 4–5.

51   See Aquinas, *Summa Theologiae* I, 39, 8.

52   Ibid., I, 91, 3; quoted in Eco, *Art and Beauty in the Middle Ages,* 78.

53   Aquinas, *Summa Theologiae* I–II, 57, 4.

54   John of Salisbury, *Metalogicon* 1.12; see the translation by Daniel D. McGarry (Berkeley and Los Angeles: University of California Press, 1962).

55   Cassiodorus, *De Artibus et Disciplinis Liberalium Litterarum,* preface; quoted in Eco, *Art and Beauty in the Middle Ages,* 92.

56   Saint Thomas Aquinas, *Quaestiones quodlibetales* 7.6.16; see the Latin edition prepared by Raimondo Spiazzi (Turin and Rome: Marietti, 1970), 76.

57   William of Auvergne, *Tractatus de Bono et de Malo,* quoted in Henri Pouillon, "La Beauté, propriété transcendentale chez les scholastiques (1220–1270)," *Archives d'histoire doctrinale et littéraire du Moyen Âge,* vol. 15 (Paris: Vrin, 1946): 263–328.

58   Wisdom of Solomon 11.20.

59   Robert Grosseteste, *Commentarius in divinis nominibus,* quoted in Pouillon, "La Beauté."

60   Saint Bonaventure, *Itinerarium mentis in Deum* 2.1.3, in *Opera Theologica selecta,* ed. L. M. Bello, 5 vols. (Florence: Quaracchi, 1934–1965).

61   See Eco, *Art and Beauty in the Middle Ages,* 9.

62   Vitellion, *De Perspectiva;* see Clemens Baeumker, *Witelo, ein Philosoph und Naturforscher* (Münster: Aschendorff, 1908), 127–178, and Eco, *Art and Beauty in the Middle Ages,* 68–69.

63   See Eco, *Art and Beauty in the Middle Ages,* 19–20.

64   See ibid., 23–26.

65   See Schapiro, *Theory and Philosophy of Art,* 20.

66   [Cuius Cartusiensis Monachi], *Tractatus de musica plana,* published as the second of four volumes of *Scriptorum de musica medii aevii,* ed. Charles Edmond Henri de Coussemaker (1864–1876; reprint Hildesheim: Olms, 1963), 434; quoted in Eco, *Art and Beauty in the Middle Ages,* 35.

67   Auguste Escoffier, *Le Guide Culinaire: Aide mémoire de cuisine pratique* (Paris: Flammarion, 1903); see the English translation of the 4th edition (1921) by H. L. Cracknell and R. J. Kaufmann (New York: Mayflower Books, 1982).

68   Madame E. Saint-Ange, *La Bonne Cuisine de Mme. E. Saint-Ange* (Paris: Flammarion, 1927); see *La Bonne Cuisine de Mme. E. Saint-Ange: The Original Companion for French Home Cooking,* trans. Paul Aratow (Berkeley: Ten Speed Press, 2005).

69   See Addison Ault, "The monosodium glutamate story: The commercial production of

MSG and other amino acids," *Journal of Chemical Education* 81 (2004): 347–355. On the nature and function of sapid (taste) and odorant molecules, and more generally the distinction between taste and flavor, see the discussion of these and other related terms in the glossary to Hervé This, *Molecular Gastronomy: Exploring the Science of Flavor,* trans. M.B. DeBevoise (New York: Columbia University Press, 2006), 337–350.

70   See Marc Meneau's discussion of this point, quoted by Jean-François Abert, *La génie des saveurs* (Paris: Plon, 1994), 92.

71   See C.-M. Hladik and B. Simmen, "Taste perception and feeding behavior in non-human primates and human populations," *Evolutionary Anthropology* 5 (1996): 58–71.

72   K. Tonosaki and M. Funakoshi, "Effect of polarization of mouse taste cells," *Chemical Senses* 9 (1984): 381–387.

73   See A. Faurion, "Physiology of the Sweet Taste," in D. Otosson, ed., *Progress in Sensory Physiology* (Heidelberg: Springer Verlag, 1987), 130–201.

74   See Chalumeau, *Les théories de l'art,* 26.

75   Lodovico Castelvetro, *Poetica d'Aristotele vulgarizzata, et sposta* (Vienna, 1570; revised and enlarged, Basel, 1576).

76   Leon Battista Alberti, *De pictura* (Florence, 1435); published in an Italian edition the following year as *Della pittura.*

77   Leonardo da Vinci, *Trattato della pittura* (Milan, 1584; editio princeps, 1651), N.2, 311.

78   See Panofsky, *Idea,* 82–83.

79   Francesco Robortello, *In librum Aristotelis de arte poetica explicationes* (Florence, 1548).

80   L.E. Pinsky, *Realism Epochy Vozrozhedenya* (Moscow: Gosletizdat, 1961), 119–120.

81   Francisco Pacheco, *Arte de la pintura,* 2 vols. (Madrid, 1649).

82   Baruch Spinoza, *Ethics,* III, 9, scholium; see the translation by G.H.R. Parkinson (Oxford: Oxford University Press, 2000), 172.

83   Anton Raphael Mengs, *Gedanken über die Schönheit und über den Genschmack in der Malerey* (Zurich, 1762); quoted by Chalumeau, *Les théories de l'art,* 19.

84   Denis Diderot et Jean Le Rond d'Alembert, eds., *Dictionnaire raisonnée des sciences, des arts, des métiers,* 28 vols. (Paris, 1751–1772).

85   Comte de Buffon, *Discours sur le Style,* inaugural address to the Académie Française, 25 August 1753.

86   Shitao, *Les propos sur la peinture du moine Citrouille-amère,* 114.

87   Ibid., 18.

88   Ibid., 9.

89 Ibid.

90 Ibid.

91 Ibid.

92 Confucius, *The Analects* 2.12; see the commentary by Simon Leys (pseudonym of Pierre Ryckmans) in *The Analects of Confucius* (New York: Norton, 1997), 115–116.

93 Shitao, *Les propos sur la peinture du moine Citrouille-amère,* 19.

94 Ibid., 33.

95 Quoted by ibid., 20, 40.

96 Hippocrates, *Aphorisms* 1.1; see vol. 4 of the Loeb edition of the works of Hippocrates, trans. W. H. S. Jones (Cambridge, Mass.: Harvard University Press, 1931; reprinted 1992), 99.

97 Quoted by Shitao, *Les propos sur la peinture du moine Citrouille-amère,* 120.

98 See the preface by Jean-Marie Schaeffer to his edition of selected writings by Goethe on art, *Écrits sur l'art* (Paris: Flammarion, 1996).

99 From Goethe's 29 January 1826 conversation with Johann Peter Eckermann; see *Conversations with Eckermann (1823–1832),* trans. John Oxenford (San Francisco: North Point Press, 1984), 101.

100 Johann Wolfgang von Goethe, "Introduction to the *Propylaea*" (1798), in John Gearey, ed., *Essays on Art and Literature,* trans. Ellen von Nardroff and Ernest H. Nardroff, vol. 3 of the 12-volume *Collected Works* (New York: Suhrkamp, 1983–1989), 83.

101 Ibid., 86.

102 Letter from Goethe to Schiller, 19 April 1797, in *Correspondence between Goethe and Schiller, 1794–1805,* trans. Liselotte Dieckmann (New York: Peter Lang, 1994), 182. [Here and below I have very slightly modified Dieckmann's rendering of the German.– Trans.]

103 See V. I. Propp, *Morphology of the Folktale,* 2nd rev. ed., trans. Laurence Scott (Austin: University of Texas Press, 1968).

104 Letter from Goethe to Schiller, 22 April 1797, *Correspondence,* 183.

105 Letter from Schiller to Goethe, 25 April 1797, *Correspondence,* 185.

106 Philipp Otto Runge, letter to his brother Daniel (May 1802), in *Briefe und Schriften,* ed. Peter Betthausen (Munich: C. H. Beck, 1982).

107 Friedrich Schelling, *Über das Verhältniss der bildenden Künste zu der Natur* (Munich, 1807); quoted by Chalumeau, *Les théories de l'art,* 52.

108 Arthur Schopenhauer, *The World as Will and Representation,* 2 vols., trans. E. F. J. Payne (New York: Dover Publications, 1969), 1:195.

109 Stendhal, *Histoire de la peinture en Italie,* 2 vols. (Paris: P. Driot, 1817), chap. 156.

110 Eugène Delacroix, *Journal,* 3 vols., ed. Paul Flat and René Piot (Paris: E. Plon, Nourrit, 1893–1895); quoted by Bouveresse, *L'Expérience esthétique,* 99.

111 Quoted by ibid., 211.

112 Honoré de Balzac, *Le chef-d'oeuvre inconnu* (Paris, 1832), chap. 1.

113 Honoré de Balzac, *Béatrix* (Paris, 1839), chap. 14.

114 Friedrich Nietzsche, *Menschliches, allzumenschliches: ein Buch für freie Geister* (Chemnitz, 1878–1880), sec. 151; see *Human, All Too Human,* trans. R. J. Hollingdale (Cambridge: Cambridge University Press, 1996), 82.

115 Friedrich Nietzsche, *Die Geburt der Tragödie* (Berlin, 1872), sec. 24; see *The Birth of Tragedy,* trans. Walter Kaufmann (New York: Vintage Books, 1967), 140.

116 See Paul Cézanne, *Correspondance,* ed. John Renwald (Paris: Grasset, 1978).

117 Claude Debussy, *Monsieur Croche, antidilettante* (Paris: Dorbon-aîné, 1921); see *Three Classics in the Aesthetic of Music* (New York: Dover, 1962), 7.

118 Charles Baudelaire, *Critique d'Art,* ed. Bernard Gheerbrant (Paris: Gallimard, 1976), 50.

119 Ibid., 67.

120 Ibid., 85.

121 Ibid.

122 Ibid., 133.

123 Heinrich Wölfflin, *Kunstgeschichtliche Grundbegriffe: das Problem der Stilentwicklung in der neureren Kunst* (Munich: F. Bruckmann, 1915); see Chalumeau, *Les théories de l'art,* 70.

124 See the catalogue of the Bauhaus exhibition jointly sponsored by the Musée National d'Art Moderne and the Musée d'Art Moderne de la Ville de Paris (2 April–2 June 1969).

125 From Klee's famous 1920 essay, usually referred to as "Creative Credo"; the name comes from the title of the anthology in which it first appeared, *Schöpferische Konfession* (Berlin: E. Reiss, 1920); an English translation by Ralph Mannheim can be found in the volume of Klee's notebooks edited by Jürgen Spiller, *Paul Klee: The Thinking Eye* (New York: G. Wittenborn, 1961).–Trans.

126 Oskar Schlemmer, *Briefe und Tagebücher* (Munich: A. Langen-G. Müller, 1958), 147.

127 Walter Gropius, *The Bauhaus Manifesto;* quoted in Bauhaus exhibition catalogue (1969), 13. [See Jean-Louis Ferrier and Yann Le Pichon, eds., *Art of Our Century: The Chronicle of Western Art, 1900 to the Present,* trans. Walter D. Glanze (New York: Prentice-Hall, 1989), 191.–Trans.]

128 Walter Gropius, *Architektür, Fescher Büscherei* (Frankfurt and Hamburg, 1956); quoted in Bauhaus exhibition catalogue (1969), 15.

129 Wassily Kandinsky, *Über das Geistige in der Kunst: insbesondere in der Malerie* (Munich: R. Piper, 1911); see *Concerning the Spiritual in Art,* trans. M. T. H. Sadler (New York: Dover Publications, 1977), 2. [Sadler locates the sense of what he calls the "almost untranslateable" German term *Stimmung,* later used by Kandinsky to signify the essential spirit of nature, somewhere between "feeling" and "sentiment"; the French translator renders it as "ambience" or "atmosphere."–Trans.]

130 Ibid., 17–18.

131 Ibid., 1.

132 Ibid., 14.

133 Ibid., 32.

134 Ibid., 54.

135 Ibid., 55.

136 Ibid., 3.

137 Ibid., 15.

138 Ibid., 23. [Italics in the original.–Trans.]

139 See Schapiro, *Theory and Philosophy of Art,* 1.

140 Klee, "Creative Credo"; quoted by Bouveresse, *L'Expérience esthétique,* 217.

141 See Schapiro, *Theory and Philosophy of Art,* 15.

142 Filippo Tommaso Marinetti, "Manifesto della cucina futurista" (Turin: 1931); published in F. T. Marinetti and Luigi Fillìa, *La Cucina futurista* (Milan: Sonzogno, 1932).

143 From Jean-Paul Sartre, *Psychologie phénoménologique de l'imagination* (Paris: Gallimard, 1940); see Sartre, *Idées* (Paris: Gallimard, 1971), 366.

144 Maurice Merleau-Ponty, *Signes* (Paris: Gallimard, 1960), 40.

145 Martin Heidegger, *Der Ursprung des Kunstwerkes* (Stuttgart: Reclam, 1960); see "The Origin of the Work of Art," in *Poetry, Language, Thought,* trans. Albert Hofstadter (New York: Harper and Row, 1971), 17–87.

146 André Malraux, *Les voix du silence* (Paris: Gallimard, 1951); quoted by Bouveresse, *L'Expérience esthétique,* 14.

147 Ibid.

148 See Pierre Francastel, *Peinture et société* (Paris: Gallimard, 1956).

149 Paul Claudel, *Journal,* ed. François Varillon and Jacques Petit (Paris: Gallimard, 1968), 473.

150 See George Dickie, *The Art Circle* (New York: Haven Publications, 1984).

151 Eco, *Art and Beauty in the Middle Ages,* 109. [Italics in the original.—Trans.]

152 Chalumeau, *Les théories de l'art,* 7.

153 Anne Cauquelin, *L'art contemporain,* 6th ed. (Paris: Presses Universitaires de France, 2001), 77. [The bracketed interpolations are Jean's.—Trans.]

154 Marcellin Berthelot, "Discours prononcé au Banquet de la Chambre syndicale des produits chimiques, le 5 avril 1894," in *Science et morale* (Paris: Calmann-Lévy, 1897).

155 Gustave Le Rouge, *La Guerre des vampires* (Paris: Méricant, 1909).

156 From Einstein's 10 June 1933 Herbert Spencer Lecture at Oxford, reprinted as *On the Method of Theoretical Physics* (Oxford: The Clarendon Press, 1933), 274.

157 Quoted by John G. Kemeny, *A Philosopher Looks at Science* (Princeton, N.J.: Van Nostrand, 1959), 63.

158 Alfred North Whitehead, *The Concept of Nature* (Cambridge: Cambridge University Press, 1926), 163.

159 Isaac Newton, *Mathematical Principles of Natural Philosophy,* 2 vols., trans. Andrew Motte and rev. Florian Cajori (Berkeley and Los Angeles: University of California Press, 1966), 2:398.

160 Denis Diderot, *Paradoxe sur le comédien* (1773), in *Oeuvres Complètes,* 20 vols., ed. Jules Assézat and Maurice Tourneux (Paris: Garnier Frères, 1875–1877), 8:339–361.

161 Ibid.

162 Brillat Savarin, *Physiology of Taste,* 177.

163 John of Salisbury, *Metalogicon* 1.11.

LIST OF RECIPES

PART TWO: CLASSICAL IDEAS OF BEAUTY

PART THREE: BEAUTY IN THE MIDDLE AGES

PART FOUR: ARTISTIC CREATIVITY UNBOUND

INDEX

culinary art *(continued)*
  symbolist aesthetics applied to, 264–
    65
  tradition in, 9, 31, 39–40, 43, 118–19,
    140
  truth in, 61, 96, 99, 102, 152, 291
  universality in, 247
  variations in, 33–35, 119–21
  and visual appearance, 11–13, 21, 59,
    60–61, 69–70, 72, 151, 153, 159, 320
    (*see also* coloring)
culinary science, 4, 36n, 38
  and chemistry, 32, 33, 158, 170, 200–
    203, 302–3
  and physiology, 97–98, 205–7
Curie, Pierre, 37
Curnonsky (Maurice Edmond Sailland),
    59, 61–63, 68, 80, 81, 96, 112, 134,
    265
cutting techniques, 82–84

Dai Xi, 238
Darwin, Charles, 111
date paste, 196
Debussy, Claude, 66, 266
decoction, 201
Delacroix, Eugène, 259, 262
Deng Chun, 236
Descartes, René, 16, 17
desserts
  Bavarian cream with coconut milk,
    15
  chocolate cake, 15
  chocolate cookies, 116–17
  chocolate cream with lavender, 131–
    32
  coffee sabayon, 164
  conger eel sponge cake, 122
  fresh figs with cumin caramel, 15

fromage blanc quenelle, 14
grapefruit quenelle, 14
Mirabelle plum jelly with pomegran-
    ate seeds, 15
pear quenelle, 14
red peppers and wild strawberries,
    175–76
red peppers with tomato pulp and
    fennel, 176
rum sabayon, 165
saffron-colored ice cream with olives
    and peppers, 174–75
Sauternes sabayon, 165
sorbet quenelle, 14
tonka bean sabayon with poached
    fresh peaches, 15
vanilla sabayon, 165
whipped cream with cognac-flavored
    tomatoes, 33
Dickie, George, 282
didactic art, 127
Diderot, Denis, 235, 310
distillation, 198, 200, 203, 291
Dobzhansky, Theodosius, 41
Dolto, Boris, 43
duck, 29, 32, 35
  with barberry mousseline, 184–85
  with mango chutney and shrimp, 91
  paired with red tuna, 73–74, 122
  See also foie gras
Dubois, Urbain, 315
Dumas, Jean Baptiste André, 37, 38n
Dürer, Albrecht, 308, 311n

Eco, Umberto, 283
eel, 121–22
egg flan, 100
eggplant, 284–85
egg yolks

Middle Ages, 63, 80, 130–31, 133, 139,
145–46, 171, 172, 191
and culinary art, 180–85, 192–94, 198
and non-culinary art, 166, 168, 169,
179, 180, 181, 191, 192–94
Mill, John Stuart, 50–52
mint, 104, 159, 161, 196
Molière, 287
mollusks, 141
with roasted peaches, endives, and
verbena syrup, 140–41
in tartare with calf's head and beef,
161–62
monkfish, 65
monosodium glutamate (MSG), 204
Montaigne, Michel de, 43n
Montesquieu, Baron de La Brède et de,
96
Moréas, Jean, 264
Moreau, Gustave, 264
morel mushrooms, 66, 229
Morocco, 104, 195
mousseline
barberry, 184–85
dace, 186
Musée Camondo (Paris), 90, 93, 108,
233–34
Musée du Senat (Paris), 212
muses, Greek, 10
mushrooms
button mushrooms with braised
squab, 210–11
button mushrooms with crabmeat,
64–65, 100–101
button mushrooms with sponge cake,
316
chanterelles, distillation of, 203
chanterelles with ratatouille, 285
chanterelles with ravioli, 269

morels with foie gras, 66
morels with licorice, 229
white truffles and cèpes (porcini),
288
music, 35, 64, 65, 66, 73, 87–88, 99,
112–13, 217, 312, 321
mustard, 26, 28, 70, 122, 162, 220

narrative, culinary, 64–65, 66–67,
249, 255, 318, 321
naturalism, 246, 259, 264
nature, 47–49, 51, 52–53, 108, 112,
212, 247, 263, 265, 268, 307
Newton, Isaac, 307
Nietzsche, Friedrich Wilhelm, 261, 265,
276
Nignon, Edouard, 31, 206, 315
numbers, 85–89, 91–92, 145

Okakura, Kakuzo, 23
olive oil, 57, 104, 122, 157, 209, 221,
285
olives
ice cream and peppers with, 175
monkfish with, 65
onions
garnish made with, 297
with giant peas, 123
in pigeon sauce, 210
in vadouvan, 70
oranges
mandarin, 116, 117
oysters
with foie gras, 220
huîtres à la louquenqua, 13
roasted in goose fat, 143
in *royale* of anchovies and shellfish,
100
with Spanish ham, 12–13

prawns, 196
prehistoric art, 77, 79–80, 278
preservation, food, 268
proportion
  beauty defined by, 136, 137–38,
    159
  in culinary art, 137–38, 151, 311–
    12
Propp, V. I., 243, 248–49
Proust, Marcel, 96, 97
psychology, 280, 282
Pythagoras, 86–89, 133, 139, 149

quails, 10, 11
quenelles, 14, 15, 27, 319
quince, 120, 253
quinoa, 288
quintessence, 198, 297–98

rabbit
  with white wine, garlic, and rosemary,
    35
Rabelais, François, 309
Racine, Jean, 113
radishes, 83–84, 326
raspberries
  with Camembert, 33, 34, 35, 44–46
  with foie gras, 57
  variations with, 33, 34, 35
ratatouille, 284–85
ravioli, 269
raw food, 48, 49, 57, 83, 324–26
red cabbage
  braised squab and red peppers with,
    209–10
  disk-shaped jellies using, 91
  with foie gras, 120
red currants, 15, 29, 91, 122, 254
red peppers

aspic with currants and watermelon,
  196
  braised squab with, 208–11
  jellies made with, 91
  with roast pigeon, 28–29
  with saffron-colored ice-cream and
    olives, 174–75
  with tomato pulp and fennel, 176
  See also sweet peppers
Renaissance, 88, 132n, 216n, 223, 224,
  226, 264, 308n, 311n
Renan, Ernest, 22–23
repetition in art, 9, 14, 24–25, 39, 64,
  95, 127, 253–54, 277, 287
rice paper, 157
rice vinegar, 71, 104
risotto, 288
Rissell, Bertrand, 306
Ritthauser, B., 204
Robortello, Francesco, 225
Roellinger, Olivier, 65
Roman Empire, 43
Romanticism, 246, 248, 252, 261, 262,
  266n
Rouff, Marcel, 62
Rousseau, Jean-Jacques, 43n
Royal Institution (London), 36n
rules, artistic, 237–38, 252
Rumford, Count. See Thompson,
  Benjamin
rum sabayon, 165
rum syrup, 316
Runge, Philipp Otto, 252

sabayons, 15, 163–65
saffron, 61, 72, 174, 176, 196
Sailland, Maurice Edmond. See
  Curnonsky
Saint-Ange, E., 202

salads
  fruit, 176
  squab salad with lasagna and zucchini
    chutney, 15
  summer truffles with crisp sorrel and
    fingerling potatoes, 15
Salon International du Livre Gourmand,
  69, 79
sarasson, 84
Sartre, Jean-Paul, 279–80
sauces
  cream, 143, 253–54
  with duck juices, 73–74
  hollandaise, 325
  mustard and horseradish in juices
    of whiting, 122
  with pigeon juices, 209–10
  rum mixed with juices of pork, 33
  tarragon, 109–10, 116
  thickened with flour, 158
Saulnier, Louis, 31
sausages
  huîtres à la louquenqua, 13
  warm sliced hard sausage with
    sarasson, 84
Sauternes sabayon, 165
scallops, 100, 117, 122, 143, 196, 255
Schapiro, Meyer, 68, 278
Schelling, Friedrich Wilhelm Joseph
  von, 260
Schiller, Friedrich von, 243, 248, 250
Schopenhauer, Arthur, 261, 265
Schrödinger, Erwin, 37
Schumann, Robert, 277
science, 36–38
  biology, 41, 43, 44
  chemistry, 32, 33, 37–38nn, 47, 158,
    170, 198, 300–303
  physics, 306–7

physiology, 97–98, 205–7
  See also culinary science
science fiction, 283, 305
seafood. *See* crabmeat; fish; lobster;
  shellfish; shrimp
seaweed, 204
Sein, Grégoire, 29
sheep's milk, 186–87
shellfish
  with cooked strawberry vinaigrette,
    57
  with sliced celery and radish, 83–84
  See also mollusks; oysters; scallops
Shitao (Friar Bitter-Melon), 21, 235,
  238, 245, 310, 313
shortbread, 116, 117
shrimp
  with duck and mango chutney, 91
side dishes, 215, 219–20
simplicity
  in culinary art, 299, 306, 315, 324
  in science, 306
smell, sense of, 157, 201, 202, 206
social relations, and food, 41–42, 44,
  319
Socrates, 54, 95, 110
sorbets, 14, 159, 221–22
soufflé
  with Chartreuse, 183
soy sauce, 57, 73, 286
spinach
  extract, as coloring agent, 72, 170
  in flower ravioli, 269
  langoustine tempura with spinach
    fondue, 104–5
  roast pigeon with langoustine and
    spinach, 26–27
Spinoza, Baruch, 227, 306n
sponge cake, 122, 316

CALIFORNIA STUDIES IN FOOD AND CULTURE
DARRA GOLDSTEIN, EDITOR

DESIGNER
J. G. Braun
TEXT
10/14 Rotis
DISPLAY
Gotham
COMPOSITOR
Integrated Composition Systems
INDEXER
Andrew Joron
PRINTER AND BINDER
Sheridan Books, Inc